DATABASED
MARKETING

DATABASED
MARKETING

Herman Holtz

John Wiley & Sons, Inc.
New York • Chichester • Toronto • Brisbane • Singapore

Library of Congress Cataloging-in-Publication Data

Holtz, Herman.
    Databased marketing / by Herman Holtz.
       p.   cm.
    Includes bibliographical references and index.
    ISBN 0-471-55187-2
    1. Databased marketing. I. Title.
    HF5415.126.H644   1992
    658.8′00285′574—dc20   92-326

Printed in the United States of America

10 9 8 7 6 5 4 3 2 1

Printed and bound by Malloy Lithographing, Inc.

Acknowledgments

I accept complete responsibility for everything I have said in these pages. Any errors of fact or judgment are mine and solely mine. At the same time, I want to express my sincere thanks to all the following who provided many valuable insights to aid me in understanding this difficult subject:

Rose Harper, Chief Executive Officer, Kleid Company, Inc., and author of *Mailing List Strategies,* McGraw-Hill, 1986.

Bill Chasse, Online Information Network, American Business Information.

Kurt and Jan Williams.

Bob McKim, M/S Project Management.

Steve Murphy.

Wayne Stoler, Letter Perfect Information Services.

Preface

We are today in the vortex of a great change in marketing. This is partly a consequence of today's economic conditions in general and partly a consequence of modern technology and what that has made possible for even the smallest marketing organization. The newest terms for these latest marketing developments are *targeted marketing* and *databased marketing,* with the latter term reflecting the more recent idea and methodology, although the two ideas are linked. We might even consider databased marketing to be an outgrowth of targeted marketing, although there is more to the latest marketing evolution than targeting alone.

Databased marketing is not exactly on everybody's tongue, but it is the subject of a large outpouring of articles in journals concerned with marketing, especially direct marketing. It is represented widely as the wave of the future in marketing: Presumably, if we are to believe the most extreme enthusiasts for this newest marketing idea, the survival of everyone in marketing today depends on getting aboard the databased marketing vessel before tomorrow comes. In line with that thought, one of my first moves in surveying opinions on the subject, as an early step in researching information for this book, was to tune in to the thoughts of a number of young, bright marketers, trying earnestly to elicit from them their own words of wisdom on this important new subject.

To my surprise, and even to my dismay, most professed to know rather little of databased marketing, other than possibly—some appeared unsure even of this—having heard the term itself somewhere. On the other hand, I soon learned from their remarks that they did not have to be familiar with the term itself to have a deep appreciation of the central concepts and problems with which it deals and essays to solve: If they had little to say about anything known as "databased marketing," they did express opinions, sometimes rather strong ones, about the most closely related subjects of today's problems with mass marketing and the state of the latter today. They also had opinions about micromarketing, narrowcasting, niche marketing, and, especially, targeted marketing. These are among the subjects that are near the heart of what databased marketing is about. Certainly, these marketers all showed a deep under-standing of the modern dilemma concerning mass marketing versus niche marketing, and of a great many closely related matters of advertis-ing and merchandising.

Following are a few of the comments and observations I thought most provocative and worthy of note. As we proceed to discuss data-based marketing you will probably recognize the problems addressed by these remarks, and possibly even have a sense of dejà vu occasion-ally. One thing is clear enough: It is not necessary to know anything about databased marketing per se to recognize modern marketing problems. Here are a few of the independent experts' most cogent observations:

A lot of people genuflect to the niche market, but I'm always amazed at how little they—even the biggest corporations—do about it, however. I think the reason is simple enough: It's complicated, laborious, and painstaking to really do anything about identifying and pursuing niche markets. It's so much easier to throw a few thousand ill-chosen words into an ad insertion than to try to find the best list(s), analyze customer behavior, design vehicles that target your product's market profile, and do all the other things necessary to find and exploit the niches.

I'm not sure the "mass market" ever really existed. The great prolifera-tion of products and choices have had a great fragmentation effect on the market. Remember Henry Ford's crack that customers could have any color they wanted as long as it was black. He could force it on people because they didn't have other choices. Now people have a variety of choices and can get what they really want instead of choking on what manufacturers decide to cram down customers' throats.

This whole micromarketing thing can get out of hand. In many cases, I agree it makes sense. In many other cases, it only seems to make sense. For example, take weekly business newspapers. Area business pubs have been hot in recent years because they make "logical" sense to media buyers. If you want to reach business people, advertise in business papers, right?

That argument helps sell advertising in local weeklies, but in reality many advertisers are better off using a mass medium like the metro daily to reach the local business readers. Editorially, business pubs get great response; in advertising, the response is often not so great. The economies of newspaper publishing are such that it doesn't really cost that much less to advertise in the business pub to reach 15,000 than in the daily to reach 500,000, including all those 15,000 and maybe another 75,000 prospects you didn't know were prospects. Certainly, on a CPM basis the business pub is 15 or 20 times more costly. My prediction: Mass marketing will make a comeback in the mid-1990s.

That's an interesting point. It dovetails with the bus and outdoor ads that our local weekly business paper is running. They show their logo with the slogan: "It's more important to reach the people who count than to count the people you reach." They're obviously concerned about the dailies taking away their base.

In the United States we haven't had "radio broadcasting" for years. We have radio narrowcasting. It's interesting for those of us in the radio biz to watch some people in other media as they go through the same change. It's also interesting to see that many of them don't realize that they are going through the same change.

In several key ways television is becoming "radio with pictures." Few people in television see it in those terms and, therefore, also don't see how to best program, promote, market and sell in a narrowcasting environment.

I'd like to test-drive a distinction between mass markets and mass marketing. It seems to me that there are still mass markets. We all shop at supermarkets, convenience stores, K-Marts, and so on. When we do, we are part of a mass market, and we are visiting mass market retail outlets. What's changed is the traditional ways of communicating with mass market participants. There are more men than ever wandering the supermarket aisles, but there is no way to target supermarket advertising to men (Does Campbell's Soup use football advertising?). So maybe what's dead are the traditional communication channels, rather than the market, or the need to perceive a mass market.

That was more than a year ago, before I began writing the manuscript itself. More recently, as I was nearing completion of this book, I went back to these sources to sample them again. To my surprise, I found considerably greater name recognition of databased marketing now and more animated discussions resulting from my queries. I cannot say, however, that the change was revolutionary or even that it reflected a greater understanding of the subject: It was fragmentary and still burdened with a great deal of confusion, as in the case of one individual who wanted to know just what databased marketing is, and how it is different from targeted marketing, if it is. One respondent remarked on the importance of database marketing as a means for cloning your best customers so as to improve the targeting of your markets. Another saw the rise of databased marketing as a serious threat to list brokers as direct marketers turn more and more to building their own marketing databases; thus a potential threat to the mailing-list business appears on the horizon.

It is quite apparent that we have no widely accepted definition of databased marketing: It has different meanings for different marketers, depending largely on individual circumstances and needs. We have, thus, a number of definitions, some in direct conflict with others, although there is agreement about a few key factors. In sum, many key questions are still unanswered:

Just what is this new idea, databased marketing? Is it a new gimmick? A fad? A buzzword? A new term for what we are already doing?

Or is it something else, something new, different, and important? As Kleid Company, Inc.'s CEO, Rose Harper, explained in her highly acclaimed and most insightful book, *Mailing List Strategies* (McGraw-Hill, 1986), whatever business you are in (or think you are in), you are nevertheless in the "customer business." *Customer business,* indeed! Important words. What is business if it is not about customers and what they want? How does databased marketing relate to that basic truth?

All marketing, including databased marketing, is about that business—about customers and prospective customers, as individuals, as groups, as the stuff of business. More specifically, however, databased marketing is about getting to know your customers and prospective customers better than you have ever known them before . . . if, indeed, you have ever known them at all before. Test yourself; try to answer the most basic questions: Who are your customers? Do you really know them . . . *who* they are and *what* they are . . . their personalities . . . their needs . . . their wants . . . their worries . . . their concerns . . . their ambitions . . . their dreams?

Businesspeople selling face-to-face get to know their customers, at least their regular ones. It's inevitable that they should get to know those buyers who are tried and true *customers* because they return to buy again and again. Such marketers learn their customers' names, faces, and favorite products and remember the names of customers' spouses and their children. They develop a relationship with many of their customers. They soon learn what to suggest to their regular customers—what, that is, are each customer's interests and what is most likely to appeal to the individual customer. For many businesses, regular customers are the backbone of their success; they could not survive by depending on their ability to generate new one-time buyers, to create a continually new customer base.

Those of us who sell by mail or through networks of distributors don't usually get to know our individual customers in this manner. We are insulated and isolated from them, and we get to know them only if and when we make a special effort to do so.

Until now it has been difficult to do this, to really *know* our customers, unless we operated small, neighborhood businesses. We have relied on our best estimates—guesstimates—of who and what our customers are. We have based our assumptions on stereotypes, statistical data, demographics, and other indirect indicators. And, in most cases, we have been right only 1, 2, or 3 percent of the time: We have had to solicit 1,000 prospects for every one, two, or three sales. If we needed 1,000 sales to meet expenses and turn even a modest profit, we have had to solicit sales from at least 300,000 prospects and be prepared to raise that to as many as 1 million prospects.

Marketers didn't make much of an effort to know their customers and prospective customers in the beginning. When the youngster,

Montgomery Ward, introduced the idea of mail order and the unconditional guarantee, he was probably launching what today is the multibillion dollar direct marketing (DM) industry. It developed quickly into a major, mass-marketing industry, mailing catalogs and other DM literature (e.g., the thick packets of sales literature of today's morning mail) by the millions. Profit resulted from the 1 or 2 percent response. Variability (e.g., profitability) of marketing with such a modest response was possible because postal costs were low, and shipping costs via U.S. mail and other means were also low.

Basing selling prices on that tiny fraction of marketing success (if such a response rate can be called a success in any sense of that word) imposes a not inconsiderable burden on the business: The profit on those few sales has had to carry that burden. With the rise in costs for labor, postage, printing, shipping, and other overhead, the strain has begun to become intolerable for a great many businesses, even the largest ones. It has become more and more difficult to support a business and turn a profit, however small, on such tiny percentages of response, so characteristic of traditional mass-marketing mail order and direct mail.

Some patches, such as charging a small fee for costly, multicolored catalogs, have been applied, but they are stopgaps: They do not address the real problem, which is one of increasing the marketing success ratio. The original shotgun approach—addressing the whole world with our solicitations, in the hopes of reaching that tiny fraction who will be interested in what we offer—has given way stubbornly and slowly, as we have refined our approach and tried to target prospects more accurately. Zip codes, for one, were a great help in sorting lists so we don't waste money offering deep-sea fishing boats to Nebraskans or snow boots to Floridians. Still, those of us who open those thick envelopes of advertising mail in the morning are often forced to smile at how completely inappropriate many of the offers are. We wonder where in the world did the offeror get the names when they offer stocks and bonds to people who are struggling to pay their rent or send a credit-card application to a small child who can't even read it.

Databased marketing is where the transition from shotgun marketing to targeted marketing stands today. Its immediate objective is to help you get to know who your customers are—what they want and why they buy what you sell. It can also help you keep your customers for the long term. The ultimate objective is, of course, to market more effectively and more efficiently in general . . . prepare materials and programs that are specific to those who are your "natural" customers . . . reduce the waste of pursuing those who are unlikely ever to be your customers . . . get to know what neglected niches in the market await you, so you can increase your sales success.

Proper marketing databases can bring this about. The trade press, especially that of direct marketing, has presented many articles on the subject in recent years, and a great many companies have invested time and money in building their own marketing databases. Yet I found a startling lack of knowledge about this among the rank and file of professional marketers and advertising specialists when I set out to do an informal investigation, even beyond that reported and commented on here already. In my early research for this book, I wrote to and talked to a great many mailing list managers and others in related services (e.g., DM newsletter publishers) asking for their thoughts on the subject. I received armloads of brochures and catalogs, but very little that pertained directly to databased marketing. (In fact, there was not much that pertained to it even indirectly, although the literature used the term freely enough.)

I signed on to advertising and marketing forums on CompuServe and elsewhere, and put out queries on databased marketing. I got a number of responses, all indicating that the respondent was not familiar with the idea. I also got a deafening silence from most, as far as discussing databased marketing was concerned.

Here and there I picked up another chain of thought. Just as the term *databased marketing* provoked from many people thoughts of niche markets, "micromarkets," abundance of choices, and the decline of mass markets, in other cases it provoked discussions of marketing databases, direct mail, and targeted marketing.

These latter three are different terms and perhaps differing views of what databased marketing is, and yet the many ideas converge on increased specialization in marketing; addressing smaller, more highly specialized and defined markets; more closely targeted markets. If there is any theme that runs through the idea, it is this.

It seems pretty obvious that most marketing and advertising professionals are not really "into" databased marketing yet, at least not consciously, although it seems to be the wave of the future in marketing. Perhaps what we are seeing is really not resistance to change as much as it is resistance to changing their views and what they call what they do, for they seem to understand the essential idea underlying the new term. Perhaps it is computer phobia, for databased marketing is more closely bound up with computers than are the predecessor marketing disciplines. There seems to be almost as much of that about as there is public-speaking phobia. In any case, this book represents my personal mission of shedding light on the subject. But a few words of clarification and reassurance are in order: For one thing, I intend this explanation, discussion, and how-to guide to databased marketing to be as nontechnical as possible. The real difficulty in learning to use computers is the arcane language used by too many nonwriters who write about computers and who have a driven need to include a wealth of detail that is bewildering and unnecessary for most of us to know. The concepts are truly not difficult to understand when they are presented in everyday English and technical details are reduced to the essential minimum.

I shall digress into technical language only when it is unavoidable, and I will be careful to explain the obscure terms I use, if any. I am fortunate enough to have long ago reached that stage where I can consider myself to be among the computer literate, if not the computer literati. I have a good layperson's understanding—that which a long-experienced computer user may be expected to have—and just enough grasp of the more technical aspects to make me wary of trying to appear to be more of an expert than I am.

That is fortunate for both of us. It spares us the trauma of struggling with such burdening and bewildering statements as ". . . each independent variable is multiplied by a weight (its coefficient) and then all the weighted variables are added to obtain a score or predicted value of the dependent variable," or of dealing with a few pages of mathematics to prove a point you (and, I sometimes suspect, possibly the author) didn't understand in the first place. (I always have misgivings about the understanding of any expert who is unable to explain the proposition in simple language.)

In any case, that is language and concept for computer scientists, not marketers, not even for computer-literate marketers, and this book is intended for marketers. We marketers may and probably will hire computer scientists to engineer our software—conceive, plan, and design our databases and other computer software—as we should: Computer technology is a complex technical subject. But the technicians are not the marketers, and we marketers must always make the decisions that affect our marketing, for example, *what* data we need in our marketing databases, and how we will use those data for our marketing. We cannot afford to be completely illiterate about computers and databases.

Perhaps you are already computer literate, or even highly knowledgeable in and experienced with computer use. In that case, you will probably be tempted to skim or even skip the earliest chapters, in which I discuss databases at the most lay level for those completely unfamiliar with computers. In later chapters I get down to somewhat more sophisticated discussions of marketing databases and databased marketing. I suggest, however, that even if you are most familiar with computers and databases and are not encountering databased marketing for the first time, it will be a good idea to spend the brief time necessary to suffer through these early discussions. In them you will learn the ground rules I observe in the chapters to follow, while I also offer my personal interpretations of what databased marketing really means. (I confess that I sometimes take issue with articles that appear in the press on the subject.) It will help you understand my rationales, even if it does not help me to persuade you to agree with them. In connection with that, I believe it is important that I offer a rationale of some sort for the views that I espouse in these pages.

As noted, definitions of databased marketing are quite broadly varied. That alone all but mandates that I decide, for my own purposes, what databased marketing is and what it is not. I can adopt one of those definitions I have discovered in my research, I can devise my own definition, or I can do neither. I have chosen to do neither. I think it is a mistake to adopt a firm definition, at least at this early stage, when all is still in flux. I think it is necessary to recognize here that there are many valid and legitimate definitions, with enough range to accommodate the marketing of all direct marketers, large and small.

One more point is in order: Theoretically, databased marketing is a philosophy that can be applied to virtually any and all kinds of marketing, retail and wholesale, or through brokerages and other means and modes. In fact, some large organizations who market in one or more of the foregoing manners are deeply involved in developing marketing databases. However, in this formative stage, databased marketing is most closely associated with direct marketing, and I will discuss it in these pages primarily in that framework.

HERMAN HOLTZ

Wheaton, Maryland
June 1992

Contents

List of Figures

Introduction to Databased Marketing

> Database marketing is much more than a corporate buzzword today.
> *Target Marketing,* May 1991

WHAT IS "DATABASE MARKETING?"

Despite the assurance of *Target Marketing* that *database marketing* is more than a buzzword in corporate offices, there is ample evidence that the term is being used glibly by many who either do not understand its significance or do not take it very seriously. They evidently do not see it or do not want to see it as the development of a serious new advance in the marketing technology of the information age that will in time make today's marketing methods obsolete. There is the typical resistance to change and equally typical fear of the unknown. Probably many perceive it as a threat to the established systems and industries of direct marketing, and perhaps especially to the stores of mailing lists; they therefore fear even to admit that it exists as a threat, much less to take a serious interest in it. Nevertheless, it does threaten these traditional practices and establishments with obsolescence, as the inevitable consequence of both advancing technology and changing market requirements.

Some of the resistance is due to true confusion, for it takes considerable study and fortitude to grasp the full meaning and significance of this new approach to marketing. Many tend to interpret it as a new term for enhanced mailing lists with greater than ever geographic, demographic, and psychographic enhancements. Such an interpretation is not entirely inaccurate, for databased marketing is that too. Still others, it seems clear, regard it as targeted marketing or perhaps even supertargeted marketing with a new and more impressive name. Whether it is or is not simply a buzzword for familiar marketing methods with a fresh coat of paint, however, the term has obviously caught on and is used increasingly in the direct marketing industry. It seems to fit best there, at least in this early stage of its arrival on the scene. It does not seem to have yet penetrated deeply into the trade literature and marketing consciousness of many other industries, although philosophically it has as much validity there as it does in the direct marketing arena. That seems logical enough: Although the concept must eventually appeal to all marketers as it proves its worth, initially it probably is a best fit to direct marketing, where its adaptation is almost a natural outgrowth of traditional systems and methods of direct marketing. (At least one writer who is also a well-known direct-marketing executive, Arthur M. Hughes, states plainly his conviction that databased marketing is a direct outgrowth of conventional direct marketing.) This apparent congruence with direct marketing becomes more and more apparent as we pursue studies of this new concept.

SOME GENERAL BACKGROUND: *WHY* DATABASED MARKETING?

The rise of databased marketing was probably inevitable. On the one hand, it is technology-based in an era of technology: Almost overnight, we have gone from an environment of manual typewriters, inkwells, and mechanical adding machines to one of computers, laser printers, fax machines, satellite communications, telemarketing, and telecommunications. How could these changes not be reflected ultimately in marketing? On the other hand, it is philosophically based in the growing consciousness that today's customer will no longer tolerate total indifference to his and her needs and wants. The business literature of recent years has increasingly explained and stressed the need of business firms to focus on the customer. ("Customer" also means *client, voter, patron, donor, subscriber,* and *prospect.*) Such best sellers of recent years as *Megatrends, In Search of Excellence,* and *Service America,* to name only three of many such books, have demonstrated the growing sensitivity of businesses to the needs of customers. How could we not recognize the need to become more attuned to the customer and prospective customer?

The general background is not difficult to understand. During the Great Depression of the 1930s, the customer became King or Queen. A seller did everything possible to satisfy every customer and encourage his or her return to buy again. Business survival was at best not easy when a full one third of the work force was idled and struggling to stay alive, living not day to day but meal to meal.

World War II changed that. The four-year hiatus in producing consumer goods and the postwar surge in demand for the gradually returning consumer goods (extended for many years as a result of the postwar baby boom) led to merchants' indifference to customer wants that survived until recent years. Now there is a surplus of goods and an abundance of places to buy, many of them discount stores. Now the baby boom is long over, and the demand has fallen sharply. The customer has become the monarch again, and those businesses that do not recognize this change and accommodate marketing to it are doomed to fail. Today's marketers must get acquainted with the customer again, learn who and what the customer is, and market *to* that customer, rather than to their own biases. That, in essence, is what databased marketing is about. But it means that this generation of marketers must be educated to understand the supremacy of the customer and their dependency on the customer.

In the meanwhile, we were developing mass marketing, elevating it to a superlative degree and creating major industries related to mass marketing. The technology helped us in this, making it relatively easy to appeal to millions of prospective customers simultaneously; mass marketing has also tended to be indifferent to the individual customer and to depend only on the numbers—probability statistics. That, too, is a decreasingly reliable approach to marketing. However, another factor has been the soaring cost increases in direct marketing: Postage, printing, and other costs related to mass marketing have made it increasingly difficult to turn a profit on a slender rate of response. It is necessary to raise the response rate, again a customer-oriented objective.

Thus databased marketing—although implemented by modern technology, primarily the computer and the many functions and facilities it makes possible for even the smallest marketing organization—is necessarily oriented to the customer. If any common factor or distinguishable characteristic identifies and defines databased marketing as a unique entity, it is that its sights are fixed firmly on the customer: getting acquainted with the customer, understanding the customer, and satisfying the customer's wants.

Aside from the philosophy, but not to demean it or deemphasize its importance, there is the technological array that must be understood and mastered, if databased marketing is to be a practical reality for you.

THE TECHNOLOGY OF DATABASED MARKETING

It is increasingly difficult to find anyone who has never encountered the term *database*. Perhaps most of those who toss the term about casually—it does roll off the tongue easily enough—do understand it fully. For those who do not, a brief explanation can only help.

We owe the popularity of the general term *database* to the computer industry, which introduced the term long ago, as mainframe digital computers (the large computers, with their false floors, air-conditioned rooms, and banks of servos with eternally spinning reels of tape) became commonplace in the business world, at least for those who could somehow afford these expensive behemoths. The word became known to virtually all of us, however, as the more recent computer explosion of the past decade placed personal computers on our own desktops: on some 28 million desktops in the United States alone, by one recent estimate. Soon enough, it was an incredibly tiny office that could not afford to replace its typewriter and mechanical calculator with a small desktop computer, originally identified as a "personal computer," and today referred to casually as a "PC." The earliest and still most popular application of the PC has been as a word processor, forcing millions of Selectrics into involuntary retirement. However, PC owners soon began to discover the database, a technology-era means for "indexing" names and addresses of all kinds, such as telephone lists, mailing lists, customer lists, and inventory lists, to name just a few of the possible uses; and that, too, has become a most popular use and reason for owning a PC.

The marketing concept known as *databased marketing* is an outgrowth of all these forces and influences.

The trade literature of the direct marketing world (e.g., *DM News, Target Marketing,* and *Direct Marketing*) and even a few other trade publications (e.g., *Telemarketing, Adult Learning, Industrial Marketing Management,* and *Progressive Grocer*) have published articles on the subject increasingly in recent years. In fact, *Target Marketing,* whose name is particularly appropriate for this new marketing concept, has for some time used the subhead under its title, "Dedicated to Database Marketing," and has recently amended that to read "The Leading Magazine for Integrated Database Marketing." (I confess that I am not sure I know just what that added qualifier, *integrated,* means here.) At least one broker of mailing lists has included the magic word *database* in its corporate title, calling itself "Database America," and using the term "DBA" (for Database America) in advertising "The DBA Consumer List" and "The DBA Business List."

There are those who evidently regard the marketing database as merely a superior mailing list with more than the usual amount of geographic, demographic, and psychographic information about those on the list. That is probably an understandable confusion because the business world has long revolved around direct marketing and mailing lists; the tendency is then to "understand" every new development in terms of the old and familiar. Moreover, for anyone completely new to the field of direct marketing, the route to understanding databased marketing does indeed require first some orientation to mailing list development and usage. Unfortunately, that background and orientation tends to dominate the definition and obscure the changes and new developments. In fact, even for those who understand direct marketing and mailing lists, a reasonably complete answer to the question "What is 'database marketing?'" is going to require more than a page or two. A definition that would cover all bases and reflect all existing expert opinions would add a great deal more confusion than enlightenment here. It is far better, I believe, to define the idea gradually, in steps. I therefore offer here an abridged definition, derived from several sources I deem to be highly respectable, and made as brief and introductory in nature as possible. I hope that it will serve as a groundbreaker:

> Databased marketing is marketing in which the approaches, strategies, methodologies, and other key marketing factors are founded on a great deal more information about each prospective buyer on the list than has normally been available in the past—based, that is, on a *consumer database* that has this wealth of information about the customer in it.

The implications of that generalized and simplified definition are many. One thing it does not stipulate—the omission is deliberate at this point—is that for the purists attempting to define databased marketing an absolute requirement is that at least some of the data about the customer come from the customer, that is there must be direct dialogue with the customer. But more on that will appear later.

WHAT IS A DATABASE?

The definition is only a partial one, as noted. It thus probably raises new questions, especially with those unfamiliar with the general idea underlying that which we call a *database,* even if the word itself is familiar. In fact, the word has two levels of meaning, one the nominal meaning, the other a much deeper meaning. That is true for many users, both those not familiar with computers and those only vaguely familiar with computers (i.e., not completely "computer literate"). Some sources assure readers that any collection of information that has a reason for being assembled together, for example, an ordinary reader file of correspondence or a list of telephone numbers, is a database. My on-line (*American Heritage*) dictionary makes two words of it ("data base") and goes a step further in defining it in a modern context as "a collection of data arranged for computer retrieval." Rose Harper, president and chief executive officer of The

Kleid Company, Inc., points out in her book, *Mailing List Strategies* (McGraw-Hill, 1986), the truism that almost any list can be considered a database, in general terms. Many list brokers today refer to their lists as databases, and author Harper points out the term *list database,* as one that refers to a collection of purged and merged lists (duplicates eliminated) having some common, unifying theme. She also points out, in connection with discussing the growing lively art of and interest in creating consumer databases, the relatively new field of "psychographics" (the book was a 1986 release), which enriches a list database with information about the personal interests of those whose names and addresses are listed. Facts about the buying habits of those on the list further enhance the database. These kinds of information add greatly to the usefulness of any database as a marketing resource.

Philosophically, that is one aspect of what databased marketing is about: knowing enough about prospects (remember that even old, established customers are prospects for every *new* marketing campaign) to target them more precisely than ever before. However, there is an important caveat here, and it concerns the enrichment of a list database "with information about the personal interests of those whose names and addresses are listed." The quoted phrase has a new and vastly different meaning when applied in the context of (i.e., with reference to) a marketing database than when used to refer to the classic mailing lists of the past. In prior usage, that phrase would mean the general interests shared by all those whose names and addresses are on the list, factors that characterize the list itself, as well as *all* the people whose names and addresses are listed. They might all, for example, belong to country clubs. But to which country club does each belong? Which ones are golfers? Which are swimmers? Which are handball players? Which are weight lifters and bodybuilders? Which use the club's facilities for parties? Which bring guests frequently? Which never bring guests? Which use the sports facilities? Which use the gym and bodybuilding facilities? Which dine at their clubs regularly? Which fancy seafood? Which prefer steaks? Which appreciate and order vintage wines? Which whiskies and brandies?

There is almost an infinity of questions to which you might seek answers that would greatly enhance the success of a country club in increasing the revenue of members and in attracting new members. Of course, for the seller of sporting goods and sporting facilities, separate lists of golfers, swimmers, handball players, weight lifters, and others can be a valuable marketing resource too.

In the classic mailing list you do not get specific information about each individual on the list; what is true for one is true for all. They are all bank presidents, all World War II veterans, all retired executives, all suburban dwellers, and so on. In a marketing database you do have individual information, and you can break the list down in that manner, for example, break out separate lists of golfers, swimmers, and party givers who happen also to be bank presidents, World War II veterans, or retired executives. That is at the root of the marketing database, the 20/20 insight into the interests of those whose names and addresses are listed, and it has many implications that we shall explore.

All of this demonstrates how broad and inexact the bare term *database* really is. It will undoubtedly continue to take on new and expanded meanings as time goes on and further work is done to make use of computer capabilities in creating and improving databases of all kinds, especially those adapted to use in marketing.

There is thus more, much more, to be said on the subject of databases generally, before exploring further the concept of the database as a marketing tool. *Database* is one of the most frequently used terms connected directly and indirectly with computers. It is also the subject of a great many kinds of computer software programs that you ought to know about. We will have to take that up in these pages too, and we shall do so. But before leaving the subject for now, it is worth stressing again that the expression is not defined in absolute terms, but only in general terms as a collection of data. Databases vary widely in their sizes, in the kinds of data they include, in the manipulations they can perform, in their completeness, and in their ancillary features: Many include editors and word processors, report writers, and sundry other features that are actually ancillary programs or subprograms. These are arbitrary measures, however: There is almost an infinity of answers to related questions: How big or how complete must a collection of data be to qualify as a database in general or, especially, as a "consumer database"? What kinds of information should a database include? How complete must the information be?

These questions never have absolute answers, except with relation to the application you wish to make of a database. You will discover, as we explore the subject, that computer software for creating, managing, and using databases are usually designed accordingly: They tend to be more general-purpose programs than specialized programs so that you may use them as you wish, designing your own databases to suit your own needs. In fact, if we are to be quite clear, we must establish definitions, at least for purposes of this book. The unadorned term *database* will not suffice in most cases; we must attach to it an adjective to qualify it for each case. Otherwise, we are not going to get anywhere here.

Unfortunately, it is most difficult to establish a brief definition of each *kind* of database, at least at this point. We will have to have brief discussions of each kind of database, referring primarily to the uses to which the database may be put, and how one relates to another. We have already discussed the general nature of that which we call a database and even referred briefly to uses. Obviously, since any collection of data can be called a database, the unmodified term is too broad to be of much use. It is necessary to use an adjective to qualify the word, if it is to be meaningful for practical purposes.

CONSUMER AND MARKETING DATABASES

Even from the little that has been written here already it should be clear that the general nature of a marketing database requires that it include personal information about all names on the list, even if only by subgroups. For example, a database of 10,000 names may be broken down into several smaller lists, identifying each as a subgroup of special characteristics—coin collectors, health food faddists, TV addicts, individuals motivated by low prices, and numerous others. Ideally, each individual would be profiled by his or her personal traits, and databased marketing zealots project that as a goal. It is possible to achieve that goal, but it would be expensive and probably serve no useful purpose. What we really want to do is learn the special characteristics, tastes, and interests that make an individual an especially well-qualified prospect for our offer, and then group together all those to whom we can assign that characteristic. In effect, we then have a set of niche markets, their number usually in some direct proportion to the amount of information we have collected about the individuals on the list: Each time we add information about certain individuals we tend to identify still another subgroup. Given that each person is unique, ultimately, at least in theory, we shall have made each individual listed a niche market! That is getting ahead of our story, however. We will return to that idea later.

If a marketing database is one that identifies special characteristics of a subgroup as indicative of how best to sell those in the subgroup our product or service, what is the main group (i.e., database) of which it is a part? That is, if a list of 10,000 names in a database can be broken down into a half-dozen subgroups, each of which is a market in itself, what is the defining name of the whole list of 10,000? That is a question never answered specifically in relevant literature, but for our purposes here we will define that total list by calling it a *consumer database*. The half-dozen lists of subgroups (niche markets) are *marketing databases*. We shall use those definitions throughout these pages. One thing, however, is an inevitable consequence of the definitions just established: First you develop the consumer database, that unstratified, undifferentiated list of people and facts about them, and

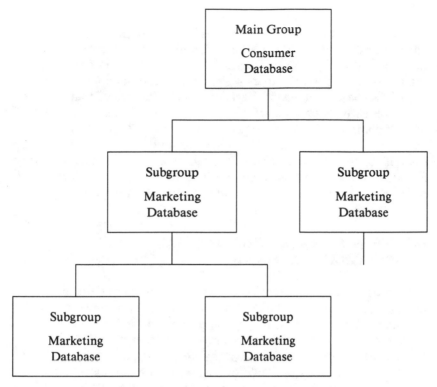

Figure I-1. Multilevel niche market development.

then you develop the marketing databases, deriving them from the consumer database as the growing information store itself differentiates each subgroup from the rest of the list. Inevitably some of the subgroups will split into additional subgroups, however, as illustrated in Figure I-1. How significant that will be depends on the uses for which the marketing databases are intended.

DATABASE OR DATABASED MARKETING?

Those in the direct mail industry and others writing about that industry refer more and more often to "database marketing." When I developed an interest in the subject and began to explore it with a few people, I found myself having difficulties immediately. I was compelled to explain the term itself, since it misled others in the meaning it suggested. When I mentioned that term to anyone, the other assumed that I was referring to the marketing of databases. That is a quite logical misunderstanding (especially for those familiar with computers and related matters): That is what "database marketing" appears to mean, just as "automobile marketing" and "clothes marketing" mean the marketing of those products. In fact—and I was compelled to explain this carefully to others—we are not talking about the marketing *of* databases but about marketing *with* databases, that is, using databases as an essential marketing tool. Therefore, it is in the interests of clear communication, not pedantry, that in these pages I will use the term "databased marketing," utilizing the adjective *databased,* rather than the noun, *database.* (I hope that others will perceive the necessity for this clarification and adopt the use of the adjective *databased,* rather than the noun *database,* to modify the noun *marketing.*)

WHERE WILL MARKETING DATABASES COME FROM?

One thing already apparent is that you cannot today rent marketing databases as you might rent mailing lists. Perhaps one day they may be available off the shelf: It may become feasible for list brokers to develop such marketing databases for rental, or marketing database owners who have developed their own marketing databases may see fit to make their databases available to list managers as they now do with their mailing lists. However, clearly the time is not yet. What is clear is that if you want to gain the advantages of marketing databases today, you will have to build your own, and it is not an easy or inexpensive task. The *Target Marketing* comment about databased marketing as a buzzword, quoted here earlier, was explained in follow-up reporting on a Donnelley Marketing survey revealing that more than one half of 65 marketing executives polled in the United States are building consumer databases, with another quarter of those executives reporting plans to do likewise. Marketing usages and planned usages of the databases were reported as follows:

Usage	Percentage
Prospecting	72
Co-op mailing	72
Testing promotions	66
Product and brand customer profiles	32
Rental of files	17
Planning advertising	15

Since these percentages add up to 274 percent, obviously most of those reporting must be making or planning to make multiple uses

of their databases. If that 75 + percent of those surveyed are representative of marketing executives generally, databased marketing is almost
a revolutionary trend. And yet, the magazine that claims preeminence
in and dedicates itself to covering databased marketing as its special
focus sees the need to assure readers that the term is more than a buzzword. They are quite right to do this: In many respects there is more
smoke than fire surrounding databased marketing, at least partly because it is a marketing methodology of great promise but still in its
infancy. Relatively few people, even those tossing the term off casually,
are truly knowledgeable and/or ready to take the first steps to implement the concept. Assuredly, there is much yet to be done to make
databased marketing a widespread reality.

Despite protestations that "database marketing is an established
practice" ("Consumer Goods Databases," *DM News,* July 30, 1990),
there is ample evidence that databased marketing is still not much advanced beyond the fetus stage or, at best, that of an innocent infant. One
instance of such evidence is the reporting coverage given each new DB
marketing initiative: Almost any item concerning databased marketing
is news, often front-page news. A recent headline in *DM News,* for example, announces that Levi Strauss & Co. is collecting data that suggests
their entry into DB marketing. (I would like to be able to refer to databased marketing as "DBM," but that term is already in wide use as a
term that refers to database management software, i.e., the management of databases through computer programs designed for the purpose.) Another is a captioned story in the same journal about Calgon
and their "database promo." There appears also to be a sense that there
is value in the presumed appeal of the word *database* wherever and
whenever possible, as evidenced by that already noted tendency of list
brokers to refer to their collections as databases. Technically, they are
correct and justified in identifying as databases their files of names and
addresses, with accompanying demographic and, in some cases, psychographic notations. But are these marketing databases or consumer
databases in the sense of this new marketing concept? That is a question
not easily answered in a marketing trend not yet matured. Yet, it
is worth noting here that some of those who support the DM industry
with services and products are well aware that there is going to be a
growing demand for marketing databases, and that many, especially the
smaller marketers, are going to need help to build their own marketing
databases.

RELEVANT SERVICES

The large organizations can and will—actually, *do*—develope
their own consumer and marketing databases with in-house staff,

although even they may need the assistance of consultant specialists; the smaller firms usually depend heavily on expert help from outside sources. It may be a bit early for predictions, but a market for relevant services seems almost certain to develop as the use of databased marketing grows. That will, of course, inspire a sharp growth in the number and kinds of services supporting marketers who wish to take advantage of this new technology. Already there are a few marketing consultants who offer a variety of useful services in building marketing databases. One such firm is Jami Data Services, of Pearl River, New York. This firm offers a variety of services, including what they call a "marketing analysis system," through which you can develop a customer profile, an essential ingredient of databased marketing. There are also some smaller, independent practitioners who can help you get started. We will peek in on these, as we proceed.

The training needed will include services to help you and your staff understand just what this technology is and how it is to be used, but you will also require specific help in the development of consumer databases and, from those, marketing databases. To date, what is or will be available to help you develop your own marketing databases is not well defined, and there is as yet only a small community of those offering services that support databased marketing directly. There are computer consultants who are ready, willing, and able to provide custom programming, help you select the best hardware and software for your needs, and train you in using the hardware and software. However, you probably really need the assistance of computer and/or marketing consultants who are well qualified in this newest field per se, and you may be hurt more than you are helped by consultants not schooled especially in this field. It is important, therefore, to check the credentials, regarding this consideration, of any specialists you contemplate using. Do inquire as to relevant experience, and ask for references you can call for verification.

OTHER MODERN DEVELOPMENTS

Not directly related to databased marketing, but concomitant with its development, is increasing diversification in related activities. List brokers, for example, are becoming more and more aware that personal computers, now almost as ubiquitous as typewriters, can be used as a more convenient and much faster medium than the mail for serving their customers. Yesterday, if you wanted to rent a mailing list or two, you called or wrote the list broker and discussed your need. He or she probably offered you some recommendations and sent you a catalog. You studied the catalog and ordered the lists you thought appropriate. Eventually, a week or two later, you got the lists and prepared your mail-out.

You don't have to do that now: You can order and have your lists available the day you order them: Today, using your PC with an inexpensive device called a *modem* and a dial-up telephone connection, you can be connected directly to the list broker's computer. Once connected, you can survey the list broker's files, specify what you want, choose appropriate mailing lists, and copy them from the list broker's computer to your own PC in a few minutes. (An example of this will be described and illustrated in Chapter 4.)

There are variants on that approach: At least one list broker, Ed Burnett Consultants, of Englewood, New Jersey, furnishes lists on diskettes, along with free software for using the lists to create labels or other suitable applications. (The disk is labeled "Pagex Systems, Inc. Direct Response Data Processing.") The disks will be mailed to you, and you can then use the lists to prepare labels, do a merge-mail, or accomplish other tasks.

DESKTOP MARKETING

In a broader view of what the PC—personal computer—has brought about, some individuals now refer to "desktop marketing." This embraces databased marketing as part of a wider view of marketing with the PC and the swiftly growing library of software programs that are making it a powerful marketing aid. The PC can be used not only to create and use consumer databases, but also to analyze data, perform research, carry out tests, make and monitor mailings, prepare reports, and otherwise support marketing in each of its phases—preparatory, execution, and follow up. One of the more interesting developments of PC applications to marketing is using your PC to "download" mailing lists, that is, to transfer the lists from a host computer operated by the list broker to your own computer over dial-up telephone lines and modems, which are devices that enable computers to "talk" to each other via telephone connections. The ONLINE Information Network of Omaha, Nebraska, for example, invites you to make their database your own database resource by subscribing to their service: "Imagine being able to retrieve mailing lists and marketing information instantly, 24 hours a day, right from your office," says their brochure, and lists two plans for using the service. You can dial their computer, scan the lists they offer, and download what you want on either of their plans. (This service is illustrated in Chapter 4.) This idea appears to be gaining more and more popularity and is likely to be offered on a widespread basis, perhaps even universally, in the future. The lists you download will now be stored in your own computer, and you can then use them to make labels, address envelopes, supply them to your mailing house, or use them in whatever way is most practicable for you.

Chapter 1

Is Mass Marketing Dead?

Rising costs are as much a business and marketing problem as they are a personal problem for everyone. They tend to make the waste inherent in traditional mass marketing intolerable, but there is also a declining effectiveness in some kinds of marketing. It is time for change, necessary change, and the technology for change is readily available and near at hand. We call it databased marketing.

A NECESSARY PRELIMINARY

What we are about to discuss might appear to be a non sequitur, something unrelated to the main subject of this book, which is the what-is-it and how-to-do-it of databased marketing. However, it will become apparent as we proceed that to understand the significance of databased marketing, it is necessary to have a clear grasp of the economics and management of marketing generally, and especially of the many challenges and problems of marketing in general and marketing in that special mode known as *direct marketing.* It is also necessary to perceive these in the light of mass marketing, if we are to illuminate how and why databased marketing is relevant and has become an almost inevitable outcome of mass marketing in the modern world. Therefore, I ask you to bear with me through a primer on marketing essentials, defining the obvious, perhaps, but nevertheless providing an essential basis for the discussions and explanations to follow in these pages.

COSTS VERSUS MARKUPS

The most basic and most necessary function of business, any business, is marketing. Without it, there are no customers, which means that there simply is no business. Business management/marketing guru Peter Drucker would defend that thesis in more eloquent terms than I can muster, but I think the argument to be a self-evident fact. And in marketing, stripped to a simple principle, the basis for success and failure is cost versus markup—cost of sales, including selling cost, for each order versus markup, or gross profit, on each order. Executive management of a business organization is nominally responsible for "cost of sales"—for buying well and managing other costs (e.g., overhead) so as to be able to set prices that meet competition and yet allow enough markup to cover all those costs and leave something over as a profit. Adequate markup is not an independent factor, but is linked closely with sales volume: Marketing management must produce sales in large enough numbers and at a small enough cost per order to cover all the fixed costs and provide a reasonable profit. It is obviously not easy to separate the responsibilities; they are closely intermingled and certainly interdependent, although also conflicting. High markup, in general, increases the margin of profit per unit of sale, thus tending to reduce the risk but also the sales volume; low markup has the opposite results, tending to increase sales persuasiveness and thus sales volume, but increasing risk. Successful business practice requires the effective balancing of these and other conflicting factors.

Cost of Sales versus Selling Costs

Selling costs and "cost of sales" are not the same thing. Selling costs are the direct costs of winning the sale, actually getting the order, while cost of sales is an accountant's term and includes a number of different costs necessary directly and indirectly to the sale. It includes the acquisition cost of the item you sell, fulfillment, overhead, *and* selling cost. Markup is the difference between what you paid for the item and what you charge the customer for it, your selling price. It represents *gross* profit, and it must be enough to cover all the costs and provide a *net* profit if the business is to succeed and survive.

Unit Selling Costs

Selling costs are the direct costs of winning the sales, the marketing costs for getting the orders. You can easily determine the gross selling costs, what the campaign costs you; but can you determine the unit cost, what each sale costs you? Do you know or must you guess? Would it not be helpful to know, as a means of determining how effective your marketing is?

Direct marketing offers advantages in trying to determine accurately the unit cost of winning sales, the cost per order. In other, more general marketing operations, it is almost impossibly difficult to establish unit costs with any great accuracy. It is easy enough to establish an average figure on the broad basis of number of sales made versus the total marketing cost. You can determine the total cost of what you are spending for advertising, samples, contests, exhibitions at trade fairs, and other public relations (PR) and selling efforts, and divide the grand total of those marketing costs by the total number of sales. That will give you a nominal unit cost. Unfortunately, the unit cost is not definitive because it does not enable you to pin down the true selling costs, the direct selling costs that actually produced the order. That is, you can't stratify total selling costs so as to determine what each of the various dollars you spent actually contributed directly to making the sale. Typically, the marketing costs have been spread broadly across a spectrum of advertising, sales campaigns, PR, and other promotional and sales activity. Some of those initiatives were effective; others were not. Some were aimed directly at winning sales; others were aimed only at image building. Therefore, how can you then calculate the true cost of finding each prospect and/or making each sale? That is the meaning of that possibly apocryphal statement credited to the great merchant, John Wanamaker, who was alleged to have said that he knew that one half of his advertising dollar was wasted, but he didn't know which half it was. In fact, it may well have been a great deal more than one half of his advertising dollar that was wasted. A great deal of advertising and promotional costs are sheer waste as far as producing orders, directly or indirectly, is concerned. For one thing, far too many copywriters and their agencies are more concerned with winning Clio awards (advertising industry peer awards for alleged art, creativity, cleverness, and other such factors in advertising) for themselves than in winning orders for clients. There are many well-known examples of award-winning campaigns that were canceled by the clients because the campaigns failed miserably to produce sales. (One advertising agency head is reported to have felt so strongly about this problem that he threatened to fire any copywriter who ever won a Clio award while in the employ of his agency.) There is also a great deal of "institutional advertising" by large corporations, the objective of which is general image building, rather than the winning of orders.

None of this is to say that institutional advertising does not have value or that organizations do not get marketing benefits from developing the right images with the buying public. These are worthy efforts, and they can be justified as useful marketing activities. At the same time, it is not necessary to lump these costs with those directed at winning orders and making sales. The major problem is the great difficulty in learning the real cost of winning orders in most kinds of marketing, or the inverse, measuring the effectiveness of each element and each marketing expenditure in producing orders.

MARKETING IS NOT ALWAYS IN DIRECT PURSUIT OF ORDERS

Institutional advertising is only one example of advertising that is not aimed directly at getting orders or winning sales, at least in the conventional sense of "sales." It is often necessary to advertise with other objectives than pulling in orders as a direct result of the advertising. There is, for one, the complicating factor that many businesses are not "one call" businesses. That is, they are businesses selling "big-tag" items, which are virtually never sold with a single, initial presentation. Automobiles, homes, large boats, building lots, and major appliances are some of the big-tag items usually sold to consumers only after more than one presentation. All kinds of contracts for construction, large capital equipment, furniture, and fixtures, as well as many items of inventory, are big-tag items sold to businesses and other organizations, also with the constraint that they are rarely sold on a one-call basis.

Selling such items normally requires at least a two-step process, the first step of which is prospecting for good sales leads. Such sales are generally won only after more than one sales presentation, and often only after an entire series of presentations. Thus, the real objective of all initial marketing promotions in these businesses is the pursuit of prospects—sales leads—rather than sales per se. And so a "sale" is not necessarily an order; it may be simply an inquiry or some evidence of interest and/or of the capability for becoming a customer. That is, "response," "sale," or "order" are not necessarily synonymous terms in marketing. In the case of big-tag sales, rate of response is probably the most meaningful measure of marketing effectiveness. (In fact, for many types of marketing, such as sales messages in radio, TV, billboards, and print media, it is probably the *only* available measure that truly reflects the value received for the marketing cost.)

The actual cost of winning each individual order in these kinds of businesses involves the cost of great sales effort—often multiple follow-ups and presentations—and so represents a relatively large marketing cost. It is easy to waste a great deal of time and money by pursuing individuals who are not true prospects, who are either not really interested in what you are selling or do not have the money (or the authority, in the case of many business-to-business sales) actually to place the order. To avoid excessive waste of marketing effort and expense in pursuing such nonprospects, in big-tag sales we are well advised to work at qualifying prospects. That means determining whether the great effort to close a sale is justified—*how good* a prospect is or, conversely, how likely it is that you are wasting your time in pursuing any given prospect. Most marketing people thus recognize the need to qualify prospects—to verify that they are true prospects and worth the expense of the sales effort—in pursuing such sales. Traditionally, prospecting and qualifying prospects have been confined to big-tag sales that require a series of sales initiatives. In today's high-cost, high-waste environment, we do or should try to qualify prospects in all kinds of marketing campaigns, even for one-call businesses.

PROSPECTING FOR ONE-CALL SALES

The notion of prospecting, much less qualifying prospects, for one-call sales, such as a magazine subscription or bottle of vitamins, may come as something of a shock to those already steeped in traditional marketing processes. An immediate reaction might be: How can I afford to spend time and money pursuing prospective subscribers to my newsletter? I would answer that by asking: How can you afford *not* to spend time and money prospecting for *any* order in *any* business today? I think that is a very fair question in this final decade of the 20th century.

The fact is that when (and if) you plan and carry out marketing activities of any kind, you are prospecting and even qualifying prospects if your marketing has been thoughtfully and methodically planned. Although you may not consciously think of it as such, you are really prospecting when you advertise, choose a mailing list, or mail out sales letters. In fact, you are trying to qualify prospects when you select a mailing list or choose a given radio station on the basis of demographics claimed: You are trying to determine which are the best prospects— which lists are worth mailing to, as the names and addresses of good, qualified prospects, and which radio listeners are likely to be the best prospects for what you sell.

Thus one of the great advantages of direct marketing is the capability it furnishes us to identify the direct, unit costs of prospecting and the direct, unit cost of acquiring each prospect and making each sale: In direct marketing (DM), you gain prospects and/or customers as a direct result of some single action, such as inquiry advertising or a mailing campaign. That enables you to link cause and effect directly. If mailing to 100,000 prospects costs you $100,000, your direct unit cost for prospecting is $1 per prospect. If you get 10,000 orders (you should be so lucky!), your unit selling cost is $10 per order. (This admittedly does not take into account the possibility of bounceback and other back-end benefits of creating customers, but counts only direct and immediate responses.) And if your campaign was in pursuit of qualified prospects, rather than orders, and brought in 20,000 inquiries, your cost per *sales lead* (that is what 20,000 of your 100,000 prospects have become) is $5 per response or lead.

In summary, you are always prospecting when you launch any marketing program or campaign. You may be prospecting for sales directly or you may be prospecting for sales leads, but every such effort, even when directed to old, established customers, is a prospecting initiative, and results can be measured in those terms.

Even so, there are still areas of uncertainty. You may assume that the success or failure of your direct marketing campaign is due or dependent on the "quality" of the mailing list you used. There is a great tendency to suspect the "quality" of the mailing list when a campaign is less effective than was hoped for, and list brokers are happy to encourage that suspicion. ("Quality" here may refer only to how appropriate the list was for your needs, rather than to any inherent characteristic of the list.) That, however, is by no means certain: The "quality" of your copy and even some less tangible or unpredictable factors may be the major influences in the results achieved.

We usually rely on testing to help us identify cause-and-effect relationships, to measure the effectiveness of the list and/or any other factor that is likely to be important in producing the result. But until now we are or have been confined to a few major considerations in our testing. We can test the list, the offer, the price, the persuasiveness of the copy, or even the season of the year, but not a great deal more, other than a demographic factor or two. Until now . . . until we turn to databased marketing. That is, until now, prospecting has depended on indirect information of questionable value for prospecting and even less value for qualifying prospects: It has depended on rough groupings, on demographics, on psychographics, and on our personal best estimates or guesstimates of how these apply to our own needs. Testing, in this approach, is almost purely empirical: We just cut and try, hoping to stumble on success, perhaps through serendipity, perhaps through pure chance—Dame Fortune. Success has long depended on mass marketing, and that meant simply "playing the numbers," trusting that statistical probability would pay off in enough hits to compensate for the usual 95 to 99.9 percent misses. In retrospect, that is a rather dismal way of doing business, is it not? What other human activity is deemed of acceptable quality with such a tiny rate of return? Surely, in an age where men have walked on the moon, where people fly halfway around the world for a weekend, where people thousands of miles apart talk to and view each other instantaneously, there must be a better way! That is another way of defining databased marketing: It is a search for a different and better way.

Costs versus Response Rates

Despite the advantage of being able to link cause and effect with some degree of certainty in traditional direct marketing, even in this milieu . you cannot usually say with any real assurance of accuracy just why certain individuals were good prospects and why certain of those prospects became customers, while others did not. You can test, of course, as noted, and you will. You will then get a certain amount of insight as to how much price, promised benefit, and other factors had to do with getting or not getting good results, but you find that even these are only rough benchmarks and "good" is very much a relative term: It is "good" only when compared with "bad," or it is "good" only when compared with last week, last month, or last year. It is not "good" as compared with the theoretically possible because we never make that evaluation. That aside, however, by what yardstick do we measure "good" and "bad?"

The direct mail industry has long tended to use that factor called *response rate* as a measure of effectiveness and efficiency of mailings. It is a useful measure in some respects, as noted earlier, and yet it is of limited utility at best, unfortunately, despite the tendency to judge results in terms of response percentages—the percentage of addressees who responded with orders, inquiries, or whatever you asked of them. In fact, we usually do not know what the response rate really means, as far as its possible use as a figure of merit. Does a 2 percent response translate into a good list? Why not an 8 percent response? Or a 15 percent response? Perhaps 2 percent or 4 percent, or even 5 percent, are really not good response rates at all, even if the campaign was profitable. How do we judge these things, other than by the black-and-white standard of profit and loss?

Actually, there is no such thing as a typical, standard, average, good, or poor response rate, despite our best efforts to establish de facto standards. What is "good" (i.e., profitable) in one case is "poor" (i.e, unprofitable) in another case, as long as profitability is the ultimate gauge. Even that is by no means fixed, however: In many ways it makes more sense to use other measures of profitability than yes or no. There is the margin of profit, return on investment, return on equity, and even other measures that are more sophisticated and more meaningful in many ways than sheer profit and loss. All can be used to reveal and reflect a satisfactory or unsatisfactory final result, without regard to response rates. There is even a measure that may reflect a successful campaign regardless of dollar considerations. It reflects a factor of potential profit called "LTV," for *lifetime value,* of a customer. (That is the subject of Chapter 11, which discusses direct marketing economics.) Still, for comparative purposes, to measure progress or the lack of it, response rates furnish at least some kind of yardstick. (They are probably the only meaningful measure available when the goal of the campaign is prospecting to develop sales leads.) Thus it makes sense to pursue basic explorations of the subject in response terms.

A Note on Testing

Theoretically at least, you can test repeatedly and so get an excellent insight into a given prospect list. Eventually, you will know precisely what is good and bad—satisfactory and unsatisfactory—in the results the list produces and what is good and bad about your offering. Practically, however, there is a limit to how much testing you can do before it becomes uneconomical. Ultimately, you may achieve a Pyrrhic victory: You will have the information and you may maximize response, but you will lose money in a "successful" campaign because the investment in testing and related costs has become too big a cost burden to overcome. Testing is important and must be done, but economics is inevitably a practical constraint that limits testing. It must not be pursued to a point where it threatens success.

DIRECT MARKETING ECONOMICS

The basic economics of direct marketing is simple enough: If your markup on the item you are selling is $10, you can hardly afford to spend $10 to get the order. (Admittedly, there are exceptions, as where the objective is to develop sales leads or to create new customers for future profits, rather than for immediate profits—i.e., when the campaign is itself part of the marketing cost—but for now let us ignore these exceptions.) The selling cost is dependent on the unit cost of reaching prospective buyers, as well as your effectiveness in converting prospects to buyers. If it costs you $0.20 to reach each prospective buyer and you persuade only 2 percent of these prospects to send you orders, your unit cost is $10 for each order. A 1 percent increase in response cuts your cost-per-sale figure to $6.66, leaving you a $3.33 gross profit to cover fulfillment costs and net profit. That, unfortunately, is probably still slender enough a gross profit to be marginal at best. But how easy is it to increase that response rate by even 1 percent? Not easy at all: Direct marketers and the DM industry generally spend a great deal of money every year trying to find means to increase that response rate by as little as fractions of 1 percent. It is a considerable factor when you are mailing millions of pieces each year, although it is small comfort to the smaller marketer, mailing only a few thousand pieces each month.

Whether you do or do not know precisely what your unit costs are, you know that it has been becoming increasingly difficult to keep the unit cost of reaching prospects down to a point where the unit costs of winning orders is low enough to enable you to turn a reasonable profit. The overall costs of marketing generally include advertising, salaries, commissions, bonuses, discounts, printing, postage, displays, conventions and trade shows, contests, and perhaps a few other items, depending on the nature of the business and how it is marketed. In winning prospects and orders in DM, for example, the principal direct costs are usually postage, printing, and advertising. All have risen steadily, often at a far greater pace than increases in prices generally and increases in profitability. Postage costs, for example, have tended to leap upward in increments as large as 16 percent, the most recent percentage rise of a first-class postage stamp, and have more than doubled in the past decade. Printing costs have also more than doubled in the past 10 years, and advertising costs generally have soared even beyond that. Direct marketing costs overall have probably more than doubled during the same period, while selling prices and markups for many items have declined.

OTHER TROUBLING FACTORS

While rates for most advertising media generally have been rising, the effectiveness of some advertising media has declined, further increasing actual cost. A prime example is broadcast TV with its advertising, which has lost much of its audience through the rapid growth of cable and the VCR. Millions of viewers now watch rented movie cassettes instead of broadcast programs, while millions of others tape their favorite programs for later viewing, during which they fast-forward through the commercials. We can only guess at how many viewers sit through, much less actually watch, commercials. Radio advertising primarily reaches people in their automobiles, because relatively few people listen to radio broadcasts at home today, further reducing the influence of this advertising medium, already weakened by broadcast TV, VCRs, cable, and stereo sound systems.

The print media have not been spared, either. Circulation figures are not always accurate indicators of readership, but that is only one factor. The moribund condition of a huge portion of the nation's newspapers and the expiration of many is not news, of course, and so print advertising in newspapers is something of a gamble: The newspaper may be losing circulation steadily, exposing your advertising to a declining number of prospects. In fact, the newspaper may expire before fulfilling the advertising contract you have with it, totally wiping out your advertising.

Many other periodicals are in a similar position. The newsstands offer a wide array of general-interest magazines and tabloids, and there are many trade periodicals that are distributed almost entirely by mail, but the attrition rate among all periodicals is a large one: Periodicals come and go regularly. Many advertisers have depended on and benefited from the cumulative effect of long-running advertisements in the same media and in the same positions: Many advertisements became classics, well-known and even famous after running successfully for many years without change. (Examples: "Do You Make These Mistakes in English" and "They Laughed When I Sat Down at the Piano. . . .") It is increasingly difficult to depend on any but the oldest, most well-established periodicals to achieve that long-term effect today, when even some of the "old timer" periodicals have succumbed to the combined blows of inflation, TV, and video toys.

In the meanwhile, more and more of the public have become educated in DM to the extent that they can spot advertising mail for what it is and discard it without opening the envelope, especially when the teaser copy on the envelope exterior makes it immediately clear to the addressee that the content will definitely not be of direct interest to him or her.

You can verify this easily: Visit your local post office and watch unopened mail being dropped into the trash bins by box holders who deliberately scan their mail there to weed out and discard solicitations and other advertising matter that do not relate to their wants and concerns. (Again, the need to address well-qualified prospects, even in direct mail campaigns.)

The result of these several influences has been a steady increase in the cost of reaching each prospect, with a corresponding increase in the cost of making each sale. But other influences are also at work, adding further to the modern marketing problem. One is the steady increase in the numbers of outlet stores and other avenues of discount sales, further increasing the price competition and driving down profit margins. Marketers thus find themselves squeezed from both directions: The unit costs of both prospecting and closing sales continue to rise, while the margin of profit on each sale continues to grow more slender, increasing the pressure to step up sales volume and find less expensive ways to market effectively.

Perhaps you cannot do a great deal directly to combat the price competition that drives down prices and, with it, markup, other than somehow to improve your buying, which will result in better markup without loss of price competitiveness. But there is something that can be done today about the unit cost of prospecting and finding buyers, that critically important cost per order. Mass marketing in the past has been done by broadcasting appeals to find prospects and create customers from the public at large. The inherent wastefulness of mass marketing was acceptable because unit costs were low enough. Print advertising (e.g., newspaper or magazine) and broadcast advertising (radio and TV) may reach millions of readers, listeners, and viewers, but only a relative handful will be true prospects. If, for example, you advertise a diet program, only those readers, listeners, and viewers with an interest in dieting are true prospects. If they represent even as many as 50 percent of the readers, listeners, and viewers, 50 percent of the cost of that advertising is wasted. The nominal cost claimed by the publisher or broadcaster may be 10 cents per prospect, but the real cost is 20 cents per prospect (assuming that the publisher or broadcaster is basing claimed costs in validated reader/listener/viewer figures). Even then, these are only a quite broad prospect pool, of which a yet smaller fraction will be true prospects. In fact, it is almost absurd to hypothesize here that one half of the original audience will be even general prospects. The real figure denoting true prospects reached is more likely to be a fraction of 1 percent of the periodical's circulation, if the medium is one reaching the general public, and still a single-digit figure even if the medium addresses a special portion of the general public as its audience.

This is bound up with the question of what you advertise and how broad its appeal, that is, what portion of the general public is likely to be interested in your advertised service or product. The case of selling a diet or related product is a better-than-average case because weight and dieting are such widespread concerns in the United States today (although that is offset by the enormous competition, the huge number of health and diet programs and preparations being advertised regularly). In other cases, the ratios are far less favorable, with tiny percentages of the total readers, listeners, and viewers being plausible prospects, so that you may triple, quadruple, or further amplify the cost per prospect claimed by the publisher or broadcaster. What percentage of the readers of any given day's big-city newspaper, for example, are true prospects for a dishwasher, a liter of gin, or the newest thing in woodworking machines? The number of actual prospects reached, that is, percentages of claimed circulation, in these cases, can become extremely small.

ALL MASS MARKETING IS BROADCASTING

The term *broadcast* was used here in the narrow sense of radio and TV, which reach audiences by "broadcasting" their electromagnetic radiation into the atmosphere where anyone who is equipped with a proper radio or TV receiver and is within the range of coverage can receive the radiated information. Mass marketing is also "broadcasting" in a more general sense: Advertising in mass media—print periodicals and bulk mail—broadcasts your sales messages. Because it addresses and reaches a broad audience of no particular qualifications except that they are all readers of the publication or fit some broad general description. They are men, women, and children of an almost unlimited spectrum of characteristics and interests, and so inevitably only a percentage, usually a relatively small minority, have needs and interests that make them true prospects for whatever you are selling. You can only hope that in that ocean of the general public there are enough individuals whose wants today are a complementing match for your offer to make the advertising program profitable.

Prospect is a term used freely in sales and marketing, and we have used it here rather freely and frequently, but this term is also widely misused. It needs definition because prospect is an imprecise, relative term that tends to mean only what the user wants it to mean. You must therefore define it in the context of your own marketing needs, plans, and strategies. If you advertise a diet product or program to one million readers of a popular magazine, you are addressing one million prospects, says the naive view (and the publisher) selling you advertising space. But if only one tenth of the readers are overweight, in fear of becoming overweight, or otherwise concerned with weight and dieting, only one tenth of the readers are even nominal or prima facie prospects (or "suspects," as one humorist sales expert has put it)—individuals who may logically be assumed to have some reason to be interested in what you offer.

NARROWCASTING

If we can somehow identify that 10 percent of the total audience who are overweight or in fear of becoming overweight and restrict our marketing efforts to reach them alone—to *target* our best-qualified prospects and "narrowcast" instead of "broadcasting" our sales messages—we will immediately cut our unit costs by 90 percent. That is a major step forward.

The idea of narrowcasting, rather than broadcasting, your sales appeal begins to approach a solution to the problem or, at least, a definition of the problem: How do we eliminate the waste of addressing appeals to nonprospects? (Especially when nonprospects constitute a great majority—even 95 percent—of those in what we consider to be the prospect pool.) Or, more directly to the point, how do we manage to select the true prospects and confine our sales appeals to them alone?

If we can do this, we obviously reduce waste and increase efficiency: We not only cut our unit cost per prospect to one tenth of what it would otherwise be but also should (logically) vastly increase our response rate, even by a factor of 10.

Unfortunately, basing our targeting or narrowcasting on what appears to be logical is expecting a bit too much. It is a misleading conclusion, based on the false premise that an individual will be interested because he or she *should* (logically) be interested. But we humans are not logical nor even reasonable: Many of those who *ought* to be interested (according to our logic) will not be. Not every overweight person is concerned about his or her avoirdupois or wants to do something about it. Some overweight people have tried to lose weight and given up trying. Others, for whatever reason, don't care that they are overweight and are not at all interested in diets and diet plans or products. Analogously, not every poor person or underpaid worker who wants to "do better" is willing to put forth the effort to make more money, nor is every uneducated or undereducated person willing to make the effort to improve him-or herself: Merely "wanting" something does not equal being motivated to make the effort necessary to get it. Some people are motivated by ambition, desire to provide more for their families, ego need for success and recognition, or other factors, and will eagerly seize any opportunity to pursue the goal. But many others are unmotivated, due to laziness, apathy, fear of failure, general discouragement, weariness, weakness of will, and sundry other factors that drive the human animal. Ergo, you are likely to get orders from motivated prospects but not from the unmotivated ones, and it has so far been difficult, if not impossible, to determine which prospects belong to which class. You can thus not count as true prospects everyone who appears to you to have a sound reason to be motivated. Your notions of what ought to be important to others are pure guesses, and often only wishful thinking.

To truly implement the notion of narrowcasting or targeting prospects more precisely, then, we must solve the problem of screening out—eliminating—the two levels of what I shall call here "pseudo-prospects" or, at best, "quasi-prospects." The first level are fairly easy to detect and screen out because they do not even faintly resemble or meet the most basic qualifications of true prospects. The second level, those who pass that first-level screening and *appear* to be true prospects, represents a far more difficult screening process, but the rewards are worth the effort. Assume, for argument's sake, that only one third of that one tenth of the original prospects are true prospects for your diet plan. That means that only 0.3333 percent of the original audience of readers/ listeners/ viewers are true prospects, those most likely to be seriously interested in your sales appeal and offer. Logically, your cost per individual prospect ought to be less than 4 percent of the cost of reaching that full audience, and your response rate ought to be many times greater than it would be if you addressed the total audience.

Of course, these are idealized approximations and really optimistic estimates, even if they appear to be modest: They reflect the realities of mass marketing. You will probably not get results quite as clear-cut and as beneficial as these projections, but you will certainly see a major improvement in cutting unit costs and increasing response rates if you can qualify your prospects more accurately before rolling out your campaign.

The term *qualify* is used here in the traditional marketing/sales sense of verifying the prospect's interest in and ability to buy/order the item before you invest too much time and money in the sales effort. However, it is normally used only in connection with the large sales that require more than a single sales call to win. To bring a significant increase in targeting sales in mass marketing, we must somehow manage to adopt the principle of qualification for even the smaller sales and adapt it so that it can be used practicably in mass marketing.

DEMOGRAPHICS, LISTS, AND TESTING

Until now the main tools for qualifying prospects and thus focusing marketing appeals more sharply have been the demographic characteristics of readers, listeners, and viewers claimed by publishers and broadcasters, and the demographics of mailing lists claimed by list brokers. The important difference is, presumably, that when you go with publishers and broadcasters you can only accept or reject their demographic claims, although you have some modest choice in the variations: You can choose, for example, between the demographics of readers of *Fortune* magazine versus those of readers of *Cosmopolitan,* or between those of viewers of wrestling matches and viewers of soap operas. With broadcast advertising you go with generalizations that may or may not be true, except as broad generalizations or popular myths with a generous sprinkling of exceptions. Not all highly educated people are intellectuals; not all intellectuals have good taste; and not all viewers of wrestling matches are beer-drinking laborers or ribbon clerks—many are women and many are intellectuals whom you might expect to be fans of grand opera and great literature. Aficionados of every kind of entertainment constantly prove to be more diverse than we think they are or ought to be. Lee Nails, a cosmetic product for women, advertised regularly for many months on wrestling programs. It was obviously profitable because the campaign continued for a very long time, but it would not have surprised anyone who had done proper market research: A visit to any of the many major wrestling matches will reveal immediately a large number of young women who enjoy watching the matches. No matter how some sneer, wrestling is a popular spectacle, whether or not it is a "sport," as sportswriters and sports commissioners of the various states define the category.

With mailing list rental you tend to have quite a bit more choice in your general prospect pool because you can specify some of the demographics you desire, for example, all engineers living in upper economic suburban areas or all members of country clubs who subscribe to sports magazines. List brokers can often customize lists for you, although you will normally pay a premium for the service of such segmentation of their lists. On the other hand, most list brokers can and do offer a wide variety of classes and categories as standard fare: The catalog of one such broker offers in its table of contents "Business Lists," "Consumer Lists," and "Other Lists," with each further categorized. "Consumer Lists," for example, include "High Income Americans," "High School and College Students," "Doctors," and "Dentists," among other categories. Another offers "Auto Enthusiasts," "Credit Card Holders," and "Families by Income." You can rent a list of corporate executives, in any of many specified industries, and even some highly unusual lists, such as one of more than 200,000 men suffering from hair loss who bought a hair-restorer, Australians who have bought good luck charms and related items, and survivalists who are good prospects for military surplus and survivalist items. And since many lists managed and marketed by list brokers are of those with known interests (e.g., they are subscribers to certain magazines, members of certain associations, or customers of some catalog house), some assumptions about their wants and needs may be made at once.

That is essentially the state of the direct marketing art today, despite the vast amount of smoke that emanates about what the industry calls "database marketing" and which ought to be and will be called "data-based marketing" here. What is essential truth is simple enough: The old methods of mass marketing are simply not satisfactory today; they do not work well enough for current conditions. Even direct marketing is no longer direct enough. It isn't enough to target all surgeons as prospective buyers of the latest information on laser technology, for example; we must find and target all surgeons for whom the latest information in laser technology is a need or at least a major asset. We can't afford to target 500,000 surgeons of whom only 20 percent want to know about the latest in laser technology (and of these most are satisfying that need already by some means). We must find that 20 percent, then that portion of the 20 percent who are likely to be seriously interested in what we are selling, and then target them further: We cannot afford to address them all when we know that only a fraction of them are true prospects. That may mean that our real prospects are only 1 or 2 percent of the entire prospect pool of surgeons, but it also means, if done well, a great decrease in wasted literature and mailings and a great increase in the rate of response.

This approach suggests that mass marketing, if even the term is to survive, must take on a new definition: much less mass and much more market than before. The latest means offered for reducing the mass and increasing the marketing effectiveness is the marketing database, the central ingredient of what we now call databased marketing. Actually, that is a rather imprecise term that must become far more exact to be useful in marketing. Its roots in direct marketing generally and in what has come to be called *targeted marketing* especially are visible enough. An understanding of databased marketing depends heavily on an understanding of direct marketing and targeted direct marketing. That latter, of course, simply restricts the marketing effort to the most qualified prospects. But it is now time to move on and take a closer look at what databased marketing represents in at least its general terms.

Chapter 2

What Is a Database?

Answering the query "What is a database?" is almost as difficult as answering the query "How high is up?" It is possible, however, to study practical database structures as designed for and used in modern computers, and answering the query in that context is most useful and appropriate for our needs here.

DATABASE DEFINITIONS AND APPLICATIONS

To discuss databases and their use and to ensure that we are communicating (i.e., that you have no insurmountable obstacles in understanding what I write in these pages), I need to establish some definitions and explain certain computer basics, at least as I understand them. In discussing that with which we are thoroughly familiar, we are usually able to cut through rhetorical vagaries easily because we automatically make distinctions according to the context of references—that is, we interpret, interpolate, and infer meanings and intentions out of our own knowledge, else the Tower of Babel (babble?) would be a daily problem. When we are in a strange field, however, it is most difficult to do that. Ergo, the need arises for the occasional digression into technical explanations to ensure understanding. I apologize for introducing and explaining computer technicalities here, which will bore those already highly "literate" in computers and probably confuse and annoy others, but I don't know how to avoid this unpleasant necessity. I promise to be merciful, however, and be as brief as possible in these digressions and excursions.

Database is a term that was spawned by the computer industry, which also gave us many other terms that became industry jargon (although much of it is now a kind of *lingua franca* among all of us lay citizens who use computers regularly). Database is one of the most commonly used and encountered—perhaps *the* most commonly used and encountered—term in all writing and discussion related to computers. The word rolls off the tongue easily with very little practice, as though it were truly definitive. In fact, it is a most imprecise term in many ways, defined more by connotation or by the user's individual intent than by any uniquely distinguishing features or precise denotation. However, as Rose Harper observed in her book *Mailing List Strategies* (cited earlier), any list may be considered a database. For that matter, almost any set of data, large or small, with even a minor unifying characteristic, may be regarded and treated as a database. Definitions of the term abound, but differ widely. The author of one database management software program defines a database as "the collection of all the individual records you keep on file." Thus a list of "Career Women in Executive, Professional Positions" is a database offered by one list vendor, as is a list of people who smoke, a list of people to whom you send Christmas cards, and a list of vendors kept by a purchasing agent as sources for the things he or she must buy. In fact, many databases are little more than lists of people, places, or things arranged in some sequence. On the other hand, the "reader file" that many offices maintain, usually a bound volume of correspondence, is also a database, as is any set of files or collection of information you wish so to designate—the shelf of suppliers' catalogs and list prices, the collections of sales representatives call reports, and the list of newsletters and trade journals.

Not everyone attempts to define a database by what it *is*. One of my software manuals defines the term by what the user does with databases. It introduces the subject by stating, "Databases offer a means of organizing, storing, and managing information." It then goes on to cite, as examples of some kinds of databases, address books, checkbooks, and telephone books, noting that databases can and do take many forms, but also remarking that "computer-based databases are particularly powerful because they are so fast and flexible."

Probably the most insightful qualification on which a useful definition of the term is based is that a database is a set of data that are so organized and structured that the user can methodically search for, find, and retrieve any wanted item, as you find a name and telephone number or a local pizza parlor in the telephone book. That is, in practical terms, each item of information (later, we will call it a *record*) in the collection has at least one identifying characteristic by which it may be searched out—a name, a number, or some identification code. (Later, we will refer to *that* as a *key field.*) The qualification of some kind of identification, preferably one that is unique, is a critically important consideration in making a database useful. However, a database may and often does have more than one such identifying characteristic for each record. If the record does not have an inflexibly unique key field, such as an identification (ID) number or other code, it may have to be identified by the unique combination of several fields, rather than by any single key field, a relatively awkward expedient that detracts seriously from the usefulness of the database.

Thus, you can easily see, the term is itself usually quite flexible in its meaning. You decide for yourself what constitutes a database. You may designate the entire contents of a metal filing cabinet a database, or you may designate as databases more than one collection of the cabinet's contents. Physically, the database may be a set of $8\frac{1}{2} \times 11$-inch paper files, a set of index cards, a Rolodex®, a strip of microfilm, a set of microform "cards," a bound volume, or almost any other kind of data in a set or package. In today's business and technological environment, however, the implication in using the term is usually quite strong that the database is in some "machinable" form—on disk or tape, in or ready to be loaded into a computer for electronic processing.

In practical terms, the connotation of the word is also that the data have at least one significant common factor that accounts for their assembly as a linked set or unit. In my own collection of databases, for example, is one file of names and addresses of organizations and individuals with whom I have some kind of business relationship. Included in that database are sources of supply, clients, sources of information, former clients, and a few other names and addresses that fit in this database file better than they do elsewhere, primarily because they have nothing in common with my other database files and they are none of them voluminous enough to merit their own, individual databases. They are thus in my general or miscellaneous database.

The terminology of computers generally is rather muddy and somewhat ambiguous, as a result of its explosive development and expansion over the past decade. New terms are invented and older terms given new meanings almost daily. Today's "chips," for example, are the direct outgrowth of "grown circuits," "modules," and especially "epitaxial circuits" of a few years ago, which represented visions and stages of development leading to what are now known as chips. They were themselves the outgrowth of transistors and the revolutionary "solid-state" electronics that transistors introduced. Discussions of databases have not been spared these verbal sand traps. This can easily become confusing for users not thoroughly familiar with the jargon. Speaking informally and as laypeople, we all tend to refer to "the database" or "our database," when we are really referring to an entire collection of databases. Nor is that the only ambiguity: Writers on the subject may refer to lists managed under one database management program (DBM) as *databases* and/or as *files*. In fact, they are both.

Computers handle data in units called *files;* a file may be almost any size, and it may be a program or subprogram of some kind, a text, or a database. So *file* is a general term, and a database is one kind of a file. A database management system or program may thus manage a number of databases, each of them a separate file. For example, among my own several databases are a list of customers for my reports, another of periodicals for my monthly column, another of editors of other periodicals for whom I write occasionally, and still others, including that general or miscellaneous list I referred to earlier. All are in and under the care of one database management system (DBM or DBMS), but each has its own identifying name and number. When I open my database management program it always asks me immediately which database I want loaded into my computer's memory, ready for work. (This morning I was honored with an order for a report from someone whose name I did not recognize. However, I scanned my customer file and found his name. Had I not found it, I would have initiated a record in his name. In this case, I entered the new information to his record, updating it suitably, and closed the file.)

Each of the several files included within this small database management system of mine is thus a database in itself, identified by a name and number that belongs uniquely to it. I must call up that number before I can work with it—add to it, delete from it, read it, retrieve from it, or manipulate it in some other way—which I can do only by first "loading" it. That means transferring it from where I keep it stored—usually on the fixed (hard) disk in my computer, although it could be on a floppy disk or even on tape, as it probably would be in the case of mainframe computers—to the computer's memory, also known as RAM for "random access memory." (It is possible to use tape storage in desktop computers too, and I do, but tape storage and retrieval is agonizingly slow, compared with disk storage and retrieval. I therefore use tape storage for long-term storage of files I refer to only infrequently and for "backing up"—making duplicate files of everything on my hard disk as a safeguard against losing important files through hard disk "crash" or other malfunction.)

There are many ambiguities and special terms that may confuse you. We laypeople tend to consider "the computer" as a monolithic unit, but that is an inaccurate view. The engineer and technician refer to only certain elements inside the metal housing as "the computer," so that although you may have the data stored on a disk that is physically inside the cabinet housing the computer, technically the data is not "in the computer" until it has been loaded into memory.

My own general database system is something of a miscellany, with records only loosely related to each other. That is, the system and each of the database files in it are rather small, making it impractical to separate the system into a great many databases, each of which would be laughably small. Were I a large organization, the various files would be broken down into many databases or files, such as different kinds and classes of suppliers (office supplies, computer accessories, delivery services, etc.), customers, prospective customers, marketing data, information resources, invoices, inventory lists, and possibly a small database labeled "miscellaneous," including items that did not fit any of these categories and yet did not have a significant common factor either. Depending on the size of the various files or databases and my needs, I might subdivide some of them into more specialized files or databases. I might, for example, have more than one customer database, more than one prospect database, and more than one marketing database.

That points out another characteristic of any database: It can vary widely in size and nature, according to individual conditions, needs, and applications. You create your databases to suit your own needs and applications, and if your needs and applications change, your database system should change accordingly. An important factor is size. I consider files larger than 50kb (50,000 bytes or characters) to be approaching the awkward stage, difficult to manipulate because of size, which slows down all related operations (e.g., entries, searches, and retrievals). I therefore tend to split files that grow much beyond that size. On the other hand, I consider files that are much less than 25kb in size to be too small to stand alone, and so I seek logical ways to combine the smaller collections of data. Manageability is another factor that acts as a constraint on size and design. I can manage my miscellaneous database quite informally because it is small enough for me to scan by eye and find the items I want. I also have another database that is a customer list and is large enough to justify its existence as a separate database, but it is too long a list for me to scan by eye; I require the help of the computer to find any individual name with acceptable efficiency. Again, were I a large organization with a customer list many times the size, I would feel compelled to subdivide the list into separate databases and I would have to determine a basis for the division. One way would be to break it into subgroups alphabetically—*a* to *g, h* to *l*, and so on. Another method would be grouping by zip codes or by geography. Another would be by types of purchase. Another would be by special identification codes. (That would require a special file to look up the codes, but in many cases that is necessary, and the computer is called upon to do that.) I would have to decide which was the most practicable and most useful way to design the system to meet my own needs. Size would be a factor, as already noted, but not necessarily the controlling or most important one.

Databases thus vary along more than one parameter. You can, for example, build and use a wide variety of databases, according to your own needs. Here are just a few examples of the many purposes for which databases are established:

- Maintain (keep up to date) mailing lists and print mailing labels, 1-up or multi-up, and address envelopes.
- Maintain price lists.
- Maintain telephone and/or name/address directories.
- Keep inventory records of all types.
- Build and maintain personnel databases.
- Build and maintain customer lists.
- Build and maintain databases to be exported for use by other computer programs.
- Import files from other systems, into your own system format.

■ Maintain "secure" information in an encrypted format. (No one can view it who doesn't know the security code.)

DATABASE MANAGERS ARE SOMETIMES KNOWN BY OTHER NAMES

The abbreviation "DBM" stands for *database manager* or database management program. (You will also encounter "DBMS," for *database management system.*) That is, it is software that calls on the strengths of the computer to help you store, organize, sort, retrieve, update, and generally manage the information in your databases. But since databases vary so widely in the kind of information they include and the ways in which it is stored, they are sometimes known by other names, especially when they are designed for a single, specialized use. For example, you can buy a mailing list manager. That is a DBM designed especially to manage mailing lists and mailings. The program design differs from the general DBM in that it is more tightly structured—less versatile—because it is a special-purpose program. It is somewhat easier to use because, as a special purpose programs, the design has made decisions for you. You can organize and design any DBM to manage mailing lists, but you must design it for mailing-list management, whereas a mailing list manager is already organized and designed for that application. Other such specialized or dedicated DBM software would include such programs as those offered to help with the management of inventories, price lists, and just about any other kind of item that is normally listed, tabulated, and arranged in some serial or hierarchical order. One of the features of my WordStar word processor is a subprogram called ProFinder. It is a relatively simple, special-purpose database that lists all the files in any directory of my computer system. Its declared function is to enable me to find any file or any bit of information in any and all files of that directory, and it does so quite effectively and efficiently. But it also enables me to sort the files to present them by date, alphabetically by title, by type of file as identified via the name coding, or by size, and in ascending or reverse order in each case. Nor are those all the features; there are several others.

Aside from that, DBM programs, even those of a general nature, vary quite widely, influenced to some extent by their missions and the sizes of the databases they are intended to handle, but due more to the designers' ideas of how to make the DBM maximally useful. All DBM software is highly flexible, permitting you to adapt it to a wide range of applications. Still, some are simple and utilitarian, along the lines of a simple passenger automobile with little more than automatic transmission and air conditioning, whereas others are much more complex, offering many more features, along the lines of a luxury vehicle with power windows, compact disk player, and sundry other special refinements.

A FEW THINGS YOU CAN DO WITH A DATABASE

Most DBM programs allow you to sort your data into almost any sequence you wish. They allow rapid access to any record in the database, with a variety of search techniques allowing comparison searches or generic searches based on any field (single characteristic or descriptive item, e.g., name, address, telephone number) in the record. (Figure 2–1a, to be introduced shortly, is a simple *record* with nine *fields.*) For example, you can list and display or print out the records of all employees over a certain age, all individuals in the same zip code, all customers who ordered by mail last year, or all items of any listed category *for which you have a field* in your database. You can print out reports, listing all or some of the fields (individual identifying items, such as names, addresses, telephone numbers) from all or some of the records, in many different sequences, with subtotals and totals of any of the categories (or *fields*). Report fields can be calculated based on information in other fields in the database. Reports can be sent directly to your video screen or to any one of many different types of printers. They can also be sent to disk (storage) for later extraction, printing, use with your word processing programs, or other uses, or even sent to your modem for transmission to another computer somewhere. (The more you work with databases and database managers, the greater the number of useful applications you will find for them.)

To conduct searches and find specific items, you need to have at least one *key field.* That, you will recall, is simply the field by which any record can be distinguished or identified, the field for which the computer is to search. It can be the name of the individual, although that, unfortunately, is not a good key field because it is not always a unique identifier; there are many John Smiths and Jane Millers in the world, and you may have more than one individual with the same name in your database. That is one reason for recording a middle initial with the name. But even that does not always help (as mistakes made by the Social Security Administration and other organizations demonstrate), and many systems assign a unique identifying code to each record. It is also possible, even highly desirable, to have more than one key field, which provides another way to identify items. If the John Smith whose record you want lives in Jonesboro, that can distinguish him from the other John Smiths. The DBM permits you to specify a unique *combination* of fields, although this is not quite as reliable as having a single key field that presents a truly unique ID. (More on this shortly.)

You can also create entire new databases from existing databases. The new database can be in a different format, and can be a subset of the database from which it was cloned. New fields can be added, old fields can be deleted, field positions can be rearranged, and field sizes can be lengthened or shortened.

You can merge together two databases that have similar definitions. Databases can thus be created and maintained on separate computers. The new database can be in a different format and can be a subset of the database from which it was cloned.

Theoretically, it was always possible to do these things with a database, even one existing as sheets of paper or boxes of file cards. Some earlier systems (some of them not really very old), consisted of data recorded on cards with holes punched in them at strategic points for "sorting" the database by inserting a needle in a hole and shaking the stack of cards, to select all of those matching some criterion, such as a common state or city. Clumsy as such a system may seem today, only a few years ago, before the desktop or "personal" computer appeared, these were state-of-the-art sorting systems. They were the only systems available to those who did not have access to multimillion dollar mainframe computers or EDP card-sorting systems.

The PC, or desktop computer, has changed all that. Even a one-person enterprise, such as I and many other independent entrepreneurs represent, can now do almost anything that only the multimillion dollar corporation or government agency could afford to do a few years ago. Almost overnight, the PC has made all those manual and mechanical systems obsolete, while it has put the most modern of facilities and resources into the hands of ordinary small businesspeople in a modern industrial revolution.

DATABASE MANAGEMENT AND STRUCTURE BASICS

The basic elements and principles of a database management program are simple enough, although the software can become fairly complex. At its most fundamental level, a database is made up of just those two elements: fields and records. Here are simple and specific definitions of these two most basic elements of any database:

A *field* is a single item of information that is part of a record, such as a date, a name, a street address, or a dollar amount, a part number, or other such information item.

A *record* is the collection of fields that describes an individual entity in a database. For example, each record might list a name, street address, and city and state with zip code; an item of inventory, with part number, number in stock, and sources of supply; or a book with title, author, publisher, price, supplier, and date of publication.

For a look at a simple database structure, see Figure 2–1a. Each numbered item—name, company, address—is a field. That these items are presented in this arrangement has no particular significance, other than that it is easier to demonstrate the concept graphically with

1. Name _____

2. Company _____

3. Address 1 _____

4. Address 2 _____

5. City/St/Zip _____

6. Tel _____

7. Fax _____

8. Notes 1 _____

9. Notes 2 _____

Figure 2–1a. A simple database structure.

this orientation. It is equally valid to present this horizontally, as in Figure 2–1b. (Some database management systems, such as dBASE, permit you a choice of two kinds of presentation of each record. More on this presently.)

Each of the numbered items in this simplest of database designs is a *field,* regardless of how the presentation is oriented. The entire item, all nine fields, is a *record.* The order seems logical enough, and it is, if the database is a small one and not likely to get a great deal larger. But it is adequate only if that is the case. Figure 2–2, the form filled out with typical entries, shows why this is so.

If you want to find Joe Smith's address or telephone number and there are only a couple hundred records in the database, it is easy enough to ask the DBM (database manager software) to stop at the first "Joseph" or display all fields beginning with "Joseph." There probably will not be more than a dozen at most, even though "Joseph" is a most common name. But if your database contains many thousands of names, that's another matter, isn't it? At that point you want a list of all the "Joseph Smith" entries, and perhaps even that will be too long a list to manage manually for a name as common as "Joseph Smith." You may find it essential to order all "Joseph T. Smith" or even all "Joseph T. Smith" entries within a certain zip code to get the retrievals down to a small enough number to be manageable.

To get your computer to do that, you must have coded the entries by establishing three fields for the name, first, last, and middle name or middle initial, and a field for the zip code (i.e., you will have to break down the address into fields for the street and number, the city, the state, and the zip code). That is, the DBM searches by fields. In the

Name _____ Company _____

Address 1 _____ Address 2 _____

City/St _____ Zip _____

Tel _____ Fax _____

Notes 1 _____

Notes 2 _____

Figure 2–1b. Horizontal presentation.

simple arrangement shown, it can search for all Josephs, all Josephs connected with Ajax, or all Ajaxes, but not for a Joseph T. Smith or an Ajax Tool and Die. If you have a large database and can remember only that the fellow you want to call or write to was named Joseph T. Smith, you may have a laborious time sifting through all the Josephs to find the Joseph you want. For the DBM to find the Joseph T. Smith who works for Ajax and lives in area code 55505, it must search through all "Smiths" to find all the "Josephs" with a middle initial of "T" living within the 55505 zip code. To do that, it must be able to find a field for each of the identifying items. That is illustrated in Figure 2–3. (Those forms you are constantly filling out are organized the way they are—so that they can be entered into a computer database.)

The graphic representation of Figure 2–4 may help you visualize the basic structure a bit more clearly. The database is made up of a number

1. Name   Joseph T. Smith

2. Company   Ajax Tool & Die Co.

3. Address   173 Prosperity Lane

4. Address   Unit A-75

5. City/St/Zip   Ball Bearing, MN. 55505

6. Tel.   623 555-1122

7. Fax   623 555-1121

8. Notes   Purchasing agent

9. Notes _____

Figure 2–2. Typical entries.

1. Last Name   Smith

2. First Name   Joseph

3. Middle Initial   T.

4. Company   Ajax Tool & Die Co.

5. Address   175 Prosperity Lane

6. Address   Unit A-75

7. City   Ball Bearing

8. State   MN

9. Zip   55505

10. Tel.   623 555-1122

11. Fax   623 555-1121

12. Notes   Purchasing agent

13. Notes _____

Figure 2–3.   Adding fields.

of records, and each record is made up of a number of fields. If the database is a list of people, the typical fields are names (last and first), addresses (street and number or P.O. box and number), city, state, zip code, and telephone number. There may be other fields, such as the individual's company, title, and fax number, and there is probably a section to enter special notes or remarks. All of these make up a record, and the records, collectively, make up the database. So you can call up a list of everyone sharing a zip code, the same last name, the same first name, the same company, and so on. Or you can search out the individual—the only Jones, Howard, who works for Tiffany Mirror Company as a comptroller. Database management programs permit you to do this if you have organized every record into all these fields.

Obviously, the items—fields—will vary, according to the nature and application of the database. A database maintained by a physician or hospital is going to be of patients, and the records in that database are going to include fields identifying each patient's history, symptoms, physical and health characteristics, and related matters. The database maintained by a payroll department will be made up of records of employees, with position titles, employment history, salary figures, taxes, deductions, and other data pertaining to the individual

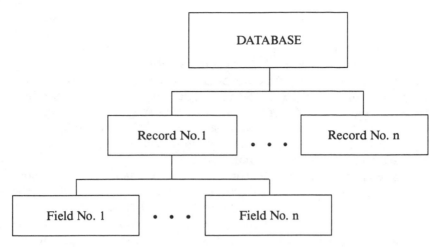

Figure 2–4. Graphic definition of a database.

employees. A database of customers ought to include in each record, after the "head" data (name, address, telephone, etc.), information on the individual's buying history (record of purchases), payment of bills, and related data. The fields ought to identify the items purchased, the sizes of purchases, and method of payment (e.g., cash or term payments), at the minimum, although there are probably many other useful items to include, depending on the nature of your business. In general, the more information included in your customer database, the more valuable an asset that database will be to you. You will find, as we proceed, that this is a crucial point in what is becoming known as databased marketing: The key to success is linked directly to the completeness of the data about each customer and each prospect in the database.

THE MOST IMPORTANT PERSPECTIVE

Never lose sight of the fact that your database is your own creation: You design it to suit your own ideas of what you need. An excellent key to understanding databases and their management is from the basic design objective. Think of a database as a card file or set of card files in a library. What form should they take? How should they be organized? The answer to that lies in the answer to the simple questions, "What do you want to do with them?" and "How will you use them?" You want to use them to find books that you are looking for or to find out what books are in the library for research. To do that you need at least one piece of information to start with: A title, a subject, or an author's name—or at least a portion of such an item of information.

Actually, you need three files: You need the collection listed by authors' last, first, and middle names; by subjects; and by titles. Each of these requires a separate file, if you are using index cards. You might want to set up even more files for greater facility. You might use dates, for example. Many catalogs are organized on an annual basis. You might also subdivide files into fiction and nonfiction, and you might then subdivide each of these broad categories into several sets of sub-categories. With a computer database, however, you need only one file or set of files, for the computer can search by any of the search terms, if they are separate fields in the database.

There is one more comparison that must be made. Let us suppose that you do not know the author's name, the title of the book, or the year it was published, but you do remember that the author's name started with a B. You also remember that the book was about the chemistry of beer brewing. Armed with these two clues, rough and inexact as they are, you can begin *browsing* in the "by author" or "by subject" card files, hoping to recognize the author's name or the book title. Later, you will find that the more advanced database managers also provide a facility for browsing the databases.

FLAT-FILE DATABASES VERSUS RELATIONAL DATABASES

Obviously, in many kinds of databases, including the well-documented customer database, each record can become quite extensive, with many pages of data and notes. In the most basic and simplest DBM, "flat-file" database management software, you have access to only the data that is in the records. That is, all the data must be in the records of the database if you wish to retrieve it or use it in any way. There is no good way to look at the information contained in different databases and files except by going into each one separately. That is true for only the flat-file DBM, however. There is a much more sophisticated DBM, the *relational* database manager, which is far more suitable for use as a marketing database manager. This manager permits you to use data in other files, in conjunction with the data in your database, so that you can keep the DBM relatively simple without sacrificing any of its capabilities for organizing and managing a wide variety and volume of information. You can, within the marketing database file, for example, call in data from other databases and files, such as your invoice files, customer files, inventory files, and others. That means you do not have to have redundant data: Your marketing database need not duplicate data already on file elsewhere, nor do you have to have marketing database files overstuffed with data that is of only marginal use. You can use data from a half-dozen or more other databases and files as though everything were in your marketing database. In effect, you multiply the amount of data in your database many times. For this reason, it is not wise to use a flat-file DBM to manage a marketing database, thus limiting its utility quite severely.

Of course, every DBM does have a basic design of its own that dictates its versatility, functions, capacities, and other capabilities and characteristics. Obviously, DBM forms and formats vary widely with different software designers. Each user has his or her own idea about what is the ideal standard format for a database record. At the same time, flexibility is inherent in the database management idea: Within the constraints of the program you design your own forms and formats, and the constraints are relatively loose. In the databases provided as part of the PC Tools software, for example, you may have up to 4,000 characters and 128 fields per record, and you may have up to 10,000 records per database. You may design virtually any form you wish in a word-processorlike subprogram. The "default" (standard) format presumes that you will want to list items vertically:

Name
Address
City
State
Zip code

However, you can set up a form that lists fields horizontally:

Name _____ Address _____
City _____ State _____ Zip _____

You can also add rules (lines) to the form or manipulate it in a wide variety of ways to get the kinds of on-screen presentation and hardcopy printout you want. The essence of database management is flexibility to suit your own desires. The DBM furnishes you a basic structure that you may modify and bend to your wishes in a wide variety of ways. However, these are primarily conveniences and relatively minor considerations in the real significance of the customer database.

In some cases you may wish to set up data as tables or matrices in your database, such as the following:

Customer Name	Item Purchased	Date of Purchase	Amount
Helen Smith	Breakfront	12/13/88	$645
Tom Jones	Bar	12/17/88	389
Erasmus Kaye	Bedroom set	1/3/89	998
Willoughby Kent	TV	1/4/89	876

A tabular presentation does not change anything. In this case, each column is a field, and each horizontal line of data is a record. The table would normally be a separate database file, unless the database consisted entirely of similar tables, such as one for each year or for each quarter. It might also be one for each department or each line of goods. Again, it is a matter of what you wish to document and for what purpose. You might use such tables to do a historical recounting of sales along any parameter—by quarter, by customer, by kind of merchandise, or other, as long as you have set up fields as key words for the software program to search. You will also find a layout of this type offered for browsing the files, as an alternative to the "edit" format.

Now let's move on to see how this applies to direct marketing databases.

Chapter 3

What Is a
Marketing Database?

Databases and database managers vary in many ways: We can find
dozens of ways to sort and classify both the databases and the database
management software programs. Databases designed for databased
marketing, however, must be special in more than one way.

WHAT DISTINGUISHES ANY DATABASE?

Many database management programs are available, probably far more
than you realize, for many are not identified as databases and database
managers. The dictionary, spelling checker, and thesaurus programs
residing in my own computer are three of a number of different kinds
of databases that are not identified as such: They are identified by their
functional purposes, they are relatively small, and they are quite simple in their design and provided functions because they have single,
uncomplicated purposes. My communications program includes a
database that exists simply to dial the telephone numbers I want. If you
have a fax machine or even a telephone in your office with automatic
dialing, it includes a simple database: You press one or two keys, and
the database takes over and issues instructions to dial the number
electronically. Thus database managers differ from each other in as
wide a variety of ways as the databases themselves differ from each
other. There are database managers designed for special applications,
such as mailing list management and inventory control. There are also
many different models of both the most basic (flat-file) database managers and the more sophisticated relational database managers, but
these are different DBM categories. Within any given category, however, and despite differences, most database managers can be used to
construct and employ fully useful databases for almost any desired
function. There are some differences of design and features, but these
are almost always relatively superficial, except, perhaps, for size. The

capacity of the DBM in terms of the number and size of databases it can manage can vary rather widely. More important is the chosen application or purpose of the database itself, which dictates the kind of information it must contain and the operations it must perform on the data to carry out the purpose. Ergo, any database is much like other databases superficially, in that it is based on the general principles and form of all database structures, with fields, records, and typical capabilities for searches, retrievals, report generation, and printing. Each database, however, is vastly different from others in what it is designed to do and what it needs in data and in special functions to accomplish that design.

That is not truly a startling idea. Form should follow function, of course. The form and even the size of the database and the DBM for it is dictated logically by what you wish to do with it and by the amount and kind of data you need to collect and install in it. A mailing list manager for use strictly within the United States has some design and content differences from one intended for worldwide use (e.g., one problem I had with such a DBM years ago was the difficulty of making labels for Canadian and other non-USA postal codes). Inventory and purchasing management of raw materials is considerably different in its data needs and database functions from inventory and purchasing management of manufactured parts.

Figure 3–1 illustrates typical entries from two completely different DBM managers. The first one is utterly simple, with a limited number of fields, because the database is so small that it may be scanned

```
                                                      Record #223

  1. Name               Harry Publicity
  2. Company            Nat. Assn Temp Srvcs (NATS)
  3. Address            119 South Asaph Street
  4. City St zip        Alexandria, VA 22314
  5. Tel-Voice          703 549-6287
  6. FAX                703 549-4808
  7. Comment            (Public Relations Mgr)



C:\WORK.DBF RECORD 2 OF 766

  1. LAST NAME: Baumgardner
  2. FIRST NAME: Harold
  3. MIDDLE INITIAL:
  4. CO: Ajax Tool & Die Co., Inc.
  5. ADDRESS: 1731 River Road
  6. CITY: Philadelphia
  7. STATE: PA
  8. ZIP: 19111
  9. TEL: 215 333-3333
 10. FAX: 215 333-3334
 11. NOTES:...................................................
 12. COMMENTS:................................................
```

Figure 3–1. Entries from two different DBMs and databases.

quickly by eye; it is not necessary to have the computer do detailed searches. The second item is an entry in a completely different and somewhat more elaborate DBM, in which the size and uses of the database require more sophisticated search and retrieval capabilities. However, the types and number of fields used were entirely at the options of the users in each case: You actually design your own database under the flexible rules of such programs. Both examples used only a handful of fields, whereas it is easily possible to have many times that number of fields. What is not apparent here is that the DBM on which the second example was based offers some special features not standard or typical of all DBM systems. In this case, the special features include word processing and notepad facilities. Both systems, however, offer a variety of typical functions for storing, organizing, sorting, retrieving, generating reports, producing mailing labels, and/or otherwise making many uses of the core data. Characteristically, database management programs are shells that you use to structure and design your own databases according to your own wishes.

THE MANY KINDS OF DATABASES

By now it is clear that there are two general categories of DBM systems: the flat-file type and the relational database type. There are also the general-purpose DBM and the special-purpose DBM. For our purposes here, we will forget about the special-purpose DBM; that type of database and its manager are irrelevant here and were mentioned purely to explain the basic nature of databases and their management. We will focus on an entirely different approach to classifying and defining databases: We will classify them by purpose and main function. Even this broad basis suggests several bifurcations, one of which reflects two major interests of any business: managing the business in general and managing the marketing especially.

We are about to consider a large number of databases normally found in any business organization today. Some of those databases are concerned primarily or entirely with managing business operations (e.g., finance, inventory, accounting, and shipping), whereas others are concerned primarily or entirely with sales and marketing (e.g., advertising, promotion, sales, and pricing). But some may possess dual significance for the organization, having an impact in both areas of concern. Keep this in mind as you read the kinds of databases hypothesized here.

Most business organizations today maintain more than one kind of database, according to the nature of their activities. In fact, as we increase the scope and depth of our "computerization" generally—as desktop computers become more and more competitive with mainframe computers, and users become more and more knowledgeable in their use—the numbers and kinds of databases are proliferating rapidly. Thus, typical databases that organizations build and maintain include such collections of data as inventories, lists of suppliers, medical records, payroll records, progress reports on projects, time records, expense accounts, payables, receivables, depreciation schedules, amortization schedules, list of capital equipment, and prediction records, according to their needs. All organizations also normally maintain databases of customers, clients, or patients. Depending on the nature and activities of the organization, such lists might be of donors, contributors, voters, members, inquirers, patrons, and even others whose names and addresses represent an asset analogous to that of a customer or prospective customer and thus information to keep on record. Other databases are not irrelevant; marketing information may come from many sources, but customer data is most certainly a prime concern in building databases to support marketing.

MARKETING AND CUSTOMER DATABASES

The problem of ambiguities and other verbal vagaries is not confined to the computer field. We are equally guilty in the marketing world of speaking in code words, however unconscious it may be. We speak of direct marketing, for example, but we are almost always referring to direct mail when we do so, making the two terms almost synonymous, although I don't think that we intend to rule out or ignore the fact of other forms of direct marketing.

The growing use of databases in marketing is relatively new, and yet it is not new. Until the concept of databased marketing came to light, databases for marketing consisted of a melange of customer lists, prospect lists, call reports, and associated data residing originally in paper files of various kinds and later in computers. According to whose computers held these data, they represented mailing lists, prospective mailing lists, subscribers, clients, depositors, patients, donors, voters, inquirers, opportunity seekers, customers, prospects, and associated data (history, purchases, demographics, etc.) that might be used, directly or indirectly, for sales and marketing. Bank customers are depositors, and hospital customers are patients. All lists of customers, depositors, subscribers, and other groups become mailing lists when turned over to a list manager/broker.

It is perhaps thus understandable that we have made little progress in developing agreed-upon definitions, especially for the newest field of databased marketing. For our purposes here, it is necessary that we make a start. Bear in mind three things about the lists referred to here:

■ They have, until recent years, resided in costly mainframe computers and so there were many restrictions on their use, especially by small, individual marketers.

- They represent a hodgepodge of data, with little uniformity.
- They represent what would be, by current standards, rather raw and unprocessed bulk data.

This latter characteristic is the most important fact to understand. By the standard of what we are striving to establish for databased marketing, the databases referred to are crude ones. To make them suitable for effective use in databased marketing, they must be refined or matured, as one writer has put it quite well. As we explore the subject, you will soon see that the databases we shall ultimately use for that higher level of targeted marketing are going to have to be quite special kinds and that they are not going to spring full-blown from your head or from any other source, but will evolve from other databases, some of which I have just listed and described, with the continuous addition of ancillary data. Perhaps some of the mature and refined databases for databased marketing will be developed from scratch, but it makes no sense to do that unless absolutely necessary: There is already in existence in most organizations a vast amount of information in machinable form that can be used, directly and indirectly, to help create the mature databases we need, both by serving as substrates for the new databases and by furnishing data to help mature the raw databases.

A FEW NEEDED DEFINITIONS

There is an apparent conflict in defining the marketing database. Many marketers insist that a marketing database includes the user's customers only, and grows only by adding new customers to it. Some say, in fact, that direct marketing is the pursuit of sales to people who appear to be reasonably good prospects for what you sell, but databased marketing is addressed only to the user's own customers. Others take the position that the word *customer* is used loosely here and actually includes prospective customers. (On the other hand, everyone you address a sales appeal to is now a prospect, whether they do or do not appear on your customer list as a result of a former purchase of series of purchases.)

I declare for the latter position: I believe that the marketing database should incorporate both established customers and prospective customers with enough data in their records to qualify them for inclusion. There are, however, at least two ways to make this inclusion: You can keep customers and prospective customers in separate databases, or you can combine both customers and prospective customers in the same database, but code the records suitably so that you can distinguish between the two and retrieve names from either or both classes. The net result is really the same. Nevertheless, I would include as prospective customers those individuals about whom I had enough information to make them equivalent to known customers in qualifications, since so identifying prospects is one of the objectives of databased marketing.

Aside from that, what we are concerned with primarily are two classes of databases. One I shall call simply "customer" databases, a generic term for those general databases of customers and prospective customers we now use in marketing—undeveloped databases of basic but raw data as just identified and described. Although most organizations make a practice of keeping their lists of known customers in separate databases for very good reasons, I will refer to any and all databases in which the names represent any of the analogs of "customer" (patient, client, depositor, subscriber, etc.) as "customer" databases, a generic term. Later, it may be necessary to discriminate among some of these classes and categories of "known customers," and especially between customers and noncustomers or prospects. For some purposes, it is critically important to separate known customers from prospects; for others, it is irrelevant. That is, everyone listed in a database is a prospect for whatever you plan to offer next, whether or not some of them have been your customers in the past. Thus the entire database is a database of prospects for your next offering. However, when it is necessary to discriminate between customers and prospects, we need to have lists we can logically identify as "known customer" lists or databases, and we also need "prospect" lists or databases of individuals who are not customers yet, but whom we hope to make customers. I choose to use the term "marketing database" or its variant, "direct marketing (DM) database" to denote that special kind of database we use to implement the concept of databased marketing.

MAILING TO A LIST IS NOT DATABASED MARKETING

One use most organizations make of their customer databases is to provide mailing lists for direct marketing efforts. Dental and medical offices may send patients reminders at the appropriate times that they are due for a periodic checkup. Others may send a Christmas card and perhaps an occasional brochure. And still others may use customer mailing lists derived from their customer databases in even more aggressive marketing efforts, in both direct and indirect marketing programs. By the new standards we are setting for ourselves, these are old and unsophisticated methods for direct marketing although, in a technical, hairsplitting sense, almost every business organization that maintains a customer database does databased marketing of one sort or another, however primitive. In reality, that is not databased marketing in the broader sense in which the term is used today and in the sense in which it is used here. It is, instead, simply conventional mass marketing via direct mail, mailing broadside to a list of names and addresses with nothing in common save that they all are or have been at some time customers of the business organization. That is not enough in itself to qualify the mailing as databased marketing, nor to qualify the database as a marketing database. It is necessary to understand this distinction if you are to understand, employ, and enjoy the advantages of true databased marketing.

Philosophically and within the meanings connoted by use of the modern term *databased marketing,* then, a DM database is considerably more than a list of customers, even if the list includes a detailed history of each customer's dealings with the organization. To understand and use this relatively new concept identified as databased marketing, we must discriminate between the literal and now traditional general term *database* and develop a new definition of the specific term *marketing database.*

TARGETED MARKETING

Marketers normally and inevitably address at least two categories of sales prospects, existing customers and prospective customers. These may be further subdivided into more specialized classes. The broad concept of databased marketing is that when a database includes enough individual information about each prospect listed in the database to determine why he or she is a customer, it becomes possible to perceive how marketing appeals ought to be tailored to the prospects. More precisely, one approach is that if we gather enough information about known customers and compare that with information about those who are not our customers, we will be able to identify the prospects most likely to become our customers. That is, we will be able to create a model of our typical customer and search among the prospects for those who match the model. This view of the process holds that we can thus clone our customers, or we can determine which of a list of prospects are most likely to become our customers. We can then target our marketing closely, aiming it directly at those with a high probability of responding with orders.

The trick is, of course, to identify the characteristics that make the difference, that enable us to identify the prospect with the highest probability of joining our community of customers.

Another view of the process pursues a quite different rationale, although it arrives at the same destination: This rationalization assumes that all sales are the result of a given sales argument, rather than of some inherent characteristics of the prospect. Thus, goes this logic, if you present the same argument to others who are of a class with your customers, you will get the same sales results.

Undoubtedly, it is possible to conjure up other rationales. Regardless of conjectures as to the objectives of databased marketing and theories as to its explanations, one fact stands out: None of the generalizations is valid for the entire population of customers. More and more we discover that what is true for John Smith is not true for Jim Smith, Jane Smith, or Geraldine Smith. We, the public, are not the sheep that mass marketing assumed we were. We are individuals, each with our own ideas. Inevitably, we tend to clump into groups, but we clump into many groups. Our message to marketers is "Don't take us and our patronage for granted, or you court disaster."

The objective of the studies and development of marketing databases is to break down the high-probability (most likely to buy) prospects into groups identifiable by the kinds of appeals they find most persuasive. That is, we must learn what motivated each group to become our customers: Which were moved by our prices? Which by the logic of our presentations? Which by the emotional content of our presentations? Which by our image as an old, reliable firm that cares about our customers? Which by our ironclad guarantees? Which by dissatisfaction with our competitors? Which by our TV commercials? Which by our direct mail program? Which by our annual trade show? Which by our contests? Which by our special events?

We have to recognize that not all our customers are moved by the same arguments and appeals, so we must abandon the mass marketing idea of one kind of marketing activity that does the job better than the others. We must identify each group so that we do not waste money with TV commercials directed to those who love our direct mail presentations and our free catalogs, or to those who participate in our contests every year.

That means dividing up our customer population into small groups and targeting each small group with the right promotion for that group to maximize response. But it carries other implications: This idea, carried to its logical conclusion (e.g., via *reductio ad absurdum*), leads some databased marketing zealots to predict that databased marketing will make it possible to develop such completely diagnostic profiles of individuals listed in a database that marketers can create unique marketing presentation for each prospect.

In theory, this is true, but the idea of building an individual marketing presentation for each individual on your list is obviously an abstraction and an economic aberration, entirely impractical except possibly for truly big-tag items, such as a yacht, a house, or a business, that require extensive presentations and negotiations with a severely limited number of prospects. Obviously, in practice some line between mass marketing and marketing to individuals must be drawn as a compromise.

MARKET SEGMENTATION

For most marketing purposes, the extended profiling of prospects, individuals or organizations listed in a database can be explained more reasonably as a method for making marketing programs far more efficient and more effective by identifying markets. One way of defining databased marketing is that it is a means of identifying your market segments by sorting and classifying the buyers, tagging them with identifiable markers (fields in each record) for retrieval. Thus a database or collection of databases may define a number of markets or market segments, depending primarily on how much data you have amassed on each individual listed. The greater the number of identifying and/or motivating characteristics you have defined in your fields, the greater the number of market segments you have identified.

HOW BIG CAN A MARKETING DATABASE BE?

Within the limits ordained by the design of the database manager, you can make each record and each database as large as you wish. The database manager provided by PC Tools Version 6, for example, is specified in the manual as having file limits as follows:

- 4,000 characters per record.
- 128 fields per record.
- 10,000 records per database.

This is not a particularly large system, but it is still the equivalent of two full (double spaced) pages of information for each record, with up to 128 separate entries for each record, and up to 10,000 customers or prospects listed for each database. Some database managers permit much larger databases, and you can, of course, have many databases within the control of a single DBM. The shareware database manager *File Express,* version 4, lists these specifications:

- 250 characters per field.
- 120 fields per record.
- 16,000,000 records per database.

These specifications thus permit 30,000 characters (the equivalent of 15 full double-spaced pages) per record, and for practical purposes the number of records per database is limited only by your preference and/or by the storage capacity of your computer.

Size and capacity of the hardware and software systems are thus not the problems in building effective marketing databases. The problem is principally one of collecting and storing the right data for your purposes, for identifying or defining your markets.

ANCILLARY RELEVANT CAPABILITIES

Modern computers, even those of the desktop variety, include a variety of sophisticated features, such as "mail/merge" capabilities. With this feature, usually found in word processor software, you may combine a form letter with a mailing list, so that the letter is printed over and over, addressed individually to each name and address on the list. Modern database management programs also offer this feature on a more sophisticated basis that permits the insertion of the addressee's name at strategically appropriately places, as in the Publisher's Clearinghouse direct mail promotions. Again, the specific capabilities vary from one DBM design to another, but virtually all offer some kind of mail/merge feature.

WHAT IS A MARKET?

To approach an understanding of databased marketing from the premise that it identifies or delineates markets, it is necessary first to define the term *market*. It is a term with a number of definitions and hence is difficult to define, except within a given context. You must define your own market(s): Where, how, and to whom do you sell whatever you sell? The answers define your market. That is, your market is the group or category of buyers who are "right" for you and what you sell. Whether those buyers are individuals or organizations—that is, whether you seek consumer or "BTB" (business-to-business) markets—is irrelevant; only the fact that they are buyers (or prospective buyers) is relevant. Bear in mind at all times that your interest in building a marketing database is solely in learning and documenting those characteristics that help you to select buyers, to identify your market.

Unless yours is a rather unusual enterprise, you probably do not have *a* market, but deal in several markets or segments of a market. To illustrate and explain this by example, consider my experience in an adventure of my own in which I created and marketed a newsletter, *Government Marketing News,* to support the consulting and training services (seminars) I offered clients who wished to pursue government contracts. Naively, I started with the assumption that everyone who did or wanted to do business with the government would want the advantages of my monthly essays and news on the subject, and would be influenced also by my physical proximity to the government market in Washington, D.C.

In the broadest of definitions, my market overall was that entire population of organizations and people who pursue government contracts of all kinds. Probably everyone knows that Lockheed, Boeing, General Electric, General Motors, IBM, and other major, well-known companies are contractors to the government, building airplanes, radar sets, computers, tanks, and other equipment, primarily for the armed forces, although not exclusively so. Despite the overwhelming preponderance of military contracts in federal procurement, in a $200 billion + procurement budget, there are many billions spent on other items: The government is also the world's largest buyer of foods, office supplies, construction, research, maintenance, vehicles, marine equipment, publications, general hardware, computers, and thousands of other kinds of goods and services. (One recent report showed about $65 billion spent annually on these latter classes of goods and services, supplied by some 250,000 business organizations in the private sector, who do business with the government regularly. (There are many more who do business with the government only occasionally, but it is a rare business enterprise that could not do business with the government more often, if the owners chose to do so.)

This can be described as a single market, the "government market." If it is a single market, however, it is one with a vast array of segments, far too broad for anyone to service more than a small fraction of it. Government procurement needs are classified into approximately 100 "supply groups," each with many individual kinds of items, resulting in thousands of *kinds* of suppliers, each of whom I could properly consider to be a market segment. I could offer general help to each of these segments, in theory, but my newsletter and my services soon proved to have much greater appeal to some than to others. My challenge was to find out which segments were my best markets: Which were *my* markets?

I didn't expect to have any trouble finding my market position. I had, after all, spent years in doing business with government agencies, as an employee of small and large corporations, and often as a consultant (technical/professional temporary) to many of them. I knew them well, and I knew the market well, despite my focus on defense, space, and related technical projects. Or I thought I knew the market well.

I was wrong. It wasn't at all easy to determine which segment(s) was/were the one(s) I should be pursuing. When I did make the determination, the answer came as a more than a surprise; it was a shock, totally unanticipated and completely outside the scope of my original calculations. I had thought that I would be able to identify my markets in terms of the sizes of the organizations, the nature of what they sold, or both. I expected the small-to-midsize electronics firm would predominate in my own market picture. In fact, I learned eventually that the size of the organization and the nature of what they sold were irrelevant for my purposes: I did business with the smallest and with the largest organizations (e.g., ITT, Control Data, Dun & Bradstreet, and even the Salvation Army). I did business with organizations selling training services, electronic equipment, and construction services. I did business with manufacturers, associations, labor unions, and government agencies.

What I learned eventually was that my main market was the organization, any organization, that felt the need for help in writing proposals and in learning to write competitive proposals. I learned that the recognition of that need was totally unrelated to the organization's size or nature, other than the fact that what they had to sell could be sold to government agencies only by writing successful proposals and subsequently negotiating agreements.

That meant that there were two major qualifiers identifying my best prospects (i.e., market segments):

■ They had to be organizations who needed to write proposals to win the government contracts they sought.

■ They had to be organizations who felt that their in-house proposal-writing capabilities were not totally adequate, but needed support or help of some kind.

In short, my original approach to defining my market was all wrong; I completely miscalculated what considerations would underlie the desire of an organization for my newsletter or other help from me in winning government contracts. My "database" at the time—before the PC—was a set of mailing lists that I had laboriously compiled, tested, and refined myself. (I found the rented lists available at that time not completely satisfactory for my purposes, since they tended to be insufficiently stratified to meet my specifications.) In terms of types of companies, I probably had more success with companies developing custom software for mainframe computers than with other organizations, but there was no really significant leaning toward any specific kind of organization in terms of their services or products. I was as likely to get a call from some executive in a supercorporation as from a tiny, newly started entrepreneur.

DEFINING A MARKET IS ONLY A FIRST STEP

You may or may not find it easy to define the market(s) or market segment(s) you believe to be "yours," and then to pursue them. It is easy to deceive yourself about this, as I did. Despite the years I has previously spent in selling to the government, I was at square one, just beginning to get an education when I struck out on my own to sell to others who were selling to the government or trying to do so. It was only after about two years of experimental marketing and testing that I began to see the light, to see what distinguished those prospective clients and subscribers who were most responsive to my offers.

Once I knew what desires brought clients and subscribers to me for help—identified the motivators accurately—I could begin to improve my marketing appeals and screen my lists of prospects more effectively, even without the advantages of computer data processing. But more important now was the question of how to find those prospects who fitted my major qualifying characteristics, both the need for proposal-writing capability and the sense of need for help in acquiring that capability. That is, I could easily enough find an almost limitless supply of potential subscribers and clients, those who *appeared* to be right for me, but how could I screen those lists to come up with the short lists I needed? It is a common enough problem, separating the short list from the long list. Perhaps that is still another way to identify the marketing database: It is the short list, and there may well be a large number of short lists to be developed as the final product.

THE CHICKEN AND EGG DILEMMA

One significant objective that characterizes databased marketing is that of identifying and addressing *your* market segments, the "short lists" just discussed. Databased marketing enables you to pursue those prospects most likely to buy from you. It is not a true marketing database unless it does address individual prospects.

That imposes on you a dual requirement: You must discover what characterizes your best customer and how to develop a list of prospects with those characteristics. A certain clothing discount retailer, Syms, has advertised for years that "an educated consumer" is their best customer. That may (or may not) constitute an effective advertising slogan, but it doesn't provide much help in building a marketing database. For one thing, how do you identify "an educated consumer?" That is much too vague a qualifier to be useful for databased marketing purposes. It is necessary to find more specific characteristics.

A kind of circular logic is involved here: Your goal is to build a list of buyer prospects that are right for you: The objective of the marketing database is to develop a profile qualifying individually each name listed in the database. The profiles will enable you to choose those prospects with the highest probability of buying what you wish to offer. On the other hand, theoretically at least, those individuals who do not match your qualifiers should not be on your list, which will include only good prospects, who are your customers or, at least, closely resemble your customers in the characteristics that count, that make them buy from you.

To put this as another and perhaps more recognizable dilemma, how do you start? Do you make initial estimates or assumptions about your markets and segments, and begin to build marketing databases based on those assumptions? Or do you commence with market testing and use the results to begin constructing databases? (But even that calls for some initial assumptions or estimates.) Or do you start with your customer list and see if you can infer some characteristics that identify buyers and distinguish them from nonbuyers? And from where do you get your initial lists?

The assumption is that you start with a customer list of your own— *your* customers. You take steps to establish a dialogue with these customers. Jan and Kurt Williams operate a Merle Norman Cosmetics and women's clothing store in Albuquerque, New Mexico. With the store, they got a card file listing approximately 800 customers. In about 1 1/2 years, they have more than doubled the list, but they have done something much more important: They have made great progress in building a true marketing database by establishing dialogue with their customers. What they have done and are doing is almost a textbook example of how to take a small business into databased marketing.

Kurt and Jan Williams were kind enough to allow me not only to cite their accomplishments, but to reprint their own comments, explaining some of what they did. The words were transmitted to me by Kurt (via computer, of course) and are reprinted here with their very kind permission:

We got into databased marketing when we bought this store back in April of 1990. Included with the store was a card file which contained customer names (about 800), addresses, birthdays, and purchasing history. Since I'm a computer nerd, I thought that this file should be computerized and my wife agreed. Once that was done, we began looking for ways to use it to help us market our products and build sales.

Out most successful project so far has been the Birthday Club. We try to get the birthday of every customer recorded in the database. We don't have all the birthdays yet, but the percentage keeps growing. Back in January we began mailing a "Happy Birthday, thank you for being our customer" letter at the beginning of each month to the customers who have birthdays that month. Included with the letter is a $5 gift certificate which expires in three months. For the eight months that are complete (January through August, all certificates have expired) we mailed 269 letters and redeemed 106 certificates for an overall response rate of 39%. (I was amazed when I saw these numbers last night.) the lowest response month was August at 34%, and the highest was March at 50%. The total sales generated are $2735.41 with an average sale of $25.81. Her average margin is 45% which means that her margin on these sales is $1230.93. The mailing cost is .50 per letter for a total cost of $134.50 and the redeemed certificates themselves were $530 (106 × $5). The remaining gross profit is then $566.43 ($1230.93 – $530 – $134.50). Low-margin sales at best (16%), but she says that they build incredible good will. When you consider the average sales per customer per year (about $100 now, but growing all time) it's a very good investment. The customers who receive gift certificates are walking word-of-month advertisements.

We also publish a quarterly newsletter with makeup tips, fashion trends, and promotions. We track the results of the promotions and record them in the database. We think that we can do direct mail promotions to those customers that respond to certain types of promotions and achieve very high response rates.

Norman Cosmetics runs some very good promotions every three months with mailings from the corporate offices. We of course track response to these promotions and record the results. We also record every time a customer makes a purchase and what the total dollars of the purchase are. Right now we don't record the products purchased, but we hope to in the future. (That's why we are looking for relational software to replace our current flat-file database.) To build the names we have on file, we do a number of things. We run a customer-of-the-month contest where every visitor to the store fills out an entry form which asks for name, address, telephone, and birth date (for the birthday club!). This gets data from customers who don't make a purchase while in the store and helps us verify our address information. We also do promotions with other related businesses (health clubs, diet centers, beauty parlors) offering their customers a chance to win a prize in exchange for filling out a brief questionnaire. these names of course go straight into the database. We haven't been doing this long enough to assess the impact on sales, but we think it will be dramatic. To expand the data we have on file, we include a short customer feedback card in the bag of every customer making a purchase. This allows the customer to express any opinions they might have and give us valuable data at the same time. We're still new at this, but we're committed to it as our long-term marketing approach. We're too small to do traditional advertising, and we prefer an approach which allows us to measure results. We would appreciate any comments or suggestions you can offer. Are you writing a magazine article or book?

You can, of course, rent lists offered commercially, choosing what appear to be the best lists, based on the demographic and psychographic data available, as a startup base. One problem with this is that in the traditional list rental arrangement you can use that entire list only once per rental. Only those who have become your customers can properly become your own names, to be used again. Or course, you can rent the original list several times or for more than one use, and in some cases you can make a deal to use a given list as many times as you like within some time period. This is perhaps one way in which you can build a marketing database, over time. But there are a growing number of exceptions to the classic list rental, at least for compiled lists, as progressive list brokers recognize that the inevitable rise of databased marketing will force changes in the industry. The immediate change that can be foreseen here is based on the fact that you may rent mailing lists, but you cannot rent marketing databases at least not at present: You must build your own marketing databases. Perhaps that will change, but if it does, it will only be sometime in the future. Thus the list brokers and others who provide direct marketers with goods and services must recognize the need to devise and develop services to support marketers who are building their own marketing databases.

Chapter 4

What Makes the Marketing Database So Special or So Especially Useful?

As in the case of a mailing list, both the volume and the quality of the information included in a database are important factors in the usefulness of the database in marketing. For what we now call databased marketing, however, that information must enable you to to differentiate diagnostically among those whose records are listed. However, it is the *source* of that differentiating information and the methods for getting it that are also revolutionary and distinguish marketing databases as such.

MAILING LISTS VERSUS MARKETING DATABASES

In this chapter we are going to have a look at what is really new, different, and distinctive—unique—about databased marketing and marketing databases. Inevitably we are going to be defining and redefining both, for there are no de facto definitions agreed upon or adopted as yet within the industries most concerned with these new ideas; we are still sorting it all out. However, getting a complete understanding of the idea and its chief instrument is necessary if you are to enjoy its advantages, and we shall be examining the concept through various paradigms, each of which will open another window on the idea of basing marketing on special databases developed for the purpose.

Databased marketing is a truly revolutionary development. Yet, it is a logical development growing out of traditional methods of conventional direct marketing on a mass basis. That is, it stems from the well-known broad approach to marketing known as *direct marketing,* or *DM,* and is perhaps best understood and appreciated by tracing that relationship to the point at which databased marketing departs from the traditional method and exploits the capabilities of the technology of recent years. There are, in fact, two broad views we need to appreciate if we are to get a good understanding of databased marketing: One is what a marketing database *is*. The other is how it gets that way: where and how the information is derived that distinguishes and qualifies a marketing database as such. We need to understand what places the marketing database in an entirely different league from the mailing list or an ordinary (e.g., customer or consumer) database, even if that mailing list or database is characterized by a mountain of demographic and psychographic information.

Figure 4–1 illustrates the evolutionary process graphically. Mailing lists, enhanced with qualifying data, constitute a list database, from which may be derived mailing lists and what we term here consumer

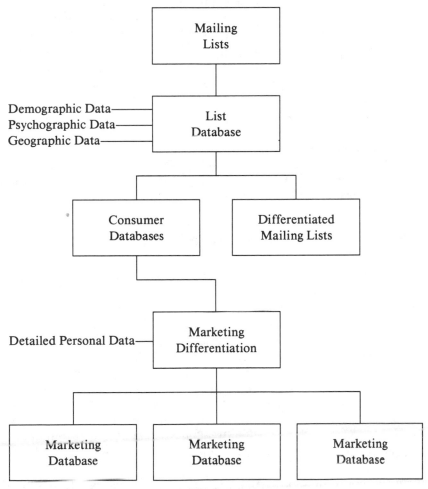

Figure 4–1. The evolution of marketing databases.

databases. The process is one of refinement, with the logical evolution, a chronological one, in this order:

1. Mailing list.
2. Enhanced/augmented mailing list.
3. Customer or consumer databases.
4. Differentiated mailing lists.
5. Marketing differentiation.
6. Marketing databases.

What we are going to discover here is that databased marketing relies on—*is* based on—profiles of the individuals listed in the consumer database. A list database may include a simple mailing list, more than one mailing list, or a store of names and addresses, with ancillary data—demographic, psychographic, and/or other data—that permit the retrieval of a variety of mailing lists. They may be lists of customers in general or they may be grouped by some general characteristics that have some significance from a marketing viewpoint: They may be subscribers, mail-order buyers, apartment dwellers, urbanites, suburbanites, rural or small-town dwellers, golfers, football fans, white-collar executives, professionals, and so on. These are typical of the many adjectives applied to and describing the kinds of mailing lists that can be retrieved from a list database that is suitably keyed with various fields, enabling differentiation along various lines, such as occupation, economic status, education, buying habits, and sundry other characteristics and qualities that are likely to be useful for marketing analyses.

THE EVOLUTION OF MARKETING DATABASES

What is the difference between what I call here a marketing database and any other enhanced mailing lists or databases used for marketing? Before attempting an answer to that, let me point out a basic principle in indexing and, especially, in searching an index or other database to retrieve desired items: The number of items you retrieve depends on the degree to which you specify what you want. It is, moreover, an inverse relationship: The more detailed your specification, the fewer items you retrieve. Search for all on the list with a college degree, and you get a certain number of items, usually a relatively large number because you have specified only one condition. Ask for all with a degree in economics, and you will, of course, get a smaller number of retrievals. Continue to add requirements, and eventually you will get zero retrievals.

View this from another perspective, that of creating and building the database. List only one field, other than those for the head data, and you can retrieve only three lists: everyone, those with, and those without entries in that one field. Add another field, and you can retrieve five lists: everyone, those with an entry in one field, those with an entry in the other field, those with entries in both, and those with entries in neither. Add still another field, and you can now retrieve nine lists. Obviously, the more characteristics or attributes listed as fields, the greater the number of lists that can be retrieved, which means the greater the number of ways the database can be subdivided.

The list and the figure depict the gradual evolution of what are termed marketing databases through successive infusions of information and successive differentiations (fields added), which must logically result in more rigidly defined and smaller lists or databases. Only three such databases are depicted in Figure 4–1, but they represent an indeterminate number that could run into dozens of successive segmentations of a market (or marketing database) into niches. Databased marketing is thus inevitably concerned with marketing to niches or segments that would be impracticable (invisible?) as targets without their close identification through database technology. Or perhaps it would be more insightful to point out that databased marketing leads inevitably, by its nature, to segmentation and the discovery of niche markets to a much greater degree than ever before.

Segmentation and niche marketing are certainly not new ideas to anyone who has had even a little direct marketing experience, but in databased marketing we analyze and define niche markets as never before. This makes a new kind of marketing efficiency possible, but before we can take advantage of it, we must identify each of these niches. One difference between these niches and those of old is size: The technology of databased marketing makes it possible to address niches that would previously have been considered to be too small to pursue profitably and possibly would have been too small even to perceive. Remember that these niches are not self-evident: They don't thrust themselves on you, but must be discovered by analysis. That itself can result only from enough data—enough differentiating factors—to link cause and effect so as to discover motivating factors and answer the question *for each niche individually:* What makes individuals in this unique segment decide to become our customers? How can we use this information to clone these customers—to find others who match them in their buying motivations? Remember, too, that a niche is an independent market segment: The customers in a niche market are not the customers in any other niche market or in any other market generally: They are customers who buy from you for some special reason or reasons. They may have special needs, special circumstances or some special combination of factors, but they are different customers or customer prospects in some way, either for the moment or permanently. You need to examine this too and make a judgment: Yesterday's customer is not necessarily today's customer.

The analysis thus includes that of identifying our customers so precisely that we can predict with a high degree of certainty which of any population of prospects are worthy of pursuit because they are likely to become customers and which ought to be dropped, as prospects unlikely to be pursued successfully.

THE PERSONAL COMPUTER HAS BEEN A PRINCIPAL PLAYER IN THE REVOLUTION

Previous discussions in these pages have already drawn distinctions between the modern marketing database and the modern mailing list. Vast improvements and increases in data enhancements of mailing lists have sparked a great and significant increase in targeting. There is much more to be said on the subject, however. For one thing, many changes that have come about in the direct marketing industry are the result of the increasing ubiquity and power of personal computers— that is, as a result of the swiftly growing power and capability of the PC. The very appellation *personal computer,* perpetuated by its initials, PC, reflected the minor significance early desktop computers were thought to have: They were little more than toys for personal convenience. No one suspected for a second that they would quite soon start to become a threat to the continued existence of the large, mainframe computer. There are still many mainframe computer loyalists who seem convinced that the desktop computer can never replace the servo-supported digital behemoths of yesterday. Despite that, the PC continues to grow in its abilities, as well as in its ubiquity: Bob McKim, of M\S Project Management, visited the most recent presentation of the annual major computer show, Comdex, and advised that he had there seen desktop computers that boasted storage capacities of 1.6 *gigabytes* (1.6 billion or 1,600,000,000 bytes). That is not nearly as much as the larger mainframe computers, but then even a small office may have a number of desktop computers linked to and reinforcing each other through a local area network, such as exists in a great many companies today. Thus, the small business organization today has in-house computer power almost as great as that formerly enjoyed by only the largest corporations, with the compensating advantages that almost anyone in the office can be trained easily to use the computers.

This great power of the modern PC alone directly affects both the users and the suppliers of mailing lists. List brokers today can furnish a great deal more information than ever before about the individuals and organizations they list in their databases. Conversely and perhaps more significantly, list brokers can offer you a wide variety of key words—uniquely identifying fields—by which you can select lists: You can have lists sorted by states, zip codes, SIC (standard industrial codes), sales volume, job titles, and by many other tags and labels, even by the past buying habits of those on the list. Here are a few examples of the kind of lists used by business-to-business marketers to identify various kinds of business firms, listed under such categories as these:

- Agriculture, Forestry, and Fisheries.
- Mining.
- Contracting.
- Manufacturing.
- Transportation, Communication, and Public Utilities.
- Wholesale Trade.
- Retail Trade.
- Finance, Insurance, and Real Estate.

Still, remember always that these are the general labels that characterize and apply to all the people or organizations on the list alike, and they are usually long lists. Here are just a few offerings of Database Management, for example, describing the lists and the number of names and addresses available from that list:

234,032 crafts and sewing enthusiasts who buy by mail.

The smokers database:

- 1,651,588 smokers, total.
- 743,245 smokers who are mail-order buyers.
- 2,609,644 Spanish-speaking households.
- 570,887 veterans who buy by mail.

In many cases, amplifying information is available, indicating what additional fields are in the database. It is possible to get lists derived from many of these categories, classified and subdivided by such characteristics as ages of adults and of children, household income, credit card users, sex, dwelling type, home ownership, occupation, and other such data.

This is useful, of course, in narrowing the field. Still, they describe general characteristics (e.g., you can order 5,000 names of veterans who are over 45, live in their own homes, and buy by mail). They do not offer the individual characteristics that are major determinants in identifying buyers individually (i.e., they do not discriminate or differentiate among those on the list by describing their peculiarly individual characteristics). The qualifiers of the list are only those that apply to everyone on the list: Any characteristic or group of characteristics would be those of everyone, so you cannot select a subgroup (i.e., a niche or segment) from that list by specifying some unique combination of characteristics. You can choose names by characteristics, as far as the data in the database permit, but they will still be rather lengthy lists, and the data will be general and not individual. The information will have been derived indirectly and so is more statistical than directly reportorial: It may be accurate in a general sense only (i.e., have a rather wide margin for error due to the indirect ways the data are gathered). However, the lists also tend to be much too lengthy to be useful for databased marketing, which is based on a highly selective process.

IS THE DIFFERENCE A MATTER OF DEGREE ONLY?

You may infer from this that the difference between the thoroughly documented mailing lists derived from list databases and those derived from marketing databases is one of degree only. That would miss the point. The degree to which the information enables differentiation of the database is one factor, but not the only one. The accuracy of the information is another important factor, and that brings in the matter of the source of the information.

THE MARKETING DATABASE AS A LOGICAL EXTENSION OF THE CONVENTIONAL MAILING LIST

One way to understand the idea of a marketing database is to view it as a natural evolution from the traditional mailing list. In many ways, the marketing database may be regarded as a super mailing list because it is an extension or evolutionary development of that well-established marketing idea, the direct-mail list. However, it is easy to become confused because the very word *database* is such a broad term (any collection of information may be referred to legitimately as a database) and is used so loosely today.

The word *database* presupposes nothing about size. The firm with millions of names on file in a massive mainframe computer may identify this mountain of data as a database, as I refer to a customer list of only 1,000 names or a subscriber list of 200 names as a database. With the advent of this newer idea of database marketing, the term has become something of a buzzword, further clouding meaning and communication.

One effect of the spread of computer jargon has been on list advertising: List brokers have more and more converted their advertising language to describe what is in their computers as "databases," where once they were universally referred to as "mailing lists." That can be misleading, even if unintentional. For list brokers to refer to their files as databases is not inaccurate, but it is confusing. Those long files of names and addresses residing in so many list brokers' computers are, indeed, databases. They are list databases, and they may include consumer databases, industrial databases, and databases otherwise categorized according to what kinds of names and addresses are listed. Many, perhaps even most, were the customer databases of the list owners.

Many—again, perhaps most—of those lists include demographic, geographic, and even psychographic data, so that they are something more than "mere" mailing lists. It is possible, even probable, that marketing databases may be constructed with much of the data coming from those mailing lists. But are they marketing databases in the sense that we use that term here?

IT IS NOT A MEASURABLE QUANTITY

The fact is that we cannot define a marketing database in absolute, measurable terms, but only in approximate or relative terms. That is, a database might be described as "a mailing list with a college education," if you want a jocular analogy that conveys a broad idea but not an accurate one. The difference between a database we consider to be only a mailing list and one that we believe to be qualified as a marketing database lies in the characteristics of the information about the names and addresses in the database. There is, however, no sharply defined dividing line at which even the most thoroughly documented mailing list suddenly becomes a marketing database, nor is there a vice versa. In fact, it is not the volume of information alone that makes the difference, nor even the relevance, completeness, and accuracy. It is, for one thing, the *source* of information contained therein that makes a mailing list of customers a marketing database: The source of at least some of the information must be the customer. Dialogue between customer and marketer, resulting in information about the individual in the database, is considered to be a sine qua non of database marketing. We can easily infer from this another sine qua non of databased marketing lists: The records of the database must include *individual* information. Perhaps everyone in a given list is a suburban dweller, but some are young couples, just starting families; some are middle-aged couples, struggling to put children through college; and others are retired, with no children at home. Some of the first class are comfortable economically, while others are straining to make ends meet. Some are one-income families, while others are two-income families or even multiple-income families. Some are white-collar professionals, while others are blue-collar workers. The variations are almost endless, but it is the individual nature of the information that is significant. However, let us briefly review mailing lists and their use to help us in drawing other clear distinctions.

TRADITIONAL MAILING LISTS AND THEIR USE

The average or typical direct marketer turns to a list broker today for a list of prospects, a universe of individuals to whom to extend the marketing offer. The list broker can offer a variety of mailing lists, about which he or she can furnish certain specific information.

Because the database manager (i.e., the software program) is capable of selecting and retrieving names and addresses by any field or combination of fields, a list catalog may offer lists totaling many times the number of names in the database. That is, each individual or organization may be represented in many lists: A bank president may also be in the "golfers" list, the "suburban dwellers" list, the "mail-order buyers" list, the "veterans" list, and so on. The toy manufacturer may be listed in a general manufacturer's list, a toy manufacturer's list, a list of buyers of metal or plastic, a list of buyers of printing in large quantity, a list of catalog buyers, lists of manufacturers or toy manufacturers by state or by city, and many other kinds of lists. (This will be illustrated shortly.)

MANY OUT OF ONE: THE MAGIC OF THE DATABASE

Despite this representation, these do not exist as separate or individual lists; they are possible or potential lists among the family of lists that can be retrieved from the list database through almost any field or combination of fields desired. Our bank president's name would appear only once in the master files that constitute the database overall, but a command to produce a list of bank presidents, golfers, suburban dwellers, mail order buyers, veterans, or any combination of these would each include his name. The toy manufacturer also may be listed only once in the database, but appear on many lists retrieved. Thus the power of the database and its manager program to make many from one. It also illustrates the power of the database to enable list brokers not only to offer a wide diversity of mailing lists, but also to assemble lists to order—custom lists—in many cases. It is another testament to the virtuosity of the database manager.

MATCHING MAILING LISTS WITH MARKETS

The individual or firm from whom you rent mailing lists is a list broker. He or she is a commission merchant who rents lists that are, in the majority of cases, the property of someone else, since most lists offered for rental are customers of publishers, retailers, banks, and others who deal in large numbers of customers. The brokers are, however, also *list managers*. They manage the lists for the owners.

An important part of the management function performed by leading list brokers is the analysis of the owner's total list and the identification of various markets to which the list might be directed. As one marketing services executive explains, traditional mass marketing can no longer reach all the markets satisfactorily. Many markets are highly specialized and are missed or bypassed by traditional mass marketing methods. (Do you have any idea, for example, how many people have rebelled against TV and either refuse to own a television set or insist on strict limitation of the hours during which it may be used? How effective are TV commercials in reaching these individuals?) Evolving demographics and lifestyles have created many new market niches that must be targeted precisely, if you are to reach the buyers in them. Databased marketing is the method for doing so.

The management function of mailing list brokers is not necessarily confined to those who own the lists: Some list brokers do little more for those who rent their lists than offer them a catalog and accept their orders. There are others who do more: They will offer renters of their lists the benefit of their experience and guide the renters in selecting the right lists. One broker who does so is Letter Perfect Information Services of Baltimore, Maryland. Proprietor Wayne Stoler is quite proud of the service he offers to help renters select the right lists to match their needs, and he assured me that he welcomes inquiries. He explained to me that he always tries to counsel prospective renters. He asks what they plan to sell, to whom, for what prices, and whatever else will enable him to offer helpful suggestions and general guidance. In fact, he also publishes a biweekly newsletter *Mailing List Tidbits,* to pass on news and useful tips to mailers.

Markets are always people, in the sense that it is people— individuals—who place orders and buy things. (You may think you sell to organizations, but you really sell to the individuals who buy for those organizations, do you not?) A market niche or segment, however, may be represented by a group of individuals, by some geographic or demographic characteristic (i.e., to be more accurate, by some set or combination of such characteristics), by some business or industrial area, or by whatever else defines the niche in such a way that you can identify and pursue it. One market niche today, for example, is that of owners of Beta model videocassette recorders. There is still a substantial number of individuals who own these original-model VCR machines and who stubbornly prefer them to the VHS models that drove the Betas from the marketplace. Probably they represent a dwindling market, but a recent sale of Beta tapes by a local video-rental chain brought out a rather enthusiastic crowd of Beta owners eagerly seeking software for their Beta hardware. A large number of these machines were sold, and they will be in existence and operating for some time to come. They are definitely a market niche for anyone offering something of special interest to owners of Beta VCR machines.

This is a simple example. Most market niches are a bit more difficult to define or identify. It is more likely that you require a fairly complex set of identifying characteristics to isolate and address a market niche you wish to serve. Let us suppose that you sell a line of collector's items related to golf. You have studied your sales records and decided that your best customer is a bank president who is not more than fifty, earns at least $150,000 a year, has a $500,000 home in the suburbs, golfs avidly for recreation, goes on golf (tournament) vacations, is a war veteran, buys by mail to the tune of at least $10,000 annually, is a football fan, collects coins or stamps, and is a joiner, belonging to at least three associations. A list of individuals meeting all of these criteria ought to produce spectacular results for you—if you can find one with all these qualifications. You would like to find a list of several thousand individuals meeting or coming close to meeting these qualifications. Can you order such a list today? Probably not. Selections would have to be made from many lists on a custom basis and even then would probably not satisfy the requirement completely. The qualifications would probably pose impossible challenges and problems for the average list broker today. The project might require too great an expenditure of computer time and human effort or produce too small a list of names and addresses to be worthwhile for either the marketer or the list broker, and so it might not be economically feasible to develop such a list. But such a capability is probably somewhere in the future as a necessity. List brokers may have to somehow meet the demand for ready-made marketing databases in the future or, perhaps, for starter lists and tools to help you develop your own marketing databases. (This appears to be a real possibility. More on the subject presently.)

WHERE DO TODAY'S MAILING LISTS COME FROM?

The Qualified Lists Corporation (QLC), a well-known supplier of mailing lists, announced recently in the direct marketing trade publication, *DM News,* that it is now the manager of the mailing lists of the Association of Catholic Senior Citizens, and that the lists include 107,521 active members, 329,740 pending members, and 235,829 former members. These lists or portions of them may now be rented from QLC as the list broker. If we pursue the advertising further in this same edition of *DM News* we can learn that the List Services Corporation can offer lists of subscribers to *Golf Digest, Tennis Magazine,* and *Snow Country.* Response Media Products offers the names and addresses of 293,819 September Days Club Senior Travelers, 767,000 auto insurance applicants, 174,600 Kuppenheimer male fashion buyers, and 1,100,000 home value consumer lifestyle respondents.

For the most part, mailing lists offered by list brokers are the customer lists, membership lists, subscriber lists, inquiry lists, and other lists that are the property of various business organizations. (They are most definitely privately held property.) List brokers manage those lists: They analyze, organize, package, advertise, and market them on a commission basis. These lists and the commissions their rentals produce are the mainstay of the typical list managers and brokers, although they may also have a few "house" lists of their own and may offer some other services. So you always know something about the individuals on any list you rent. Subscribers to *Golf Digest* are obviously people with an interest in golf, usually golfers. Senior travelers are retirees indulging their desires to travel in their leisure years. The interests of insurance applicants are equally apparent, of course.

On the other hand, the immediate interests of members of the Association of Senior Catholic Citizens are not as clear. Their interests, other than their Catholicism, are not suggested by their membership, and may be of the most diverse and general nature.

Of course, certain demographics are apparent from the individuals' addresses alone. The lists can be broken down by cities, states, and zip codes. Anyone familiar with the areas can determine the nature of the area thus designated and, from that information, the probable economic status of the individual. But this is not nearly enough for even a well-documented mailing list, let alone a marketing database. Data is collected for mailing lists by specific effort, and the process is even more intense in building a database.

There are other criteria on which to base such decisions, such as size of purchases, frequency of purchases, recency of purchases, buying habits (e.g., buys newest styles, never buys new items, fond of appliances and gadgets), credit history, and other useful items of information. You may also wish to develop special databases, according to such information as this (e.g., a list of buyers of kitchen gadgets).

MANAGED LISTS VERSUS COMPILED LISTS

We have been talking about managed lists offered by commissioned brokers who market the lists for their owners as part of a list-management contract. The lists are usually supplied to the renter on labels of one sort or another or on tape. As a user, you pay a fee for each use of the list, that is, you *rent* the list for each use. Although there are some variants of this pattern, this is the usual arrangement contracted by the parties. Copying the list and using it again without paying a second rental is taboo—stealing, in fact. (Exceptions would be the name and address of each individual who buys from you and thus becomes a customer and goes on your own customer list, or an inquirer, to whom you respond appropriately.)

Note carefully that this standard practice applies to the rental of mailing lists belonging to others and being handled by list brokers on a commission basis. There is another species of mailing lists, the *compiled* lists, which are compiled primarily from directories, such as the yellow and white pages, membership lists, and other such sources, and sorted into categories. They are then entered into databases, and subjected to merge-purge processing to eliminate duplications and erroneous entries. Such lists are sold to buyers by a growing number of list vendors for unlimited personal use: You may use the list over and over for your own marketing and related purposes, but you may not resell the list or portions of the list to others and may not include the list or portions of the list in products to be sold to others.

In general, compiled lists are deemed to be of lesser value for direct marketing than are managed lists because compiled lists are "cold" lists: Virtually nothing is known about those listed on them but statistical or "head" data, the cold facts of the individual's or organization's existence. However, many people do have uses for compiled lists. There are list brokers who sell both managed lists and compiled lists, and there are specialists who deal primarily or exclusively in compiled lists. (There are also those who will compile lists for clients on a custom or contract basis.)

Parallel forces are at work and exercise their own influence on the industry and its practices: In recent years, the swift proliferation of the omnipresent PC has resulted in an equally swift proliferation of computer literacy. The numbers of those adults who come into contact with computers and learn something of them is swelling rapidly: We are all or virtually all becoming computer literate. That has made it viable to base many businesses today on the abilities of ordinary lay people to operate a PC. One such development has been the appearance of a business selling compiled lists in machinable media (e.g., floppy disks) and via online databases (i.e., via PC-to-PC communications via modem and telephone line).

Database America offers compiled lists through Ed Burnett Consultants, of which it is the parent company. Ed Burnett Consultants offers compiled lists on floppy diskettes, magnetic tape, and in other media. The company also offers to supply the necessary software with the diskettes to print the lists in various formats as labels, cards, reports, or other presentations. Moreover, the company appears to recognize the utility of using their compiled lists as the basis for building your own marketing databases and makes mention of that application in their advertising brochures.

Online Information Network of Omaha, Nebraska, advertises Online Databases, offering to provide their lists through online transfer: You dial up their computer via your own computer and modem, scan their offerings, and download—transfer to your own computer—the business or lists you want. You can retrieve lists by such fields as state, zip code, SIC code, and other factors. You also have a wide choice of diskette formats and other services, such as profiles of those business organizations you specify.

In a tryout of this system I called and ordered a list of Maryland manufacturers employing up to 249 people. I asked for the list to be displayed on the screen, and set my system to capture the data. I received a listing of 273 names of firms, with their addresses, telephone numbers, name and title of the chief executive officer, SIC code number, number of employees, and sales volume. I chose to have the list so sorted and retrieved, although I had many other options available. Figure 4–2

```
                      <<<<<<<<<<<MAIN MENU>>>>>>>>>>>

(A) U.S. BUSINESSES--9.2 Million U.S. Businesses, including:

                              * Owner/Mgr/CEO Name
                              * Employee Size
                              * Sales Volume

(B) U.S. MANUFACTURERS--551,000 Listings, including:

                              * Owner/Mgr/CEO Name
                              * Employee Size
                              * Sales Volume


(C) CANADIAN BUSINESSES--1.6 Million Business Listings

SELECT FUNCTION:
(A) Retrieve Lists by S.I.C. Code
(B) Retrieve Lists for All Manufacturers
(C) Find SIC Codes
(D) Retrieve Counts Only
(E) Company Profile
(P) Return to Previous Menu
(X) Logout


Enter Selection :B

<<< MANUFACTURERS MENU >>>

Demographic Selections:

(A) Employee Size
(B) Sales Volume
(C) Ad Size
(D) No Selection
(P) Return to Previous Menu


Enter Selection :A

Code A Number of Employees: 1-4
Code B Number of Employees: 5-9
Code C Number of Employees: 10-19
Code D Number of Employees: 20-49
Code E Number of Employees: 50-99
Code F Number of Employees: 100-249
Code G Number of Employees: 250-499
Code H Number of Employees: 500-999
Code I Number of Employees: 1000-4999
Code J Number of Employees: 5000-9999
Code K Number of Employees: Over 10000


Enter Employee Size Code or Range #1 (<RTN> if done) :F
Code F Number of Employees: 100-249
Enter Employee Size Code or Range #2 (<RTN> if done) :
```

Figure 4-2. Sheet 1: Selection and downloading of online network information files. *(continued)*

```
Geographic Selections:

(A) 3 digit ZIP Code or Range
(B) 5 digit ZIP Code or Range
(C) State Abbreviation
(D) County Code
(E) Area Code
(F) MSA Code
(G) Total USA
(P) Return to Previous Menu
(X) Logout

Enter Selection :C

Enter State Abbreviation # 1 (<RTN> if done) :MD
Enter State Abbreviation # 2 (<RTN> if done) :
Do you wish to review your entries? (Y/N) :Y

   NUMBER     State Abbrevs
     1    MD

ENTER: A TO ADD MORE ENTRIES.
       D TO DELETE AN ENTRY.
  OR: Q TO CONTINUE :Q

Retrieving names. Please wait.
Final count will appear when complete.

Total names in this selection = 273

(A) List all names retrieved
(B) List part of names (by record #)
(C) Nth-name sample
(D) Description of B & C
(E) No list desired-Delete File
(P) Return to Previous Menu
(X) Logout

Enter Selection :A
Please Choose Sequence Desired :

(A) ZIP Code Sequence
(B) Alphabetical by Company Name
(C) No Sort
(P) Return to Previous Menu
(X) Logout

Enter Selection :A

Select Format Option :

(A) Screen Viewing Record--Stop Every 3 Names
(B) Prospect List (Non-stop)
(C) Mailing Labels--One-Up
(D) Diskette/Hard Drive Formats
(E) Send File to ZIPNET
(P) Return to Previous Menu
(X) Logout
```

Figure 4–2.   Sheet 2. *(continued)*

```
Enter Selection :8

Processing files. Please wait . . .

                           ** IMPORTANT **

             If you wish to save this information
             to a diskette or hard drive, be sure
             your communications software is set to
               receive (capture) names. If sending
             to your printer, be sure it is on and
                         ready to receive.

             Press RETURN--To Begin Receiving Names,
             Press N--To Return to Format Menu :


------------------------------------------------------------

JENSTAR STONE PRODUCTS        SIC: 275999
250 ACTON LN
WALDORF MD 20601              Employees: 120
Telephone: 301/870-6200       County: 24017
DON DEAN, President           Sales: E ($5,000,000-$9,999,999)


SOUTH COUNTY CURRENT          SIC: 271101
7 INDUSTRIAL PARK CIR
WALDORF MD 20602              Employees: 150
Telephone: 301/645-9480       County: 24017
KAREN ACTON, Manager          Sales: F ($10,000,000-$19,999,999)


EMBASSY DAIRY INC             SIC: 202498
MATTAWOMAN DR
WALDORF MD 20604              Employees: 225
Telephone: 301/843-1212       County: 24017
JAMES POWERS, Manager         Sales: H ($50,000,000-$99,999,999)
```

Figure 4–2. Sheet 3. *(continued)*

illustrates the main menu and a typical listing downloaded in my test. The set of choices shown is only the first of many such: The system presents a progressive series of choices by which you define the list(s). You can preview the lists too, if you wish, before making choices.

I chose simply to log the lists on my disk, as they scrolled across my screen, giving me a file I could use to make up labels or process in some other manner if I wished to. I could, had I chosen to, have sent the list to one of my printers, instead of to a disk, and printed labels or hard copy directly as the list arrived. It is more efficient, however, to log the data to disk and do your printing later.

The download took about 11 minutes and cost 20 cents per name plus 30 cents per minute for connect time, for a total of slightly over $58. Together with telephone tolls, the cost per 1,000 names is not inconsiderable. However, these are lists that are yours to use again and again without further charges, so the cost is actually quite modest when averaged out over repeated uses. Too, the convenience of ordering and receiving a list within minutes is a consideration that has great value.

BUILDING A MARKETING DATABASE

The simple fact is that as of today you can rent mailing lists of a great many kinds and with an almost unprecedented volume of geographic, demographic, and psychographic qualifiers, but you can't rent a marketing database. In fact, you may never be able to do so because marketing databases may well prove to be always too individualized to be made into anything resembling a standard commodity that may be sold or rented to all. In any case, at present it is necessary for those who want to start using marketing databases to build their own. But where and how to start?

STARTING DATABASES AND THEIR SOURCES

An obvious place to start is with your own customer, inquiry, and prospect lists, if you have them. If you do not have such lists or wish to add to and expand from them, you can turn to at least two alternative ways or sources: One is to build new lists from scratch, through such methods as inquiry advertising and promotions (e.g., contests and lotteries) of various kinds. Another way is to start with conventional lists—not rented lists for they are yours to use only once per rental, but compiled lists, which you may use over and over, building them into a marketing database.

Each approach has its advantages and disadvantages, as you will appreciate when you consider the most distinguishing characteristic of the marketing database. It is this: The detailed, personalized information that makes the mailing list a marketing database comes primarily from those on the list. We can gather certain data from observation and perhaps from public records, and we can *infer* certain individual characteristics from these data, but we cannot be sure that the inferences accurately reflect the individuals' choices. That accuracy derives only from information "from the horse's mouth"—from the individual. That is, databased marketing involves a *dialogue* between seller and buyer. To build your database you must be deeply interested in everyone on your list and in your general database. Traditional inquiry advertising and other lead-generating programs are designed to produce a list of prospects nominally qualified as interested and, possibly, as capable of becoming buyers. Gathering information from which to build a marketing database is a different proposition: You design your promotions and advertising to elicit information from prospects that does far more than merely qualify them as potential buyers; it must provide individualized information about the prospect's interests and motivations such that you can identify market niches from that information and tailor your sales appeals to those interests and motivations. Establishing the dialogue to get that feedback is a main objective in building a marketing database. One important qualification must be made about this approach, however: Demographic and psychographic information is as broad as possible so as to provide a broad basis of possible uses for the list. The information gathered for a marketing database, however, is individualized in more than one sense: It is individualized first in terms of the personal interests and motivations of the subject, but it is also individualized in terms of what you, the marketer, are trying to sell.

Consider this carefully. There are practical limits to how large you can permit each record in your database to grow or how large it ought to be to serve your needs well. You want only the data that indicate the kind of prospect the individual is for what you sell, and not for anything else. If you sell cosmetics, you don't care what make of automobile the subject prefers, and any effort producing the latter information is wasted. You would discard that information. Thus you need to have a well-developed set of specifications for your marketing database.

In this light, the advantage of using commercially available compiled lists is that you start with a base of information, easily entered into your system as a beginning database, which has at least some data relevant to your need. However, much of it is not, and thus you may be getting not much more than a list of names and addresses.

Building your lists and your beginning database from scratch is laborious and expensive, but it is a direct attack on the problem and, if well handled, begins directly to produce the marketing database. In the final analysis, you will probably use a combination of methods.

NICHE MARKETS

A subgroup having characteristics especially favorable for your marketing needs or for some portion of your marketing needs is, in fact, a potential niche market for you. There are several ways to identify such subgroups. One method, using databased marketing, is to determine, in some manner, what the ideal characteristics are for some market niche you have identified and then work to develop a matching list of prospects. There are alternatives, however, such as to study the lists you have and try to identify those having the ideal characteristics. Another is to study your total list and see how many niche markets you can identify. Still another is to study your customer lists critically in search of clues to niche markets.

For example, I learned by experience that firms devoted to developing custom software for computer owners were an excellent prospect for my services as a marketing consultant and proposal writer/manager. I learned further that within this general class of firms I had great success with minority-owned firms trying to become established in a competitive field. I learned also that, among these firms, the ones that needed and welcomed my help the most were those in pursuit of government contracts. Thus those characteristics identified one market niche for me. But there were others: I learned that many firms that had for years enjoyed "sole source" advantages with certain government agencies were no longer to have that special largess, but would be compelled henceforth to compete for their contracts. They also needed and welcomed my help. These were two market niches I discovered by experience and benefited from.

In selling my writing services to government agencies I soon discovered two important facts:

- Many agencies had major training responsibilities.
- They knew how to create training programs, but they needed writing assistance.

Thus I soon found myself offering and selling writing services to training departments of the agencies.

I discovered another fact that appears to be counter to logic without an understanding of the government and thus the true logic of the condition: Prospecting for contracts with agencies that had specific training and publications departments (and appropriate staff) was far more productive than prospecting with agencies that had training and publication responsibilities, but no specific departments for these. (They assigned these as ad hoc or ancillary duties to their personnel office.) The reason this was true is simple enough, once you unchain your mind from conventional thinking: The agency without specific offices or departments for training and publications has only occasional need for the function. The agency with specific offices or departments for the functions has the need consistently enough to require special personnel. Government agencies, however, are almost always understaffed and therefore contract out the bulk of their work. (This is not entirely untrue of the commercial world also, where organizations frequently get overloaded and contract out much of their work as a consequence.) And so the agencies (and companies) with training and publications departments were always higher on my lists of prospects than those without them.

DATABASED MARKETING AND DIRECT MARKETING

We have been discussing databased marketing primarily with reference to mailing lists and direct marketing. Conceptually, however, there is no logical reason for confining the idea of databased marketing to direct marketing: If databased marketing is valid for DM, the idea is valid for all marketing. (Eventually, we will discuss it in the context of that broader universe.) However, there are good reasons for having discussed and explained databased marketing in terms of DM, at this point: For one, it is the DM industry that has first embraced this idea and ought to be credited with popularizing it, and perhaps even inspiring it originally. Most of the literature that has been and is being published on the subject appears in DM trade publications and books by specialists in that field. At this early stage, databased marketing lends itself best to DM. And, finally, the principal tool and medium of DM, the mailing list, is the analogue of databased marketing that offers the most convenient means to both understand and appreciate the idea of databased marketing (by its parallels with and even roots in the mailing list and related demographics and psychographics technologies) and furnish the most viable seeds from which to build a marketing database. It would not be outrageous to consider the marketing database to be a kind of super mailing list, in the sense of the accompanying data that qualify the list.

Chapter 5

Source of
Data for the Database

There is rarely a single source for all the information you need for your marketing database: It is usually an agglutination of data from many sources. It may even be an "Acres of Diamonds" situation, in which much of what you need is already in your possession and under your nose.

THE PRIME SOURCE OF INFORMATION
IS THE CUSTOMER

It is not only the thousand-mile journey hypothesized by the ancient Chinese philosopher Confucius that begins with a single step; the building of a marketing database, too, must begin somewhere with a first step. Whether you begin to build your marketing databases with your own customer* list, with rented or purchased mailing lists, from a combination of these, or from absolute ground zero, the source of the most important information is the customer. In the end, it is the customer who tells you how to sell to him and her!

CUSTOMER-BASED DATA VIS-À-VIS
MARKETING SUCCESS

There is really nothing new about this idea: We have always known that successful marketing results only when the marketer succeeds in learning or anticipating what the customer really wants. You can't sell a blue automobile to a customer who is mind-set on buying a white or red one, unless you manage to change the customer's mind about his or her

---

* In most cases, the term *customer* is used broadly here to refer both to those who have bought from you in the past and are truly customers and to those who are only prospective customers. Usually, the context will make it clear to which the reference is made, where it is necessary to make the distinction.

wants. You may be able to change a customer's want by showing him or her a blue car and offering some special inducement that is more powerful than the customer's original want, but you would have to conceive and offer the inducement that would do the job: You would have to know or successfully estimate the customer's priorities vis-à-vis a red car, a white car, and any special inducements to decision. In the final analysis, only the customer knows what it takes to motivate him or her to buy, so only the customer can pass on that necessary information to you. Lacking that certainty, we can only make our best estimates of what the customer is most likely to want. We gamble our marketing success on those estimates, and the history of marketing (including, significantly, that of business bankruptcies as well) is replete with examples of disasters resulting from misguided judgments of what customers want.

An example of that is documented in a recent book, *Taurus, the Making of the Car That Saved Ford* (Dutton, 1991). According to author Eric Taub, the Ford Motor Company was in rather desperate shape at the beginning of the 1980s, losing market share on a grand scale, as a result of Ford's conviction that it knew better than its customers did what the customers wanted and ought to have. Or, probably more accurately, the customers had no choice but to accept what Ford force-fed them. (I am one customer Ford lost many years ago because of its defiant refusal to honor its warranty.) The Taurus, however, revolutionized not only Ford but the American automobile industry. More significantly perhaps, it represented a revolution in thinking because, for the first time, Ford management (and probably a great many others in American automobile manufacturing management) began to listen to what customers thought and had to say about their wants, rather than what their executives thought. That is credited by Taub as the key ingredient in the Ford Taurus success story.

VALUE MARKETING

"Value marketing" is a new buzzword in the business world. Its basic premise is that customers know and appreciate real value, and in these somewhat straitened times are far more discriminating in seeking values than they were in the easier times of the past. Ergo, according to this rationale, today's business must offer true value if it is to survive. The explanations, however, are rather vague, and they fail to demonstrate that the average customer really knows or even has any way of determining how to measure or judge value. Some of the explanations suggest that changes in language make a difference: One suggestion, for example, is that changing the MasterCard appeal from the romantic "master the possibilities" theme to the more practical argument of ready access to cash via omnipresent automatic teller machines that accept MasterCard represents greater value to the customer. Thus the clues to value that customers supposedly use include guarantees, competitive pricing, and practical applications.

For the most part, these explanations vary from weak to unconvincing, except for pricing on known brands, where the customer is indeed able to make price comparisons and judge value on some objective basis. However, where the explanations suggest that the seller ask Mr. and Mrs. Customer what they want or, at least, demonstrate some concern for what the customer wants, they begin to make sense. Giving customers what they want and have asked for is likely to be accepted by those customers, whether they even consider the question of value. (In fact, most marketing theories are based on the premise that emotional appeals are far more effective than are rational appeals, and there is ample evidence to support that argument and orientation.) In that respect, some explanations of what "value marketing" means are often echoes of what we hear offered as definitions of databased marketing. The article, "Value Marketing," a cover story of the November 11, 1991, issue of *Business Week,* defines it, among other things, as building relationships with customers through frequent-buyer plans, 800 numbers, and membership clubs, among many devices. Sound familiar? See the reference to Kurt and Jan Williams, with their cosmetics and clothing shop (Chapter 3). More important is a story reported about a problem Toyota encountered and how the company handled it.

Toyota ran into a problem with its Lexus, a luxury automobile, that required issuing a recall. That is obviously a potential public relations (PR) problem that could have disastrous consequences. Wisely, Toyota handled the problem with such panache that they turned this threatened catastrophe into a PR coup: They had the dealers telephone each Lexus owner personally, offering to pick up their cars and provide lenders.

A major asset of databased marketing is that it reduces the amount of guesswork in deciding what customers want and replaces it with validated information because it turns to the customer as the prime source for the information. The 800 telephone numbers help because they are toll-free and thus encourage customers to call with their questions, complaints, and suggestions. All other means of reaching the seller help also. As fax machines become more and more widely used, invitations to use fax for messages can be offered, for one. And as more and more people buy and learn to use personal computers, the PCs can become another convenient means for dialogue with customers. Therefore, many companies in the computer business have established electronic bulletin boards to afford their computer customers a communication link. When I found my printer driver, the software program that helps me print out information on my NEC printer, to be less than totally effective, I rang up the NEC (Nippon Electric Corporation) BBS (electronic bulletin board system) to see if they could help. I was able to download—transfer from their computer to mine—another printer driver that worked far more effectively for me. NEC made no charge; the cost was only that of the telephone line, which was a dial-up call, the same as an ordinary voice call. Nor was this the only occasion on which I was able to use a supplier's BBS to help me solve a problem, which certainly has endeared me to the company.

The value of databased marketing must also depend directly on the quantity, accuracy, and relevancy of the information. Presumably, in the normal course of research, that data will be furnished by the customer, directly and indirectly, but that does not always ensure its accuracy and relevance. In the case of the automobile customer hypothesized earlier here, it would enable you to discriminate among various customers in identifying the one to whom color is all-important, the one to whom price or some other inducement is all-important, and the one who can be persuaded to trade one want for another. It thus offers the avoidance or, at least, the minimization of marketing disasters resulting from bad guesses.

That latter consideration raises another interesting and important point: Databased marketing can prevent marketing disasters, which is as important a consideration or objective as increasing marketing successes. Most companies are far more likely to survive the lack of great marketing successes than they are to survive great marketing disasters.

METHODS FOR GATHERING INFORMATION FROM THE CUSTOMER

Despite the many examples of marketer–customer interfaces and methods of dialogue, especially feedback from customer to marketer, we have not exhausted that subject by any means; there are still other methods for getting valuable marketing information from customers, both direct and indirect. Ironically, in some cases it is the difficulty in closing a sale that offers the greatest opportunity for valuable feedback.

In face-to-face selling, especially in that situation involving a big tag item, the typical customer is going to do at least some investigation— some looking about and shopping—before making a decision. That is not a drawback. Quite the opposite: It gives you, as the seller, the opportunity to do some probing to find out what the customer really wants. That may require a bit of patience. The truly professional sales approach is not to attempt a sale immediately, but rather to find out what it will take to make that sale, to find out what kind of sales presentation to make. Those pleasantries and conversational gambits a skilled salesperson offers a prospective customer are not merely small talk, although they may appear to be so; they are research, marketing probes asking the customer, in effect, "Tell me, what are your interests and desires? What motivates you? What must I do to sell you an automobile/house/boat/diamond ring? What is it that will induce you to buy from me?" Apparently casual questions about the customer's interests in color, price, operating costs, features, delivery, guarantees, financing, and other matters are anything but casual: They are bricks that build an individual customer profile: a prescription for a sale. Nor is the feedback always verbal: One of the most effective salespeople I have ever known got the bulk of his feedback—his clues to the customer's state of mind, desires, and intentions—by watching the customer's eyes, expressions, and body language as he made his step-by-step presentation.

On more than one occasion I have encountered the salesperson who is ready enough to take my order, but who does not take the first step necessary in making me a customer—that is, to finding out what it will take to make me a customer by probing to discover what I really want—what motivates me, relative to what the salesperson wants to sell me; what he or she must say, do, and offer to erase the glazed look from my eyes and replace it with the sparkle of interest. The sales record of such employees is typically undistinguished.

Today, the establishment truly interested in building a marketing database must be willing to do whatever is necessary to gain the data necessary to build the database. Perhaps that will be to have telemarketers call all customers and chat with them. Perhaps it will be to have the salesperson immediately make out a report—actually a data sheet or form—recording the details of each interview of a prospective customer: the customer's name, address, purchase, expressed interests and biases, method of financing, and a host of other details that will be entered into the record of that customer prospect in the establishment's database. Perhaps they will have interviews recorded on tape for later transcription and analysis. Perhaps they will ask prospective customers to fill out questionnaires or attend a demonstration or free seminar, at which data may be gathered. Many contests, trade show exhibits, and other such PR activities have, as one of their main goals, the collecting of customers' own preferences to help in gathering data for the building of marketing databases. All these are based on the notion of getting the database information from the prime source, the customer.

By far the best way to find out how to sell anything to a customer is to ask the customer. It is the entire key to marketing success. It *is* the essence of marketing. (Who knows better than the customer what motivates him or her to buy?) Did I say that before? Yes, I am sure that I did, but it needs repeating: It is a message that seems to get lost, somehow, and thus needs repetition.

MARKETING DATABASES ARE NOT BUILT OVERNIGHT

Procter & Gamble, GE, GM, IBM, Ford, Sears, and all those other major corporations and supercorporations can afford to mount huge programs, with platoons of staff experts, to build marketing databases. An increasing number of them are doing so today. However, the typical small business, whether a list broker or a small to medium-size seller of goods and services, cannot sustain such large programs, especially since the return on investment is not only not immediate but also not at all predictable or certain. It is a long-term, highly speculative investment at this time, and no one has yet figured out how it can pay back investment in the short term or even in the long term.

For that reason alone, many of us, if not most of us, must make the development of marketing databases and their use for databased marketing a gradual process: The data will accumulate steadily but by degrees from our traditional marketing activities and whatever ancillary special activities we can mount to speed the process. Still, it is a way to get there eventually, if not immediately. And gathering the necessary data is not something new or unusual; the things we normally do in preparing any DM campaign are entirely relevant.

Most of us normally run tests before rolling out a campaign as a matter of standard practice. We test our lists, we test our offers, and we test our copy. In effect, when we are testing, we ask a representative group of prospects what will persuade them to buy—which price, which headline, which feature, or which other major factor of our campaign he or she likes best, which least, and by which feature or factor he or she is best motivated. It's an indirect way, unfortunately, trying to find out what it takes to sell to only 1, 2, or possibly 3 or 4 percent of those prospects to whom we plan to make an offer. We hope that they are truly representative of the entire population of prospects, and we do what we can to maximize that probability, but we can never be sure. Moreover, we can ask only a quite limited number of the important questions in such testing, but that is the best we can do in that marketing milieu. It would be self-defeating to try to develop more information in a simple prerollout test. Still, we can record the data and add to them constantly, as we find opportunities to do so, and so build our databases steadily.

ASKING THE QUESTIONS AND GETTING THE ANSWERS

There is a certain advantage in selling customers by the direct face-to-face means, whether we are selling an automobile, a house, a yacht, a refrigerator, a diamond ring, or anything else, even a can of soup. We can ask questions over a rather broad range, much more so than by that indirect means we call direct marketing. (The anomaly here is, of course, ironic.) But in selling a can of soup in today's self-service supermarket merchandising and mail-order systems, you normally "meet" the typical customer only through the in-store displays or the advertising and direct-mail literature you send out that happens to draw a response. And, of course, for everyone who becomes your customer, there are dozens you "invited" (i.e, solicited at great expense) to become your customers who resisted your appeals. That means that all those others fall into one of two classes: Either your appeals were not attractive enough, as far as they were concerned, or those addressed were not true prospects for what you offered, and would not have been under any circumstances: It was a sheer waste of time and money to pursue them at all.

Thus, to improve your batting average, you must find other, preferably far less expensive, ways to ask the customer what it takes to sell him or her. You also need to get answers to more than one or two key questions if you want data that will be useful for more than the immediate purpose of your current program. It is time to depart from the common denominators of low prices, catchy slogans, or free gifts as the main appeals that will capture a tiny fraction of the population of prospects. Each individual is unique. Customers and prospective customers do not constitute a uniform sample about which a single rule applies; what will sell John Doe is not what will sell Jane Doe or John Roe. Nor are customers' buying decisions necessarily based primarily on any single factor, such as price or color. Far more often the decision is based on a combination of several factors, some practical but often quite subtle emotional or subconscious ones. Even the customer whose prime motivation is price and financing, for example, is not unmoved by considerations of convenience, delivery, service, guarantees, and other factors that he or she must balance against the appeal of favorable price and financing. Where low price or convenient financing alone may not move him or her to a buying decision, low price plus another inducement or two may do the job. But how to know what those inducements ought to be?

THE BUILT-IN HAZARDS IN QUESTIONNAIRES

If you have ever asked for a free subscription to a trade journal of any kind, you have had to complete a questionnaire of some sort. Some of these are rather lengthy, some are relatively brief, but all are aimed at the same purpose: They are collecting data to explain to prospective advertisers who their readers are, that is, whom the advertisers will reach with appeals published in the journal. This information is the only price of subscription required of you, and it has specific value to the publisher: It is the basis on which he charges advertisers whatever rates he charges, and with which he wins their advertising in the first place.

Perhaps you are the proprietor or chief executive of a small business, wearing a half-dozen hats. You must decide which is the appropriate box to mark to answer the question asking you to identify your role:

☐ Chairman of the Board
☐ Chief Executive Officer
☐ President
☐ General Manager
☐ Sales Manager
☐ Comptroller
☐ Chief Engineer

You decide that Sales Manager is most appropriate in this case, and you check off that box. Or perhaps none of the choices really reflect your status, so you sigh and check off the one you think is closest. Then again, you may be a junior executive and fearful that you won't be granted a free subscription unless you inflate your role somewhat, so you appoint yourself to a high-level job in the company.

Those are the automatic hazards to accurate information when relying on questionnaires, whether in specific applications such as this or in more general surveying and polling. Respondents often choose alternatives to strictly objective or accurate responses for any of several reasons:

- None of the options offered in a multiple-choice questionnaire is quite right for them. No issue involved is important (not to the respondent, anyway) so they choose one that seems to be fairly close.
- They often tend to judge what answer is desired (especially in face-to-face interviews) and try to satisfy that perceived desire.
- Sometimes the question (i.e., the nature of the answer called for) is unclear, compelling the respondent to guess at the kind of information desired, with predictable effects on accuracy.
- Some items call for judgmental response by their nature, rather than by uncertainty as to meaning. Then the information furnished reflects the respondent's biases, emotional state of the moment, and the tendency of many of us to compromise and find a middle-of-the-road choice. (This is especially the case when the respondent is uncertain of the most appropriate choice.)

QUESTIONNAIRE DESIGN

Questionnaire design is a field in which there are expert consultants. It may be worthwhile to seek one out if you are planning a serious effort to gather data with some sort of questionnaire or polling program. However, there are a few broad guidelines to consider if you plan to develop your own data-gathering instruments. These reflect the implications of the hazards just enumerated.

Two Kinds of Data Are Needed

In the case of gathering data for a marketing database, you will want both objective (i.e., factual) data and subjective (i.e., judgmental) data. You want to know how respondents, who are prospective customers, *feel* about many things; that is important information for marketing. At the same time, you don't want the respondents' emotional reactions clouding the accuracy of factual data. You must be clear in your mind as to the *kind* of data you want as a response to each item of your questionnaire, and you must tailor the item accordingly.

Avoiding the Hazards

Following are some suggestions to bear in mind when designing a questionnaire or other data-gathering instrument:

- Include an "other" category in each listing of choices in multiple-choice questionnaires, inviting the respondent to write in an appropriate response if none of the choices offered are quite right.
- Try most earnestly to eliminate or at least minimize questions calling for judgment by making the question require unemotional, objective responses. For example, don't ask whether the respondent lives in a "large" or "small" city, but offer categories to check off, such as sizes of population—"Less than 50,000," "100,000 to 500,000," "500,000 to 1,000,000," and "more than 1,000,000."
- Edit the items closely to eliminate ambiguity and other threats to clarity.
- Avoid invitations to middle-road answers. Don't ask respondents to use a scale of 1 to 10 in making a judgment, for example. But don't use such quantitative choices suggested in the previous item when the choice calls for judgment, rather than reporting. Do not, for example, use that method to elicit a responses to such a question as "In what size city would you prefer to live?" You are much more likely to get a true and useful answer if you put the question along the lines, "Would you prefer big-city life to small-city or small-town life?"
- When you want a subjective response, design the item to call for a yes–no choice, as in the preceding suggestion. This calls for an unequivocal response, which is much more likely to show the respondent's true feelings than any item that would invite a fence-sitting response.

THE SIGNIFICANCE OF ALL THIS

By now you may be asking yourself why the emphasis on all this individualized data. Why do you need to know what each prospect wants? Why the individual want, rather than the group want? Obviously, we are not going to mount a separate campaign for each respondent. So why efforts to all but personally interview each possible customer individually?

The answer lies in today's economics. It is simply no longer viable to pursue or make presentations to a million prospects to win 1,000 or 2,000 orders. We must narrow the field in bracketing the group wherein our best prospects, our customers, lie. We cannot identify each and every one individually in advance, but we can and must identify that 10,000 or 20,000 prospects in which we shall find our 1,000 or 2,000 customers. We can, that is, identify the *niche markets* containing those customers, while we screen out the vast number representing waste and futility. That is a discussion unto itself.

NICHES OF THE MARKET

To maximize marketing results, we must address customers as individuals, appealing to their specific desires. And if it is not practicable, in a literal sense, to appeal individually to each prospect, we can at least sort our prospects into the many smaller groups that represent the different market niches. We can identify and prepare appeals to the ones who want to get the most possible value for their dollars, the ones who seek something with a glamorous image, the ones who are looking for something "new," the ones who want something public figures endorse, the ones who have special needs, and all the other small groups that will become your customers if you understand their wants and can thus offer to satisfy them.

That is the kind of information you need in the marketing database: what the customer says he or she wants to buy, even when the desire is not entirely a conscious one and not necessarily the product per se, but a feature of the product or conditions of the sale (i.e., price, service, bonus, or other). But it is also necessary to find out whether a prospect is indeed a prospect, and to select from your lists those who are true prospects. Those who cannot be qualified as real prospects should be dropped from the database or, at least, transferred to some other list. That is itself a prime objective in building marketing databases: An important part of the process in developing a marketing database is qualifying the prospects to maximize the value of the list. A true marketing database includes only those who appear to be real prospects for what you are selling, enabling you to avoid wasting money and effort in sending your offer to others who are not really good prospects for you.

TWO OBJECTIVES IN BUILDING MARKETING DATABASES

It does not require a great deal of initial thought to realize that there are at least two ways to approach the development of and set objectives for a marketing database. They are implicit in the concept. One objective is finding model prospects or identifying your typical customer, the archetype. The other is finding the most suitable niches in your market spectrum. In fact, except for those selling impressively large-tag items that justify and even require special marketing presentations to individual prospects, these are effectively a single goal: For most products and services other than those large-tag items, it is impracticable to pursue individual sales, and so it is really grouping prospects of similar buying motivations—niche markets—that you must pursue as the object of your marketing database development. There are, however, various complications possible, according to variants in what you sell and your own peculiar marketing requirements (e.g., the difference between selling costume jewelry and fast-food franchises). These also affect your approaches and processes in building your marketing database(s).

Finding Model Prospects

In the first case hypothesized here, you are in quest of better qualifiers for your prospects. You sell a single item or closely related line of items, and you want to profile your typical customer: You want to develop a profile that defines the best prospect for what you sell. You have therefore somehow decided what the criteria and characteristics are that identify your customers. That information constitutes a model. If the model is a true representation and you can use it to build a list of prospects that match the model, your response rate ought to go through the roof. On the other hand, because of this accelerated response rate, your marketing cost, the cost per order, ought to drop through the cellar. In substance, you will have the model to ensure continued marketing success in your business. You can now examine the characteristics and qualifications of every prospect in your general database to screen out those who do not conform to the model and make a first-priority list of those who do conform. Your can thus build a marketing database that represents high-grade ore: It ought to produce orders at a very satisfying rate.

Finding Market Niches

Not every marketing problem lends itself to building a single model as the pattern for a successful marketing database. In fact, it is probably the rare exception that this proves to be the case, and the example just described is useful more for illustrating a principle of modeling customers than to represent a typical situation. In the more probable case, you must develop a number of models, customers with different reasons for buying what you sell, each representing a niche market.

Building a marketing database or set of databases to identify and pursue niche markets is thus really more of the same. Typically, niche markets are market segments that have been neglected by your larger competitors as unfeasible ventures because the markets are relatively small. However, they are niches in which you can sell effectively whatever it is that you sell. And they can be niches in a market where you normally sell to individual consumers or they can be niches in some kind of BTB (business to business) marketing where you normally sell to organizations. In either case, each market niche will be some identifiable group of individual consumers or organizations.

For example, suppose that you sell a diet preparation of some sort. What are the possible market niches? Let's hypothesize a few different prospects, as defined or identified by just a broad generalization of their characteristics (as distinct from the more detailed ones we would normally seek to identify in building a marketing database) and see what they might represent:

1. The experienced and somewhat disillusioned dieter. He or she has tried them all and is skeptical about all.
2. The spasmodic dieter. He or she periodically goes on a crash diet, loses some weight, and abandons the diet until the clothes no longer fit or there is some special occasion to attend (a wedding, a testimonial dinner, etc.) and it is time to diet again.
3. The first-time dieter, who knows next to nothing about dieting.
4. The eternal optimist dieter, eager to believe that this time he or she has found the Holy Grail of diets.
5. The dyed-in-the-wool, dependable dieter, who has no illusions about dieting and will diet all of his or her life, but will always be looking for new diet ideas and new diet preparations to try.

Each type dictates a different marketing strategy, a different appeal. One might be attracted by "the *different* diet," another by "the *speedy* diet," and still another by "a *new idea* in diets." Knowing the history and biases of the dieters is the key to selling them, but you must segregate them into their proper niches and make appropriate offers and appeals to each niche.

Among those listed and described in your general database are many who would be excellent prospects for items or services you sell, although they are merely small segments of the market overall. This presupposes that you have a large general database so documented that it is possible to segregate the entries into small groups, each representing a market.

If you sell a wide and disparate variety of items, rather than a single item or a narrowly specialized line, you may or may not be in a situation in which all your customers will be prospects for all the items you sell. If you sell a complete line of office supplies, for example, you are marketing a widely diverse line, from paper clips, to office machines, to computers, and even to office furniture. It is quite likely that customers for some parts of your line will not be customers for other parts. Your niches will appear in terms of customers segmented by different kinds of characteristics, and there are many ways in which customers may be so segregated. There is the general nature of the customers: the independent freelance or self-employed individual, the home-based business, the rural small business, and the urban large corporation. There is the diversity of what the customer does. In my own case, I am closely tied to my computer so most of my buying is of equipment, accessories, software, and consumable supplies for my computer system.

Niches may be characterized by motivations, but the motivations of any individual on your list may vary, according to the item and how the individual views the item and its importance; he or she may be motivated primarily by price, with respect to one item, but by service or some other factor, in the case of another item.

I am probably typical of most customers in the variance of my motivations. I perceive different considerations in each case: I buy a full year's supply of toner cartridges by mail because there is only one make and model that I can use, and a certain mail-order house offers the best price for this expensive item if I buy at least three at a time. Since the item is unique, the only possible differences among sources are price and service, and price is really the only significant factor. I buy paper for my printer and fax machine in a local warehouse store, motivated by both price and convenience. I have no pattern or basic principle for buying computer software and accessories, however, but buy them wherever it is convenient, if the price is at all competitive. On the other hand, I buy my computers and upgrade enhancements from a local computer builder whose prices are by no means the lowest. I buy from him because I have great confidence in his products and because he provides unfailing service when I need it and backs up his guarantees cheerfully and willingly.

There is thus possible segregation in terms of what the individual is a best prospect for—office furniture, computer supplies, general office supplies, and/or office machines. There is also segregation in terms of motivation—name brands versus generic brands, quality versus economy, and discounts versus free gifts or bonuses. But a given customer may have entirely different motivations for different kinds of purchases (as I do), according to his or her rationales about the best principles to follow in buying each kind of item. It is thus hazardous to generalize that any customer is always motivated by the same considerations.

Your marketing database thus ought to identify individuals for each segment with which he or she ought to be associated. A database of 10,000 names, for example, might actually include several dozen database files totaling far more than 10,000 names and addresses. That is, the actual file might include 10,000 names and addresses, but you could easily compile several dozen selective assortments (niches) that would total several times 10,000 names and addresses if you created permanent new files. (In practice, that is not necessary. Each database file exists only as an individual search-and-retrieve command, executed spontaneously when you wish to make a mailing to the names constituting that niche.)

Defining Market Niches

This feature of marketing databases means that any given customer may belong to or be representative of more than one market niche, but not of all. It also means that market niches need to be identified in different ways. For example, you might identify one niche as that of buyers who always prefer to order by telephone, while another niche may be that of those who prefer to order by mail. There are those who prefer to pay in cash, others who prefer to use credit cards, and perhaps another group who pay in full by check, but insist that they thus merit a special discount. Then there are the senior citizens who are interested in the senior citizen discount that so many businesses offer today. (Only yesterday, such a discount saved me well over a hundred dollars on an expensive automobile repair. On the other hand, the senior citizen discount would save me $30 in a membership fee, but it is then a limited membership, so I prefer to pay the full price for an unlimited membership.) Of course, a niche defined by one motivation does not tell you for what goods or service the individual is a good prospect; the niche needs to be identified also in those terms, that is, at more than one level or by more than one criterion or field of the record. (More on this in the next chapter.)

ACRES OF DIAMONDS

Unless you are only now launching a business venture, you have already built more than one database. You have a customer list, for example, which is a bare-bones database, even if it contains no information other than the name and address of each customer. You have an invoice file of some sort, another bare-bones database. Putting the two together yields a database of customers with data on what each one bought in the past.

You may have several other databases. If you have salespeople on the street making calls, you have call reports. You may have credit applications and credit reports on file. Depending on your systems, you may have correspondence files, individual folders for each customer, and many other kinds of records. You may, in short, already have more than a little of the data you need to expand your customer list into a marketing database. Give first priority to that possibility. It may be laborious to sort it all out and compile it, and it is almost surely not enough by itself, but it is probably the least costly way to begin. On the other hand, it is not the only way. You can also begin with conventional mailing lists that you have compiled yourself or bought from a compiler, as explained earlier (Chapter 4). Here, too, you have a reasonably complete set of beginning data, primarily of a fairly general nature, as per examples of the previous chapter, but still a good base.

OTHER SOURCES OF DATA

There are numerous ways of collecting information. As suggested earlier, the primary source is the customer, but such information may come from the customer directly or indirectly. Here are some ways others gather data from customers, many of which may be suitable for your own purposes:

■ You may use such direct means as surveys, questionnaires, and application forms, but you may also get information from secondary sources, such as credit reporting bureaus and published directories.

■ There are a number of alternative means for getting such information directly. When you fill out an application for a rebate or a specially discounted or even free book or other item, you may wonder why some of the questions seem to be rather outré, as far as the rebate or item is concerned, but the offeror is collecting personal data not normally available in any other medium. (Now you know!)

■ Pace, the warehouse store, for example, furnishes brochures inviting customers to submit suggestions for additional items they would like to find in Pace outlets. This is a common practice, and many such brochures and pamphlets go well beyond simply asking for recommendations and pursue a wide range of facts and opinions from the customers.

■ If you apply for a free subscription to a trade publication you generally must respond to a rather lengthy set of questions, but that, too, provides data not usually available otherwise. (On the other hand, if you advertise in one of those trade publications, you will reap the benefits of that data as the publisher furnishes rather well-detailed profiles of readers.) The many ways you can contrive to elicit such information from customers and prospects are limited only by your own ingenuity and resourcefulness.

■ Not long ago my wife, an inveterate dieter, bought several packages of *Lavosh,* a flatbread cracker produced by Adrienne's Gourmet Foods of Santa Barbara, California. To her dismay, she discovered the calorie count on the package reported as 18 calories per cracker. The package listed an 800 telephone number, and my wife promptly called. She was treated most courteously, and the company apologized for a mistake on the label: The proper calorie count was 18 calories for *two* crackers. Publishing that 800 telephone number saved them the loss of a customer. Of course, it probably has saved them the loss of many customers. It also provided exclusive input for the manufacturer's marketing database.

■ You may use conventional advertising media to induce customers and prospective customers to call and write. One way to do this is to use a special form of inquiry advertising. Originally, inquiry advertising was used as a method for generating leads and compiling mailing lists, which are, of course, leads en masse, to be followed up by mass mailings, rather than by telephone or personal visits. In its simplest form, inquiry advertising consists of small, classified advertisements offering something free, such as a special report, a newsletter, or a sample of some product. But it is sometimes even more effective to use a variant of this, the loss leader (an item sold below cost).

■ The Walter Drake mail order company has for years sold stick-on personal name-and-address labels for a nominal sum as a leader. The names of respondents—customers for these labels—were added to the company's mailing lists and sent catalogs of the entire product line. There are many other ways to employ this basic idea to elicit inquiries and thus identify prospects. Some marketers have taken this idea further and used it to gain information from prospective customers by inserting questionnaires and survey instruments in popular magazines and newspapers or even packaged with their products.

■ Quill Corporation, a leading mail-order vendor of office and industrial supplies over a wide range, includes a special kind of newsletter, *The Quill Pen Pal,* in its monthly catalog of specials, offering useful tips and inviting letters from readers.

■ More than a few other companies are publishing free newsletters for customers today, encouraging letters from readers as an effective means for generating data for their databases. Some companies have even launched more ambitious such projects, customer magazines, usually at subsidized prices. In the past, when such ventures were undertaken, it was usually only by companies manufacturing high-priced items, such as IBM and its *Think* magazine. Today, however, Olin Chemical offers pool owners its *Poolife* magazine, and cat lovers can subscribe at nominal prices to *The Morris Report*. Such magazines are growing in number. Many accept advertising that does not compete directly with the company's own product, which helps defray the costs of publication.

■ Many companies have taken to sponsoring customer clubs. Burger King and Woolworth, among others, have clubs for youngsters. Miller Brewing Company, Seagram, Warner-Lambert, and others have clubs also, generating a good bit of dialogue with customers.

THE DESIGN OF THE DATABASE

Two of the points made so far in these pages have been these: Your needs depend on a great many factors, of which at least a few are peculiar to your own business and your own situation. Database design is highly flexible and can be readily adapted to your own needs. We will discuss this in the next chapter.

Chapter 6

Designing the Database

Designing a database is a collaboration among the marketer, the technician, and the designer of the database management system—the software program you use. Yet, in a large sense the responsibility for the
final design rests on you, the marketer, and the design is much more an
ongoing process than a single action: Like people, databases are born as
crude beginnings and must grow to maturity.

GENERAL PREMISES

For the purposes of our discussion here, I will assume that you will be
working with a late model PC, and our DBM will be a hypothetical
one, although I will confess to being heavily influenced in this concept
of a hypothetical DBM by the latest versions of the classic DBM software. I am not, however, even going to attempt to be highly technical in
discussing the design of database files and the manipulation of DBM
software. In fact, I will deliberately minimize technical coverage for it
is not only unnecessary, but it is also a digression that would serve the
purposes of this book badly. My chief interest in this chapter—in this
book, for that matter—is to address the *marketing* significance and
methodologies related to database use and not the technicalities of
computers and database design. They are the means and not the end.
In fact, I will even bypass the traditional mathematical disciplines
such as regression analyses, which are mathematical modeling processes that purport to link causes and effects or show straight-line relationships between and among various factors known as "dependent"
and "independent variables," in the jargon of the math. If, for example,
most of your customers with incomes of more than $100,000 annually
buy more frequently and/or spend more money with you than those
with incomes of less than $100,000 annually, you may assume that this
correlation is a fixed one. That is a sometimes truth: There will be
many exceptions, but it furnishes a pretty good rule of thumb for you,
at least for the moment.

Mathematical disciplines have their virtues and are even a necessity in the case of the large marketing operation. There are, however, a few problems with this kind of data processing. First, because it has many exceptions—is not an unvarying truth—it has most limited value for small operations. Its chief value lies in large numbers, where the exceptions are a small percentage of the total. In fact, the correlation is not at all reliable unless it is made on the basis of a very large sample. Thus it has a large element of doubt and uncertainty for the small business.

A second problem is that the correlations found, even for a very large sample, may not be true for wider applications than the one at hand. That is, relying on the correlations found may produce great results for the campaign of the moment, but may prove to be entirely unreliable a short time hence, when there have been changes in economic conditions, competition, or products offered.

For these and other reasons we are going to shun the sophisticated techniques and technical terms that the magna-marketers use and remain strictly laypeople. In this chapter we are concerned principally with the development, organization, and use of the customer data for marketing effectiveness, rather than the most able technical management of DBM software, database files, and data manipulations. These are really technical matters for experts of various kinds, not marketers. Focusing unduly on this aspect of database design and development has sometimes led users into the trap of relying on the experts, computer and otherwise, to design the database files and related procedures and processes. That is to be avoided here, as an unacceptable weakening of your overall control as the marketer.

The abandonment of managerial control to the technical expert is not an unheard-of problem, especially in relation to creating computer systems. In one sizable company where I served as the manager of one of its many branch offices, the home office acquired a large, mainframe computer and installed therein a database system to handle the payroll, a major task that had to be performed weekly. The system was designed by the company's computer experts, with occasional meetings with the comptroller, who had managerial responsibility for the work, of course. The payroll checks were run and sent out without difficulty every week thereafter. However, when vacation season arrived, the home office, with all the employee records in its giant computer, had to ask each branch manager to supply figures on the vacation time due each employee of the branch. This information was, of course, information the home office should have gotten as a report from its own computer's database files and distributed *to* branch managers, rather than the reverse. A properly designed system would have printed out a simple report listing the names of all employees, by location, jobs, or any other designator desired, along with earned vacation time. Unfortunately, the colloquies that had taken place between the comptroller and the computer experts had been somewhat less than perfect: The comptroller did not really understand the nature of computers and databases, and had therefore never really thought out his needs or how a computer could help to satisfy them. The company's computer experts had not a clue as to what the comptroller of a large company needed to know and what information a payroll program ought to be able to produce, over and above that necessary to print a check and make the proper tax deductions. Each operated from the base of his or her own interests and gave little thought to what the other needed or cared about. So the resulting system produced the payroll checks but failed to keep track of and calculate vacation time for each employee or to provide any of the other routine information that should be supplied by such a system.

Problems such as these can be overcome later by reprogramming, using 20/20 hindsight, but that wastes time and is expensive. Far better to spend a little more time in advance planning, deciding just what you are most likely to need and want from your system, and even anticipating that you will fail to anticipate future needs and so create some reserve capacity to cope with this eventuality when it comes to pass, as it almost surely will.

PLANNING AHEAD

One thing all of us who use computers soon learn is that we must choose software to meet not only our needs of today but also tomorrow's needs as we anticipate them: Too often, characteristically often, we learn that we have grossly underestimated our needs of tomorrow. The wisdom of many in everyday life dictates that on a personal basis you can never be too thin or too rich. There are analogies here. When working with computers generally, you learn that you can never have too much memory. When working with databases specifically, especially for marketing, you learn that you can never have too much available capacity for adding data. We appear always to underestimate future needs and opportunities for new breakthroughs, whether dealing with computers or designing and building highways. The needs, the challenges, and the opportunities of the future also prove, almost always, to be far greater than you ever dreamed they would be when you started. A rule of thumb often offered as general advice in planning anything connected with computers, is to estimate your probable needs as generously as possible, and then double that estimate. That should apply to your estimated needs for analyses, list compilations, and list retrievals, as well as for reports. The DBMS is the perfect or at least the near-perfect tool for this, but it is still a tool that is under your control.

THE ROLE OF THE DATABASE MANAGEMENT SYSTEM

You will remember that one of the major characteristics of database software is that it is inherently highly flexible, structured in only a most general sense, structured for versatility, in fact: The database management software is much more a shell or a template for your use as a designer of your own database program than it is itself a program per se. It furnishes the overlay or template for your design and does all the tedious detail work of sorting files, selecting names you want, compiling lists for you, generating and printing out labels and reports, and otherwise carrying out all the other laborious duties. You, however, decide how the many and various files are formatted and what goes into them. Moreover, not only does the software relieve you of a lengthy roster of tedious chores you might otherwise be forced to perform but it does these things almost infinitely faster than you or an entire battalion of clerks could do them by the old-fashioned "manual" means. At the same time, it assists you in designing all the files, labels, and reports you will need. It lays out the guidelines and furnishes a most general format and suggestions as "default" options, but *you* are free to design the specific program (e.g., formats of records and reports) for your specific application. Ergo, our discussions of database design in this chapter are going to range widely, exploring ideas gleaned from many sources, but to offer specific designs would be a contradiction of the entire idea of marketing by database. So bear in mind always that you are the designer, ultimately, and that you must design in strict accordance with your own imagination and your individual needs, constrained only by the limits imposed by the DBMS. We will discuss this, but first let me refresh your memory on a few matters discussed briefly in earlier chapters.

The DBM program software does lay down some basic designs and rules; you must function within those constraints. They are, however, not at all confining: DBM design is highly flexible and adaptable to your own desires, although it is not, of course, completely formless. Within the broad constraints of those guidelines and limits, you are free to design and organize your various files, labels, reports, and forms as you perceive your own needs. In fact, the DBM even helps you by furnishing a number of "default" options—standardized forms and designs you may opt for as suggested (i.e., by default) or that you may modify to suit your own tastes.

Still, despite this typical great flexibility and openness of all DBM software design, there is a great deal of variance among DBM programs; some of the most basic differences (e.g., permissible numbers and sizes of fields and records) were mentioned earlier, and to a large extent those constraints are the principal ones of interest. At the same time, there are other considerations. Database management software runs the gamut from the simplest flat-file programs to the most complex and sophisticated relational database management software, such as dBASE IV, which is probably the quintessential DBM, and the best-known name, although there are other database programs of equal sophistication.

The specific designs of marketing databases are as much the proper domain, and the proper responsibility, of the marketers as they are the responsibility of the computer mavens. If you have computer experts putting your system together for you, be sure that you make all design decisions in terms of what you want the system to be able to do and make those decisions clear to your computer expert, whether he or she is your own employee or a consultant. Be absolutely sure that you understand each other. The computer expert will either figure out how to implement your idea or will tell you that it can't be done the way you want to do it. In that case, you put your heads together and work the problem out so that you get what you want. The technician may do the technical design, but you do the practical design, the *marketing* design. If you do not do it, it will almost certainly not get done, and your system will not do what you want it to do.

A common problem in this is that you, the expert marketer, may not only know little or nothing about computers but are awed by the computer and the computer expert; too many marketers are so awed. If you are one of those who are overwhelmed by computers and by computer experts, dismiss that fear now. Do not accept the "authority" of the computer expert as something that overrides your decisions about what you want or your own wisdom and experience in making marketing decisions. Try to remember that you are the marketing expert, and that the computer is simply a more efficient way to get your job done. It is up to you to specify what you need and want as a capability, and up to the expert to provide it. If he or she demurs, you must require him or her to explain the problem *in terms you, a layperson, can understand.* You must never accept an allegation that the matter is too complex for you to grasp; that is nonsense, a copout by experts who either are too lazy to do that part of their jobs or aren't too sure what their jargon really means, after all. Such an allegation reveals only that the expert either is not truly expert—does not him- or herself really understand the problem— or is trying to "snow" you. Do not infer that you are incapable of understanding such technical stuff. The most complex matter can be presented in simple lay language. Even Einstein's sophisticated theories were eventually translated into lay terms for the world to understand. It is part of your expert's responsibility to provide that kind of translation for you: You have a right to expect your experts to make issues clear in simple language that any intelligent adult can understand, and you should refuse to settle for less than that.

The converse is also true, however: As a marketer, don't allow yourself to become overly concerned with the technicalities of computer and database management designs, other than to understand their use and capabilities in practical terms. It is also unnecessary to lecture your experts in the marketing aspects of what you want: They do not need to become marketing experts. Tell your computer experts what *results* you need, not why you need them nor how to achieve them. Call on your computer experts to guide you in the choice of database management systems most suitable to your needs and, if necessary, in setting up the records, fields, reports, and labels. You may wish to have an expert install your system, answer questions you have about operation and maintenance, and even train people in your organization. However, as the marketer, you must make decisions about basic approaches to your marketing database design. That should become self-apparent shortly.

MAIN OBJECTIVES

You cannot pursue the development of marketing databases in a vacuum: You must have some clear idea of your specific objectives—what you are trying to accomplish. There are two possible main objectives to address: One is identifying the best possible prospects for your proposition through developing one or more profiles of your typical customers to serve as diagnostic models. The other is determining whether there are groups of individuals or organizations within your database that represent one or more special segments or market niches. The database manager you elect to use and the design of your database files should be geared to accomplishing both of these objectives. Bear in mind, however, that distinguishing between customer profiles and niche markets may be academic (i.e., they may be the same thing or, at least, closely related to each other). If you can identify several distinctly different customer profiles, you may be, in fact, identifying niche markets (depending on that basis for identifying a niche market, about which there will be more to say shortly). That is, you want to distinguish between different kinds of customers for different kinds of items and different kinds of customers for the same item or line of items. The latter kind of distinction reflects different market niches; the former kind of distinction may or may not signify niches in the market. That is, modeling your several sales prospects may be a subobjective, the real objective being the identification of the niche markets revealed by those models.

A BASIC DESIGN PHILOSOPHY

Before you design your database, you must decide what the basic design principle or philosophy is to be. Even though you have a computer expert on staff or retained as a consultant to advise and guide you, *you* must choose the basis for your records. You have two choices: You can set up records on a transaction basis or on an account basis. That is, you can create a new record for each individual transaction, regardless of who the customer or account is, or you can create a single record for each account or customer, and record each transaction in that record. (With a system set up by accounts in a flat-file database manager, each transaction would have to be literally accounted for or at least identified in the record. With the same system set up in a relational database manager, the transactions can be installed elsewhere but retrieved as though they were in the marketing database. More on that subject shortly.)

There are arguments for either basic system design. You can design a database system recorded by accounts or a system recorded by transactions. Both system designs can be made to work. However, it is probably easier or at least more efficient to have your database system set up on a customer or account basis, with each record a running narrative of transactions with that same customer. You can thus get a complete history of your relationships with that customer by accessing his or her account. That seems to be the most relevant approach if you are building a databased marketing system. The philosophy of databased marketing is, after all, based on the notion of maximum information about each individual customer and prospective customer. However, aside from the fact that the focus of the marketing database we are discussing here is customer oriented, there is the question of efficiency: Suppose that you have one database in which you have a separate record for each account or transaction, as in the (simplified) record shown in Figure 6–1.

If a given customer buys from you frequently and/or buys many different items from you, you will have a constantly growing number of records such as that shown. If the account number is constant, the same for each transaction, you can identify each purchase made by the same customer and, if your DBM has suitable features, collect and consolidate all those records. You will, however, have a great multiplicity of records that are redundant in many of the fields, rather than a single record for each customer. On the other hand, if each record has its

Acct # _____

Cust Name _____

Address _____

Item Purchased _____

Date Purchased _____

Amount of Purchase _____

Figure 6–1. Records filed individually by account number.

Acct # _____

Cust Name _____

Address _____

Item Purchased _____

Date Purchased _____

Amount of Purchase _____

Item Purchased _____

Date Purchased _____

Amount of Purchase _____

Item Purchased _____

Date Purchased _____

Amount of Purchase _____

Figure 6–2. Growing records by account numbers.

own ID (i.e., identification by account number) you will have a problem compiling a history of purchasing by each customer. It can probably be done, using the customer's name as a key field, but it would be rather laborious, slow, and probably not completely accurate, given the likelihood of some duplication of names. Whichever alternative you choose, you will do well to assign a unique ID of some kind to each customer, that ID to appear always in any record pertaining to that customer.

On the other hand, suppose you do have a unique ID for each account so that there is simply a lengthy and constantly growing record, to which you add new information each time the customer makes a new purchase, as in Figure 6–2. Obviously, in time the records will have become so long as to be quite unwieldy. They will strain the capacity of the system before long, and will become a definite problem in searching and retrieving information. Fortunately, there is a way to avoid this Hobson's choice.

THE RELATIONAL DATABASE MANAGER

The practical solution to the problem described is to establish separate databases for various kinds of records, as your organization has probably long since done. Your accountants require a database of accounts to which they can refer as necessary to gather figures, determine the amount of receivables outstanding, the current status of any given account, the creditworthiness of a customer, and many other such data. A production department must be able to track the movement of various kinds of goods to estimate inventory needs. A marketing department needs to know what items sold best last year or the results of an earlier promotion of some sort. A purchasing department has to maintain lists of supplies normally needed, suppliers, prices, delivery times, and other related information. Other departments and functionaries in the organization must have other kinds of information to do their jobs efficiently and accurately.

A great deal of redundancy is suggested here, since business inevitably revolves around customers. What a given customer has inquired about, ordered and bought, returned, complained about, paid for, neglected or refused to pay for, or otherwise communicated and transacted with you, may show up in a dozen different databases or database files. Fortunately, there is a way to minimize the redundancy of a new record for each such transaction, while avoiding the overload problem in the marketing database. The solution is the *relational* database.

As explained briefly in Chapter 2, the relational database system permits you to import information from other files into your marketing database files, so that you do not need to centralize all the information in one massive database. You can thus set up a marketing database oriented strictly to individual customers and including only that data pertaining solely to marketing effectively to those customers. In a sense, you might consider this to be the master database, which permits you to examine data in other fiels and databases and to import any of the other data into the master database and its files. You can actually add this other data to your master database or you can simply include it, suitably integrated, with other data you are printing out as a report, mailing list, or other output. Having set this information up in a relational database, you can establish each record with a unique ID, the head data (name, address, etc.), and room for the addition of pertinent data collected from many sources, including imports from other databases. The latter source includes your own databases and those from outside sources, a growing number of which are offering services designed to assist you in building your own marketing databases.

PROFILING THE TYPICAL CUSTOMER

In principle, profiling the typical customer is simple: It consists of determining which relevant and distinctive characteristics your customers have in common. In practice, it becomes a bit more complex, especially in deciding which common characteristics are relevant to the profile.

As David Shepard Associates point out in *The New Direct Marketing* (Business One Irwin, 1990), the two main sources of data are from the customers themselves (referred to by those authors as "primary research data") and from other sources ("secondary research data," in the authors' terms). They then divide secondary data into the four categories, demographic, psychographic, behavioral/lifestyle, and financial. Let us try to assess the value of these before we get down to assigning them to an actual database.

SECONDARY DATA AND HUMAN JUDGMENT

What is the value or potential value of demographic data? Let's consider geography first: Does it matter to you whether the prospect lives in California, in Arizona, or in North Carolina? The answer is "Maybe. It depends on what I am selling." Almost everyone in the country (with a few exceptions) might be a reasonable prospect for a VCR or a diet supplement, for example, but I would not expect the Arizonan to be especially interested in a fish finder for big-game fish.

"Why not?" you ask. "Even Arizonans go to California, Oregon, and elsewhere to pursue the big ones."

True, true, true, but these are exceptions, not the rule. Marketing to exceptions is a fast highway to disaster. Success in mass marketing, even in the more sophisticated and more sharply focused milieu of databased marketing, means marketing to the typical, not the atypical, prospect within whatever constitutes the market addressed.

"But wait," you say. "This is not to say that the above is a hard and fast rule. Quite the opposite, the base idea of databased marketing argues against such a rule. Perhaps there *are* enough Arizonans traveling to fish the oceans to make up a viable niche market."

Absolutely true. Maybe there is a niche market here. You must first find those big-game fishermen, however, and determine whether you have identified a large enough group of prospects to be worth pursuing. In conventional mass marketing you would not even make the effort because you would assume, as an obvious premise, that the exceptions are not numerous enough to make a market. In databased marketing, however, the niche may find you by falling out of a routine analysis of your database. (The size of the mass in "mass marketing" is a variable; in a way, niche marketing *is* still mass marketing, but on a small scale—i.e., the meaning of "mass" has changed.)

Aside from this, and still recognizing what this means in today's marketing environment, I would consider Arizonans and some other westerners (e.g., Californians and Alaskans) to be good prospects for a gold-panning kit and instruction book on the subject, but would not expect this item to sell very well in New England or the deep South.

Thus we have first examples of what we must always bear in mind: There is no substitute (so far, at least) for human judgment. (Artificial intelligence, the ultimate goal in computer design and capability, may come one day, but the time is not yet.) We may start with emotional biases and preconceived notions, but unlike computers, we can change our minds and adapt our thinking to new information. We know that few truths are really general or absolute truths. They are truths only in given circumstances and under given conditions. So you must apply your judgment to the situation in each case. You must consider circumstances that the computer program could not possibly have considered in a completely objective, uninstinctual analysis. We shall miss some of the brilliant inspirations, such as Joe Karbo and his *Lazy Man's Way to Riches,* and Gary Dahl with his "Pet Rocks," if we abandon the old-fashioned mass marketing by applying probability statistics to large populations of prospects, and utilize computers to initiate the new mass marketing to far smaller masses.

That variability in what is truth applies elsewhere, but unfortunately one of the more critical places it applies is in human judgment: The assumptions on which judgment relies—that which we call "conventional wisdom"—are not always valid premises, as is apparent by considering the financial factor.

The normal assumption is that the prospect's financial picture furnishes a clue to his or her potential as a buyer for what we sell. We may, for example, assume that only buyers with medium-to-high income are likely to be able to afford that super-duper, $2,500 45-inch TV receiver we sell. We thus rule out as a prospect the factory worker earning only $35,000 and living in a modest row house. Instead, we address the white-collar yuppie couple in a $250,000 condo earning $90,000 between the two of them. Sensible? Maybe. Fact (all too often): The HFW (humble factory worker) paid off his house long ago, has modest living expenses, substantial savings, and a wife who also works as an HFW. The couple can easily afford the payments on the super-duper TV, whereas the yuppie is often "house poor" and cash poor, and could not possibly handle it, no matter what his or her net worth on paper or potential. Far too often we are concerned with a prospect's net worth, when we ought to be concerned with his or her "disposable income," as we are also often more concerned with external appearances than with substance.

This example is not speculation, but represents facts verified on the street by knocking on doors. It is typical of many premises. Examine your premises most carefully. Are they fact or opinion? What is the evidence for them? Where, how—and if—verified or validated, as the socioeconomic professionals prefer to put it? Skepticism is most definitely an order of the day here. Unquestioning acceptance of dogma is an invitation to disaster.

The tendency of many in the mass marketing of the DM world today is to put their trust into statistical analyses, assuming always that they will work with great numbers, in which their statistical analyses are a security blanket, protecting them from the hazards of judgmental error. There seems to be a great reluctance to call on managerial judgment or marketing instincts to make important decisions, despite the track record of these latter factors. We must be careful to use our computers to do only that which they can do better than we humans can do, and not abandon our responsibility to *think* and to exercise the judgment that is unique to the human brain—unique so far, at least. There are still many situations in which human judgment is far superior to computer analyses.

The gathering of demographic and other secondary data in general relies principally on external sources: the U.S. Census Bureau, as probably the most important resource for such data; other government agencies (federal, state, and local); the dozens upon dozens of vendors of such data (Dun & Bradstreet, Donnelly Marketing, and R. L. Polk are among the best known of such vendors but by no means the only well-known ones); and the owners of mailing lists who can provide certain information about those listed. (The federal government is a rich source of information of many kinds. It was once possible, for example, to buy the list of subscribers to the federal government's *Commerce Business Daily,* a daily announcement of federal government contracting opportunities and awards, and the Navy once made available a list of its contractors.) Among the vendors of lists and associated data, unfortunately, the reliance on mass-processing methods—statistical analyses of many kinds—is even more dominant than in in-house systems.

Databased marketing, by its nature, must in the end rely on human wisdom—critical judgment based on experience and introspection—if it is to be effective. For it to depend entirely on preconceived premises and statistical analyses of huge numbers is to preordain its failure. Such an approach is, in fact, a direct contradiction of the basic concept, which is treating each individual listed as an individual and not as a statistic. But let us now look at this as a real problem, in practical, everyday terms.

THE RAW DATA

A first obligatory item and usually a first field in a marketing database is a customer ID. You can use the customer's proper surname for this, of course, as we do in everyday life, but it doesn't work well in large databases: There are many John Smiths and John T. Smiths in our society, but there are also dismayingly large numbers of Gunter Grunbachs and Bat Bunghas if the database is large enough. Proper names do not furnish absolutely distinctive identifications, especially in large databases. And so the first item of a database entry in a large database is normally a unique customer ID—usually a number, often modified by the customer's initial. Thus my own ID for one database in which I am listed is H4385. Even if there are other Herman Holtz's in the database, I can be singled out from others of the same name. Ergo, unless yours is a very small database, you will do well to assign some unique ID to each individual listed therein and include that unique ID whenever that customer's activity is recorded in any of your databases and database files.

Following this you need to install the normal "head data": the individual's name, address, title, and/or whatever else is part of the ID and data necessary to prepare labels or envelopes for mailing.

Demographic/geographic/psychographic data follows, ordinarily. But which data are relevant and necessary? Is the type of residence and its value or cost pertinent to your marketing approach? Does the size of the family, the ages of the members, its gross income, the clubs to which it belongs, the places where it vacations, the size of its garage, or the number of automobiles parked therein affect your marketing problem?

If your answer to these questions is "I don't know," you are in good company. Most of us do not know the answers to such questions as these. At least, we do not know the answers before we do a great deal of work to find those answers. And for that reason we have to construct at least two databases before we can undertake databased marketing seriously: The first database includes every kind of data we can acquire, from whatever sources and with whatever apparent significance or relevance. It is a database we might label "customer" or "consumer" database and is probably roughly equivalent to the first, rough draft a writer makes. In it is included everything, every data item, no matter how irrelevant it may seem at the early stage of database building.

THE REFINED DATA

The second database includes only those data items, or fields, that we decide are useful and necessary to market successfully, using the databased marketing philosophy. It is a second draft and not necessarily a final one, but it is at least the first stage of refinement or maturation of the data and the database.

All the initial data needs to be screened objectively. You may think that the age of a prospect to whom you are trying to sell computer software is not relevant, but you do not *know* that—not yet, anyhow—so you cannot be sure, and you certainly do not wish to reject it before you are sure. You must rely on experience or other references to produce some real evidence, one way or another, before passing final judgment. Here are just a few of the kinds of raw data that you might gather before refining or "maturing" the database and the categories in which they might be organized:

Demographic
Sex
    Male
    Female

Age
    Younger than 18
    19–25
    26–65
    65+

Education
    Graduate degrees
    Undergraduate degree
    Vocational school
      graduate
    High school graduate
    Grade school graduate

Occupation
    Blue collar
      Skilled
      Semiskilled
      Unskilled
      Student
      Retired
      Other _____

    White collar
      Professional
      Physician
      Lawyer
      Accountant
      Engineer
      Architect
      Technician
      Office worker
      Other _____

    Executive
      Company officer
      Senior position
      Junior position
      Other _____

Annual Income
    Over $250,000
    Over $100,000
    Over $50,000
    Over $25,000
    Less than $25,000

Hobbies
    Golf
    Stamps
    Coins
    Models
    Woodworking
    Computers
    Other _____

Residence
    Area
      Urban
      Suburban
      Rural
    Type
      Private home
      Garden apartment
      High rise

Purchases
    Kinds of goods
      Kinds of goods
      purchased
      Typical sizes of
      purchases (in $$)
      Number of purchases
      Frequency of purchases
    Methods of purchasing
      By mail
      By telephone
      Across the counter
    Solicitation responded to
      Direct mail
      Telephone
      TV commercials
      Radio commercials
      Print advertising
      Catalog

These are by no means all the classes and categories of data or all the items you might wish to identify, nor must all those listed here be weighed: Many items are simple facts—name, age, address, education, and occupation—and need to be retained as head data. Most of the others must be weighed to determine their value to your marketing database and so whether they are to be retained or discarded.

Many of the items are dictated by availability: what your first efforts dredge up from various sources. Others are dictated by the nature of your own business—what you sell. Depending on that, you may or may not care about your prospect's hobbies and personal interests. But that does not depend entirely on what you sell or what you care about. In my own fields of activity, I would not, for example, normally care about my prospects' hobbies. I would be concerned only with their business interests and concerns. That, however, is a first reaction; perhaps I spoke too soon: Were I a golfer, I might think differently: I might consider how many good business contacts I might make on the golf course, since such "contacts" are important in my corner of the business world. Too, the individual's personal interests and hobbies are often an excellent indicator of the individual's motivations: They may furnish a useful clue to a marketing strategy. If you had a large number of coin collectors listed in your database, you might consider an advertising piece that featured a photograph of a most rare and valuable coin with a message along the lines: "Our service is as rare as this coin . . . " as an attention getter.

In general, then, what belongs in your marketing database is up to you, and probably no one, no matter how expert in his or her own field, knows as well as you do what really belongs in your database, what you *need* there. You must be the final judge; no one else can do the job. As computer scientist John E. Gessford states rather plainly in his book, *How to Build Business-Wide Databases* (John Wiley & Sons, 1991), "The information requirements of those who do the marketing for the organization is what should be described, not the data that information systems analysts think marketers should want. . . . Only data that will actually get used by those doing the marketing for the company is relevant and the experts on this data are the people in the marketing function and subfunctions."

MATURING THE DATABASE

The methodology for choosing the data to be included in the marketing database is essentially a screening one: First you collect all data possible, as many items and as many kinds of items as you can. You sort and organize them into their various classes and categories. After careful thought and after experience in selling to those listed in your database, you eliminate items that are not germane to the notion of modeling individual customers and thus do not help, and you try to find more of the kinds of items that do help to describe those with whom you are most likely to do business. But you don't do all of this in one session, one campaign, or one year: It is ongoing, as you run your marketing campaigns, but you monitor results constantly, and you refine your database continuously. Year by year, month by month, day by day, it gets better and better.

THE AUTODEVELOPMENT DATABASE

In a sense, this means that you run a never-ending test, even when you have rolled out the campaign. You monitor results continuously, constantly increasing the size of still another, special database, the feedback database. In this database you collect only results of your tests and campaigns. The fields might include such items as costs, gross and by units; response rates, stratified by such factors as unit prices, types of items, types of prospects, market niches, and sundry other factors; profit and loss analyses, also stratified appropriately; and whatever other fields will produce that data that enable you to judge the effectiveness of your marketing database. You then design reports that your DBM can produce to document this data and furnish the clues to improvement of the marketing database. In short, you can thus use the computer and its databases to monitor the entire campaign and report on it to help you in developing and refining your marketing databases. In effect, this is an autodevelopment database: You use your computer to help improve its own efficiency.

IDENTIFYING MARKET NICHES

Profiling customers and identifying market niches are not necessarily different marketing activities. We can identify markets in many ways, but a market is composed of people: People do the buying. However, there are various bases on which to identify or isolate a market niche. Here are just a few possibilities, based on data about individuals, some of the data quite specific, but some quite general and calling for further subclassifications to achieve maximum utility:

By Type of Individual
    Age group
    Occupation
    Economic status
    Hobbies

By Geography
   State, city, or region
   Type of area—e.g., desert, mountain, seacoast
   Nature of region—e.g., industrial, vacation, rural

By Organization
   Industrial corporation
   Small business
   Nonprofit
   Membership association

By Personal Characteristics
   Eager for anything new
   Responds to discounts and bonuses
   Is motivated by the word FREE
   Responds to anything different

By Personal Interests
   Sports fan
   Sports participant
   Physical fitness enthusiast
   Ardent TV watcher

This is intended only as a starter list to trigger your own imagination. You will, of course, find many of these inappropriate to your own needs and will select your own identifiers, as you should.

Chapter 7

Putting the Marketing Databases to Work

The ultimate objective of databased marketing is, of course, greater success in the marketplace. Marketing databases offer several approaches to increasing that greater success.

CUSTOMER MODELING

We have by now narrowed the focus of databased marketing objectives. In general, the idea postulated has been to gather relevant information about each and every *individual* listed in the database and use that information to model customers. The models are useful in several ways, according to circumstances: For all businesses, the models are keys to finding the right prospects and the right marketing strategies and tactics to make sales. In those businesses in which each sale is so large as to constitute a minimarketing campaign in itself, the individual is the direct object of the data gathering. For other businesses, those which have traditionally used mass marketing methods, modeling customers serves several purposes or objectives:

- It helps us identify our most typical customers and so become more effective in our prospecting.
- It helps us identify our *best* customers, another aid to prospecting.
- It helps us identify niche markets to add to our marketing universe.
- It helps us develop more effective marketing tools (materials and media).

So far, I have discussed customer modeling only on a simplified and rather shallow basis, looking at it philosophically, rather than in any practicable way. In one example I looked at only one attribute, income, as an indicator of what characterizes a good customer. Obviously, a model will have to cover a range of characteristics to have any validity, a range that will enable you to scan the characteristics of prospective customers and judge which most closely resemble your customers. Among the characteristics may be some or all of the following:

Age range	Life style
Education	Marital status
Occupation	Hobbies
Income level	Family
Residence type	Purchase habits

I have so far made no distinction among customers or tried to classify them in some way, other than to identify them as customers and establish a customer database. That implies that all customers are equal in what they represent to you as business assets. That is obviously not a useful concept nor is it a true one: Some customers are of much more value to you than others are. Here, for example, are a few most basic and most important characteristics of customers that should be of direct interest to you:

- *Frequency of Purchases.* How often does the customer buy something from you?
- *Size of Purchases.* How much does the customer spend on a typical transaction?
- *Recency of Purchasing.* How long has it been since this customer last placed an order with you?

To ignore such factors is to distort the model. It makes the model an average or mean derived from a widely variant set of samples. Neither average nor mean is helpful in finding a useful model. If you pursue such a model, you will pursue only a fraction of all your customers and prospects.

The 80/20 "Rule"

There is a belief that in many, if not most, things, 80 percent of the result is produced by 20 percent of the effort, and vice versa. The figures may or may not be reasonably accurate estimates of actual values for all cases, but the principle has been demonstrated to be valid in many cases. It means here that for most businesses, 80 percent of the sales are made to 20 percent of the customers, and the remaining 20 percent of the sales are made to the remaining 80 percent of the customers. A gloomy idea? Perhaps. But a realistic one. Its significance here is that you need to model that customer representing the 20 percent who produce 80 percent of your business.

It is not an easy task, and it may require you to develop more than one model of even your best customers. A best customer is one who produces some portion of that 80 percent of your business, of course, but that may be the result of buying frequently, buying in quantity, buying the most expensive items, or a combination of these. Thus you may easily need to develop four separate models of your best customers, and you may even want to establish four separate marketing databases corresponding to these models. Depending on your business, you may even want to set up categories and subcategories of good customers, along the following lines:

Best Customers

By purchase volume
Groups (minimum spent each year), several levels

By average order size
Groups, several levels

By frequency of purchases
Groups, several levels

By price and quality of items
Groups, several levels

Poorest Customers

By purchase volume
Groups (minimum spent each year), several levels

By average order size
Groups, several levels

By frequency of purchases
Groups, several levels

By price and quality of items
Groups, several levels

Medium-Grade Customers

By purchase volume
Groups (minimum spent each year), several levels

By average order size
Groups, several levels

By frequency of purchases
Groups, several levels

By price and quality of items
Groups, several levels

You might also want to track customers by recency of purchases, pursuing the philosophy that the more recent the purchase, the more responsive is the purchaser to new offers and solicitations. Here again, you might code the records to indicate the recency of purchases—less than one month, less than three months, and so on.

Even these classifications are not absolutes, however, but are probably merchandise-dependent. That is, a good or best customer for jewelry may be a poor customer for furniture or cosmetics. If you handle a broad variety of items, you may very well find it profitable to differentiate customers according to what they are good and poor customers for. That will call for some kind of cross-referencing system, depending on how you wish to use your databases. A multidepartment or multibranch business might find it best to set up databases by department or branch, for example. This suggests, however, the complexity that the entire system of marketing databases can assume for large organizations. It also illustrates the need for expert help for this aspect of the problem (i.e., for doing the complex analyses and cross-referencing of databases).

Of course, these characteristics of your customers are subject to change. People's buying habits change, they move, they change occupations, they get divorced, they remarry, and otherwise undergo changes that affect their status as your customers. At the same time, you lose some old customers and you acquire new customers. That means that you must reassess your marketing databases periodically and update all records. This is a laborious job that can be automated, and it is the point at which you would probably do well to retain someone to write a procedure and program to do this for you.

Why the Need to Discriminate

The small business owner may see no need to discriminate among customers and assign them some kind of code or figure of merit to identify their status as customers. The small business owner probably addresses each campaign and promotion to all customers equally. There is some waste in that, of course. If you are running a promotion that offers an expensive luxury item to your customers, there are some who are first-class prospects for sale of the item, but there are others who are most unlikely to buy the item. If you had the models, you could probably identify those on whom you are probably wasting postage, printing, and other costs. If you have such a large database that you plan to address only a part of it with a special offer, you need to be able to distinguish the right part of it—to select the right list or the right database. Thus it is not enough even to choose the best customers; you need to choose the *right* best customers.

The same logic applies to any promotion you might want to run; a special sale, a discount, a closeout, a new item, or other. If you model your customers according to the several classifications by which you will want to address them, you will have an increasingly powerful marketing tool. With enough effort, you can compile lists of customers who buy lots of costume jewelry, those who buy lots of clothing, those who want to buy and try every new kitchen gadget, and others whose buying habits become readily apparent after a bit of study. Discovering what each customer is most likely to buy and documenting the customer record accordingly represents a most powerful sales tool, indeed. Consider just a few of the potential uses of such a tool:

- You are offered what appears to be a great opportunity to buy a lot of goods at an excellent price. In trying to reach a decision you search your databases to gauge your existing potential market for the goods or franchise.
- You are considering expanding and opening a branch office or store. You go to your databases to map the physical locations of your customers, as an aid to selecting a site for a branch.
- You are considering a merger with or buyout of a competitor. You use your databases to compare your customers with those of the competitor to judge their compatibility and/or value to you.
- You study the appropriate databases in planning each campaign, from choosing the mailing lists and timing of mailing, to finding the right copy strategies and media.

Note that here again we encounter the idea of niches in your market, in your customer databases, in fact. All roads in databased marketing appear to lead to niches in the markets.

NICHES IN THE MARKET VERSUS NICHE MARKETS

Narrowcasting, to refresh your memory of this rather new term, is rifle shot targeting, rather than shotgun targeting of markets. The uncovering of those identifiable market segments or niches that are defined by the prospect and customer models is an important and integral element in narrowcasting: The whole idea is a reversal of mass marketing, which does not attempt to make other than the roughest of discriminations among prospects, and even those on a large group or mass basis. However, we must find groups of prospects that represent large enough numbers of potential customers to constitute niche markets worth pursuing with individual programs. The latter is very much a consideration: What makes a niche in the market a niche market? Are they the same thing—is a niche in a market automatically a niche market? And what is a niche, for that matter? Do we really know what it is? Maybe we do. But maybe we do not. We do need a few answers, and some of them may be rather surprising.

However, let us consider the process of gathering information increasingly to identify niches in the market.

Philosophically, the database-building process is one of steadily increasing the definition of the market through the increasing definition of customers. (Remember that markets are people, not things, for it is people, not things, that buy what we offer.) That is accompanied by a decreasing breadth of markets: As the data accumulates and the models become more and more well defined, the groups to which the various customer models belong become smaller and smaller niches. The logical extreme is, of course, the niche market that exists as a single customer. Nor is that necessarily a *reductio ad absurdum:* The narrowing of market definitions to single individuals is one of the many goals projected by databased marketing enthusiasts, mentioned earlier, and it is a viable extreme for certain cases. We toss the term *niche market* around rather casually; have we ever really identified it? What *is* it? Is it any distinctive group within the total market spectrum? Or is there some special qualification? Is a niche in the market the same thing as a niche market—when is a niche itself a market and when is it not a market? How can we know the difference, if there is a difference?

VALIDATING PROSPECT PROFILES AND NICHE MARKETS

It does not take a great deal of study to realize that the size of the perceived niche is a critical consideration in deciding whether the niche does or does not constitute a market. But "size" is a relative term, as we shall soon see: A group that might constitute a viable niche market for one business might be too small to be worth pursuing, for another business. In short, a group of prospective customers is not necessarily a niche market. It is not a market at all, niche or otherwise, unless it is a large enough group to represent a market worth pursuing (i.e., justifying an individual program or campaign to capture it).

We thus need to discriminate between a niche *In* a market and a niche that *is* a market, that is, to *validate* a niche as a market. Suppose, for example, that you have managed to identify a group of 5,000 individuals with attributes or characteristics that, you believe, identifies them as unusually well-qualified prospects for what you sell. You estimate that marketing to the group by direct mail will produce a response of perhaps 15 to 20 percent. That is a fairly optimistic estimate by conventional standards, but possibly it is a realistic one under these special conditions of an unusually well-defined market. On the basis of what you sell and your own economic estimates—cost of the program/campaign versus net profitability—you see an almost assured breakeven and a good probability of a net profit even if you get as "little" as an 8 to 10 percent response. This definitely adds to your degree of comfort with the prospect of addressing this group as a market. Is this or is it not a true niche market? How can you validate your premise that you have found a niche market? Or, as an alternative question, how do you arrive at a figure of confidence in your estimates?

Of course, you do not know how reliable your estimates are, and you should not assume that even the most well-developed marketing databases eliminate all uncertainty and all risk. You must operate on high and low estimates and perhaps on wishful thinking too, albeit on far better diagnostic data than ever before. Statistically, you have reduced the risk materially by narrowing your group of prospects and qualifying them more thoroughly and, you hope, more accurately. You have not, on the other hand, eliminated all risk. You have not eliminated the need for testing, analyzing, and adjusting your estimates and your market approaches—your program/campaign designs—accordingly. We need to recognize and accept that as a condition with which we must contend, despite the computer and the marketing databases it enables us to build. Let us also operate on the assumption that you will have identified a few niche markets and decided to address them with specially designed programs and sales campaigns.

Databased or not, testing any niche is a good idea. You can probably get a pretty good idea of how well your estimates hold up by testing about 20 percent, 1,000 names and addresses, of the group. For a group of 5,000, that ought to give you statistically significant results so you can get a good idea of the worst- and best-case probabilities. (For larger niches, you may wish to consider other media for testing.)

WHAT, THEN, DOES THE DEVELOPED DATA DO FOR US?

Testing the niche market—and, to be sure, also testing the customer/prospect profiles that define the niche market—requires a campaign package of some sort, of course. The design of that package will necessarily be based on the data in the marketing database. It is from the data that you infer what benefits, prices, and inducements you must offer the prospects. You might also wish to examine the data furnished by the marketing database to judge which are the most appropriate media for reaching each of those niche markets with your sales messages, if you are not totally committed to direct mail, as suggested for testing. It will be on the basis of the information identifying these market targets, individuals and groups constituting niche markets, that you design the radio and TV commercials, the direct-mail pieces, the print ads, the contests, the "clubs," the coupons, and whatever other sales campaign and promotional material you devise.

THE COSTS OF NICHE MARKETING

Niche marketing introduces certain added costs. In the typical mass marketing campaign you would run one or two tests, perhaps, and then roll out the campaign. You would have creative costs for the test packages, and perhaps for only one (as a split run of some sort) package with several keys and then a single package for the rollout. However, if you pursue niche markets, you will have the test and rollout packages for each niche, even if you can standardize portions of the package. That is part of the economic problem of narrowcasting: You must amortize the creative costs across a relatively small market. Here your desktop computer can be the answer or at least a large part of the answer of keeping those costs down to acceptable levels.

There is also the matter of collecting data gathered through the tests, making analyses, and doing these things for a number of niche markets, rather than for one large, general market. This is again a costly multiplication of efforts.

Fortunately, your PC is an asset in many ways in helping you carry out most of these functions in-house. It can be instrumental in making niche marketing more viable an option than it might otherwise be. Hence, let's make a brief digression to discuss computers and their capabilities vis-à-vis the needs of niche marketing.

COMPUTER CAPABILITIES

For convenience in these discussions I refer to various functions and ways in which we use computers today as "computer capabilities," which is how laypeople conceive the functions of computers. That is not entirely accurate. In fact, the computer itself is a mere machine carrying out orders mechanically. The orders are issued by the software programs, so it is really the functions of the software that do so many things for us today: It would be more accurate to refer to "program capabilities." Each program has its own set of functions and capabilities, and these grow constantly as the software-design geniuses invent newer and better ways to use the computers. The computer itself is a general-purpose device; the software programs are special-purpose entities, each of which makes your PC, in effect, an entirely different capability.

Merge/Purge

Two phrases that describe computer capabilities highly relevant to our discussions here are *merge/purge* and *mail/merge*. Merge/purge refers to computer functions in which two or more lists are merged and purged, that is, the resulting combined list is purged of duplicates to eliminate the waste of redundancy. Different strategies are used, but that it is not used as often or is not always as effective as it should be comes home to me frequently when I receive two or more identical mailing pieces. Sometimes they are addressed identically to me, revealing, probably, that merge/purge has not been done on the list. Sometimes there is some slight difference in the address, which may account for the failure of the merge to purge: The program was unable to discover that the two records were, for practical purposes, duplicates. This alone furnishes a good argument for the need to establish a unique ID for each record. This morning's mail again brought me two identical packages of literature. The apparent cause was a difference in the address: Our zip code was changed at the beginning of this year. However, that has been going on all over the country, and the Postal Service is quite willing to help mailers update their lists with regard to correcting zip codes. (On the other hand I also received three copies of a form letter from the IRS, each in its own envelope, and all absolutely identical with each other in all respects.)

Presumably, merge/purge is up to the list broker, if you rent lists: He or she is morally obligated to rent you a merged and purged list that has no or at least minimal redundancies and nixies (undeliverable names and addresses). There is the probability, however, that at least some of the names and addresses in such lists are duplicates of customers and prospects on your own, in-house, lists.

That is not the only source of redundancies: If you rent more than one list, and especially if you rent lists from more than one list broker, you are likely to encounter duplicates. (Almost everyone whose name finds its way onto one list being traded will eventually be included in dozens of other lists.) Thus, if you wish to eliminate the redundancy or at least minimize it, you must do a merge/purge of your own. You must combine all lists for a merge/purge to produce a single clean list for a one-time mailing.

List-Cleaning Purge

While merge/purge is normally designed to eliminate redundancies when combining two or more lists, there is another purging operation that must also be performed regularly. That is "cleaning" the list by purging it of "nixies," which are undeliverable names and addresses resulting from incorrect addresses, deaths, marriage, moving, and other such changes. The computer can be programmed to do this also when the list of nixie names or identification codes is provided. That it is an important matter is demonstrated by typical list-brokers' guarantees of some minimum percentage of nixies, usually on the order of not more than 3 to 5 percent. Whether you are the list broker or the mailer renting lists, the minimum-nixie guarantee is important to you. Ergo, list cleaning ought to be equally important.

Mail/Merge

Mail/merge is a much different computer capability. Briefly, it is the capability of the computer to merge a list of names and addresses from one computer file with a form letter from another computer file so that the letter is addressed personally to each individual on the list, rather than to "Dear Respondent" or Dear Resident." We all receive such letters in the mail today, many of them even addressing us personally in the body of the letter, as well as in the salutation. In modern contest promotions, each addressee finds his or her name being inserted frequently in the package of literature, greatly personalizing the presentation.

There is a hazard in this because computers and their programs, even the most sophisticated ones, are still unable to make judgments. So a letter addressed to HRH Communications, Inc. has sometimes begun, "Dear Mr. Communications," or even "Dear Mrs. Inc." If you use this feature of your word processing software, you must be careful that each name on your list is that of an individual. I have observed this kind of error to be occurring much less frequently, as time passes, so the lesson has struck home apparently or the capability of the software to discriminate and reject the absurd salutations has been improved. (It is possible to program computers to minimize this problem.)

Enter the PC

Until the advent of the PC, only the largest firms had their own computers, owned or leased. Even so, many large firms found it expedient to buy computer time (i.e., pay computer centers for time on their computers to run programs) rather than to have computers in-house. Mainframe computers were expensive and so the cost of running them was high, no matter what the arrangement, making computer use practicable only for projects of substantial size. Small projects were never favored with computer support. In many cases, mere preparation for computer support (e.g., the cost of keyboarding the mailing list) was itself prohibitively high for any but the largest campaigns.

The desktop or personal computer, the PC, has changed that, and on a revolutionary scale. Even the smallest firm today enjoys computer capabilities because the modest PC has grown rapidly to a point where it is as powerful as the largest mainframe computers of a few years ago, while it costs hardly more than the electric typewriter and printing calculator it has made all but obsolete. Too, modern software makes it possible for anyone to operate a computer, whereas a few years ago specially trained technicians were required to operate the large, mainframe computers of that day.

ECONOMIC CHANGES

Not the least of the changes are the changes in the economics of use. In addition to the obvious savings in original investment and the training of clerical personnel to use desktop computers, other economies have evolved from the PC.

The PC has changed the significance of the concept expressed as "economies of scale." Projects that would have been too small to be economically viable for a mainframe computer are eminently practicable for a PC and run routinely. Let us take, for example, a market for which you would have planned a 500,000-piece mailing a decade ago, in the hopes of garnering 2,500 to 5,000 orders. Even at an optimistic $0.30 cost per name, the initial mailing would have run $150,000. Had you managed to win a full 1 percent return on an order size of $30, your gross income would have been $150,000, considerably less than your total costs. You would have needed more than a 1 percent response to have covered your costs of getting the orders alone, but you would also have needed to recover fulfillment costs before you could hope for even a break-even situation, much less a profit. (You would probably have needed a 2.5 to 3 percent response—12,500 to 15,000 orders—in the case hypothesized here.) That is how fragile the mathematics of success and failure can be: A difference of 1 percent and even a fraction of 1 percent may spell the difference between success and disaster.

There is virtually no way to decrease the costs of running the campaign (e.g., printing, postage, and list rentals) or the associated costs of fulfillment, and there are only three ways to increase the probability of success in this campaign:

■ Reduce the cost per order.
■ Increase the profit per order.
■ Increase the rate of response.

These all say the same thing. If you increase the response, you will reduce the cost per order and raise the gross profit per order. And the way databased marketing increases the response per order is by improving the targeting. If, for example, you can screen out one half of the mailing as being poor prospects for what you offer and thus get that 12,500 to 15,000 orders from a mailout of only 250,000 pieces, you double the response rate. At the same time, you cut the cost of the mailing by one half, from $150,000 to $75,000. That is, if you screen your prospects more effectively, you reduce the wasted mailings—by one half, in this hypothetical case. That alone doubles the rate of response. But there is more to this. There is the matter of better sales literature, owing to a clearer picture of the prospect. Because you screened out the poorer prospects, you also had a more accurate view of the prospects to whom you were mailing, and you therefore wrote far better copy that appealed directly to these better-defined prospects. We ought, however, to take a look at just what *that* means: What *is* better targeting?

TARGETING IN GENERAL

When I went in pursuit of prospects for information and other help in selling to the government, I assumed certain things as facts without in any way verifying that they were facts; I had no way to validate my assumptions except by test marketing. I assumed what appeared to me to be logical, that anyone who was currently selling to the federal government or who was in a business where (I thought) they should be selling to the federal government, was a first-class prospect for me. It was an erroneous assumption: The fact that these organizations were in constant pursuit of government contracts did not mean that they would buy what I had to sell—information on the subject of how to sell to the federal government, in the form of newsletters, reports, and seminars. What I soon learned was that what most organizations wanted (and not consciously either, apparently) was not the promise of information and education in winning contracts, but the promise of actual *help* in doing so. That was in itself a most valuable lesson in the true meaning of "benefits" in the sales appeal: Prospects are motivated far more by the promise of their desired end-results than by the promise of some benefit that is only the means to that end, in this case learning the means of achieving those results. That was only one of two lessons learned, however, and the other lesson was no less important to me. It was that while electronic companies were interested prospects of some merit, they were not the main prospects, as I had assumed; the many computer-software developers, even the largest among them, were by far the more eager and willing prospects. I could get far better results by targeting them especially.

If you keep your mind open and do not permit your judgment to be clouded by your preconceived ideas—your biases—you are going to get many surprises. Things are not always what they appear to be in marketing, as in many other things. Databased marketing often gives you leads to the truth, but not necessarily truth itself. It is important to remember that this is a field yet in its infancy. Do not expect more of it than it can deliver.

THE SUBNICHE CONCEPT

Paul and Sarah Edwards, in their CompuServe work-at-home forum, publish a kind of electronic newsletter on a monthly basis, *Making It on Your Own*. In it, they recently reported the emergence of an idea of subniche markets, crediting the information to The Public Relations Exchange International, a network of PR firms. The difference between a niche and a subniche is not defined, and probably it is not possible to define it in measurable terms: Niche or subniche, it can only exist as a relative quantity. It fits the notion offered here earlier of a spectrum of markets, with the mass market at one end and the individual customer at the other; niche markets fall between the two extremes, and the subniche markets would then fall between the niche markets and the individual customer, as illustrated here:

Increasing detail: Decreasing market size →

|–Mass markets—Niche markets–Subniche markets—Individual customers–|

← Decreasing detail: Increasing market size

What might be a viable market to some small firm, such as a home-based business, might be too small to qualify as even a subniche to another, even only slightly larger business firm. However, the idea that niche markets might be viable at even smaller sizes than any of us have customarily thought of as the smallest practicable markets is an interesting one, suggesting that we have not yet made a full analysis of what constitutes a market. Still, in the absence of anything better as definition, we must conclude that there is no significant difference between niche and subniche, except relative size, as perceived by the marketer. Pursuing the same logic, however, there is no difference between a niche market and an individual customer, except size.

LARGE COMPANIES AND SMALL NICHES

I made it clear earlier that a group or class of prospective customers should be considered a niche market only if the group is large enough to support and justify the expense of a campaign especially designed to exploit it as a market. This consideration is itself relative to the size of your own business, that is, the size of the sales potential you assign the group vis-à-vis your own size as a business is a determinant. There is a minimum startup cost to prepare and launch a campaign, and that cost is largely dependent on the size of the business overall—if the organization has only one modus operandi for starting up a program. This can be a limiting factor that prevents you from taking advantage of many possible niche markets, let alone subniche markets, unless you take special measures to overcome the problem.

The Small-Orders Suborganization

There are at least two ways for the large organization to attack the problem of handling small niche markets profitably. In one approach, you borrow a leaf from industrial companies that are often too large to handle small orders; for example, if their normal mode of operation is assembly-line production of custom-designed items in large quantities, they cannot set up an assembly line to mass produce some custom-designed item in small quantities. Nor can print shops equipped with large presses that normally handle very large print runs of magazines, thick brochures, and other such items handle small printing jobs efficiently. They must turn down the customer who wants 5,000 single sheets of a circular printed because they cannot run such an order on a 36- or 48-inch press economically. But they can have a special, short-run shop, equipped with small presses to handle such work, and many do have such special shops. Similarly, large manufacturing firms often set up special shops to accommodate customers with small orders. The special shops are equipped for the purpose and can process small orders profitably. It is easily possible to do this in marketing. The large marketing organization can establish a special section to respond to niche and subniche markets profitably with accelerated, lower cost methods for preparing materials and rolling out small-scale campaigns.

Integrating Niche and Subniche Markets

Another way for the large organization to handle the problem of responding to small markets, or niches, practicably is to integrate the various niches in its promotional campaign. That is, it is necessary to search out the practical compromise between the mass-marketing concept (apparently an almost obsolescent idea now, although not everyone accepts the idea that the days of mass marketing are numbered) and the ultratargeting base idea of databased marketing. To do this, you must perform an analysis to identify all the common factors among the many niches and subniches, on the one hand, and the distinguishing factors of each individual niche and subniche, on the other hand. The objective is to establish a standardized set of materials that can be varied easily and inexpensively to customize them for each niche.

It is not as difficult to do this as it may sound at first. There may be exceptions where this is not a practicable idea because there is too wide a divergence of interests among the perceived niches. Usually, however, only one or two major distinguishing characteristics identify a particular group as representative of a niche in the market. "Major" is an important qualifier here: You must recognize that each individual, as an individual, has many characteristics, some of them unique. However, you cannot, if you are to operate on a practical basis, respond to each and every quirk and preference of each and every individual. Instead, you must decide what *major* characteristic distinguishes the individual and identifies him or her as an element in a niche market. It is the ability to do this—to identify and utilize that one major difference—that enables you to take advantage of the niche-market idea.

This takes courage as well as wisdom. The almost automatic instinct of many of us is to include a multiplicity of items to justify our decisions and our approaches. For example, we often tend to lard our sales messages with promises of many benefits, rather than focusing on one or two major ones (and preferably only one dominant theme). Unfortunately, we can't or at least shouldn't try to divide our market according to every distinctive characteristic exhibited by individuals on our lists for at least two reasons: One, we do, indeed, thus make ourselves impotent by creating far too many minuscule niches if we allow every minor individual quirk to move us to create special appeals and special programs. Two, "polypharmacal" remedies (prescriptions with many ingredients specified, in the hope that at least one may work) do not work in marketing any better than they do in medicine, and can be as dangerous as they are in medicine. The correct prescription is the one that works, not the many that may or may not include one that will work.

Thus we must have both the wisdom and the courage to base our decisions on single major characteristics that distinguish individual groups of substantial size from others of substantial size. That is the key to identifying and using niche and even subniche markets profitably. Suppose, for example, returning to our simplified example of selling a diet preparation, that you identify niches distinguished from each other primarily by the following major characteristics:

- *The Eternal Hopeful.* Tries every new diet idea.
- *The Impatient One.* Looks for overnight success.
- *The Hungry One.* Can't tolerate self-denial or discomfort.
- *The Thrifty One.* Wants the most inexpensive program.
- *The Uninitiated One.* Has never dieted and has an open mind.

You need a different lead—different motivator—for each one, obviously. The leads in your presentations must feature appropriate appeals:

- A *new* kind of diet.
- *Fast* weight loss.
- *No-hunger* dieting.
- *Low* cost.
- *Educational* approach that explains dieting.

If you use this method, only the opening message, the lead, must be individualized. The rest of your copy can be standardized for all the niches that constitute the whole market. (However, it must be written with full consciousness that it must support all the various leads you will use as prime motivators.)

THE OFFER: WHAT DOES THE TERM MEAN?

What constitutes an "offer?" Just what is this item we call an "offer?" Those in marketing tend to speak of "the offer" routinely and regard that as the description of the product or service and the terms under which the sale of that product or service is offered (e.g., "the EZ diet plan at only $49.95 in 12 small monthly payments").

That is the accustomed orientation of many, and if history teaches us anything, it teaches us that we have great difficulty in learning new things when the new learning requires that we abandon old learning: We are all of us most reluctant to cast off the old, conventional wisdom with which we are now so familiar and comfortable. Yet, progress invariably requires that we do learn new truths and abandon old ones that are made obsolescent by the new ideas. Databased marketing is itself a new truth, and we must abandon our old ideas of mass marketing if we are to benefit. Hence, no matter how difficult, we must try to embrace and understand new wisdom.

In this vein, I find it helpful to think of an "offer" as what I, the advertiser, am going to do for you, the consumer—the major benefit I promise as a result of doing business with me. I offer, for example, to make you slim and attractive so you will have dates and a romantic life. I offer to make you proud to wear a bathing suit at the beach. I offer to make you the envy of your friends and family. I offer to make you beautiful. I offer to make you feel good about yourself again. I offer to give you the courage or inspiration to go out and enjoy life. I offer you freedom from your old fears. The product or service itself and the terms under which I suggest you buy is thus not my offer; that is my *proposition.*

The importance of this distinction, this definition of an *offer,* is that it forces us to think in terms of the major promise that we believe will induce our prospect to become a customer. In my view of marketing, the *benefit* is the offer because it is what the customer really buys. Customers never buy *things*—products or services; they buy what the products or services *do* for them—or, at least, what they hope and believe the products and services will do for them. Ergo, that is the real offer. Think in these terms, not in terms of offers and benefits, but in terms of offers as benefits.

That definition of the offer, as prescribed here, has more than one special advantage for us in our struggle to reason out how to turn databased marketing to the greatest advantage: It is the definition of the niche itself: It defines what the individuals constituting the niche want as an offer, what will motivate them to buy. That alone solves a problem for us. It also identifies the chief distinguishing characteristic of the presentation as customized for each niche or subniche: It tells us what we must do to customize the presentation for the niche. Finally, it serves well as the factor for integrating niches into a single market spectrum by identifying the sole, major difference between the niche and the rest of the general market. None of these are minor considerations. They are the instruments by which we can make databased marketing a reality to survive the new economics of this era and the coming one.

STILL ANOTHER KIND OF NICHE MARKET

If we are to be truly open-minded about the new marketing, we ought to recognize the possible uncovering of still another kind of niche market, representing those who want something a bit different from the service or product we have been selling. For example, if you are selling a line of vitamins and food supplements, you may discover a number of customers interested in one or more products you do not normally carry. You may have arbitrarily decided earlier that the demand for this/these product/s was minimal, or the demand may be for products you were not aware even existed. Of course, the same thing applies to services: You may discover a large group of people who want a service slightly different from the one that you offer.

In my own case I made a discovery when publishing a newsletter I called *Buyers and Sellers Exchange.* I thought I was sending out my copies every month to *subscribers,* but after a while I discovered that a great many of my subscribers referred to themselves as "members" of *Buyers & Sellers Exchange.* I discovered that this was not a phenomenon: It is a common characteristic for people to want to *belong.* (I suppose this is a manifestation of the all-too-human reluctance to be frighteningly alone in this awesome world.) I soon turned that to advantage: I created "BSE Associates" (I had long since called my newsletter *BSE* as a convenient abbreviation) and invited all subscribers and others to join for an additional annual fee and certain benefits I promised. The results of the appeal were quite gratifying.

Note here that my customers did not ask directly for that which I soon devised for them. I had to read between the lines of their many letters, but the message was there, and it came to me because I encouraged the feedback that is so critically important to the development of marketing databases. (Actually, this was a rather substantial niche, if it is fair to call it a niche at all: At least one half of my existing subscribers and considerably more than one half of new subscribers opted to join my associates program.)

It should be noted, in this connection, that what you often uncover are unconscious desires of your customers. You would never learn of many customer desires by asking such direct questions as "What features do you like best?" or "What new features/services would you like to see added?" Feedback from customers must be studied carefully and analyzed to gauge its true meaning, and often new offerings must be made experimentally to test customer reactions.

Opportunities arise for everyone in business—manufacturers, dealers, brokers, and others—to read their customers' minds. Coca Cola miscalculated the reaction of their customers when they made changes to their basic product, and quickly backtracked. On the other hand, when the late Joe Karbo conceived the idea of writing and publishing his small book, *The Lazy Man's Way to Riches,* he wisely decided to test the market first. He did this by advertising the book as a mail order item to see what the public response would be. Had it been negative, he would have returned the orders and money sent him with his regrets. But when the response proved positive, he quickly proceeded to have the book manufactured and planned an extensive advertising campaign.

This kind of niche market has variants. Some customers who are favorably disposed to the product or service will not buy it because it comes in only one size, which they deem to be too large and too costly for them. Borland, a software producer of Quattro® Pro, a popular spreadsheet program that sells normally for $495, is well aware that many potential buyers are shut out by the price. The company therefore developed and offers an abbreviated program that does not have all the features of the original version, but does provide the basic functions of a spreadsheet program. (So appealing was their literature and idea that I found the Borland offer most tempting and even contemplated ordering it, even though I know of no use I might have for a spreadsheet program.)

Packaging changes or additions can cater to a niche market. Some manufacturers of household products that are sold in costly dispenser packaging (e.g., glass cleaners in bottles with spray attachments) have begun to provide their products in refill packages, so that the consumer can reuse the original dispenser package and save money. (They then multiply the impact of the addition by using it as a main sales argument.)

Some firms have found a large niche of individuals who care about environmental issues, and these organizations focus on arguments about changing their packaging to biodegradable materials. (McDonald's is an outstanding example, but many, including those who have taken to packaging their product in refill containers, have also used environmental issues as a sales argument.)

Note, from these examples, another significant result of finding important niche markets: In many cases, changes inspired by the discovery of niche markets can be used effectively in sales promotion generally. Be alert for this possibility also as you search for useful niches in the markets.

ALTERNATIVE DEFINITIONS OF DATABASED MARKETING

The discussions in this chapter and earlier have tended to define databased marketing as a method for narrowcasting or identifying and selling to niche markets, recognizing that a niche market may be as small as one customer. Obviously that latter niche is a special case: The limiting factor is the nature and size of the sale, which must be large enough to justify a specific marketing effort directed to a single prospective customer. There is at least one other fair definition of databased marketing, however, and it may also be fairly defined as a method of superqualification of prospects. It is, in fact, qualification of prospects to a greater degree than we normally qualify customers.

Chapter 8

Databases for Prospecting

Rising costs of marketing are one major influence inspiring the development of databased marketing. The same consideration encourages a trend to using databased marketing principles and practices in prospecting. Improvement in prospecting is itself an attack on the high cost of marketing.

WINNING SALES VERSUS WINNING CUSTOMERS

We have been discussing databased marketing in the framework of developing marketing databases by building on our existing customer databases. We have talked about measures to use our customer databases more efficiently, through targeting our campaigns and promotions more accurately and so pursuing greater sales return from our customer databases. That is the immediate and most obvious utilization of the whole idea. However, the whole notion of databased marketing is still in its infancy and must be developed more fully. Perhaps there are other ways of using customer databases than for the direct pursuit of sales. We have just discussed, in the previous chapter, a number of ideas for using your existing customer database more effectively, to improve your sales volume both directly and indirectly.

That is certainly not a new idea. To many, the prime significance of databased marketing is that it represents more efficient ways to pursue and win sales, presumably the essential goal of marketing. But is it? Is the main goal of marketing making sales or is it making customers? Perhaps it depends on the business. Two successful businessmen referred to in earlier chapters and to be referred to again, Joe Cossman and the late Joe Karbo, focused entire promotional campaigns on selling single items, with great success, earning a great deal of money thereby. The nature of what they were doing, the business of promoting a single item on a grand scale, compelled them to concentrate their efforts on making sales. They are not alone in this kind of single-item promotion. Gary Dahl did it with his "Pet Rock" novelty and Ken

Hakuta with his "Wall Walker" toy. These are modern versions of the carnival barker kind of sales pitch, and many successful businesses are so conducted.

One factor that makes this business strategy workable is that the promoters have no immediate competition: They are generally selling a unique item, sometimes a novelty, sometimes something new. (Many of the standard kitchen gadgets you take for granted and can buy in thousands of stores were originally introduced to the market with such merchandising methods as these.) Still, on the larger scale of business generally, these are exceptions: Most businesses rely on getting repeat business—making customers who will come back to buy again and again. Unfortunately, the art of making customers has been largely neglected for many years by American businesses. Only lately has the need to resurrect the art begun to be recognized, under the pressure of an increasing number of bankruptcies and other business failures. The basic marketing problem is thus not how to make sales per se but how to make customers. We need to shed some light on the problem and possible solutions. Thus the question becomes: How can we use this new technology to win new customers more efficiently?

DATABASED MARKETING VERSUS DIFFERENT NEEDS

Nothing is perfect, and even those of us who have unrestrained enthusiasm for databased marketing must acknowledge that it is a far better fit to some marketing situations and business needs than it is to others. Certainly, it is not a panacea for all marketing ills. Although databased marketing is undoubtedly one of the most important new marketing ideas of recent years, revolutionary in the degree to which it enables identifying and targeting markets and market segments, its appropriateness and fit are better for some marketing problems than they are for others. In some cases the quality of the fit is obvious; in others it is not. But let's look at a few general considerations first, and then we can look at more specific examples of where databased marketing is most appropriate and offers the greatest promise in winning customers.

Companies of all sizes have been discovering more and more in recent years that the long business boom and the years of business arrogance, are rapidly drawing to a close. For many years after World War II, it appeared to be almost impossible to do wrong in business: Many business owners treated customers with contempt, exploited them mercilessly, and were at the least indifferent to their customers' interests. That was the result of the postwar boom and general shortage of goods and services: No matter how badly many customers were treated by business owners or how poorly they managed their businesses in general, they were able to survive in those years, and the occasional recessions were not very painful for most of them. But then came the reckoning, finally, as a flood of new products, a surge in the growth of small companies, and foreign competition gave buyers the wide breadth of choices they had not enjoyed before. Business failures became more and more common, and many well-known and apparently well-established companies (e.g., W. T. Grant, Robert Hall, and E. J. Korvette) suddenly and surprisingly collapsed, while Chrysler Corporation narrowly avoided the same fate that had finally overtaken all the smaller, independent automobile manufacturers. Many new books, such as *In Search of Excellence* and *Service America* offered explanations: Companies that had rediscovered the value of customer loyalty and those who had always recognized it were surviving, while those who thought the customer was someone to use, rather than someone to serve, were disappearing, bankrupt, liquidated, or acquired.

Mark Keefe delivers a message that recognizes the problem and the need for solution in introducing his recent article, "Tips on Developing a Double Duty DM Database" (*DM News,* 9/23/91). He makes it clear that at least one objective of a marketing database is to help the marketer foster and nourish a continuing relationship with customers as individual patrons.

Databased marketing at its heart depends on dialogue with customers, on getting information for your marketing databases directly from them. Thus it draws the marketer—the business—closer to the customer inherently and inevitably. The activities necessary to developing the marketing database reflect your active interest in the customer, in learning what he and she thinks and wants and recording that information in your databases to be acted on in whatever ways are possible. That is an important element in not only making sales, but in building customer loyalty, in *keeping* your customers. I have my own example as a customer to help me understand this.

I take my car back to the dealer from whom I bought it, and have it routinely serviced every 6 months, as the manufacturer recommends. I know that it costs me more for service there than it would at the local service station, but this dealer has gained my confidence by the obvious professionalism of his service department and by my reception there. I am always treated with courtesy, and all recommended repairs or replacements are explained to me carefully by the service manager, seeking my permission to proceed with the repairs. A week or two later, I invariably get a telephone call from the dealer, questioning me on my satisfaction and soliciting any comments or complaints I wish to make. I also get reminders in the mail periodically. The service is expensive, but the comfort of personal treatment, the confidence in the dealer that has been instilled in me, and my need to have peace of mind about what represents to me a substantial investment and an important property brings me back every six months.

Still, despite the excellent relationship, the dealer cannot count on my patronage forever. Someday it will end, for one reason or another, no matter how well I am treated and how well satisfied I am for the present. Keefe points out this truism that no customer is forever: Your hard-core, steady customer of today is likely to be your occasional customer or even former customer tomorrow. That can happen for any of dozens of reasons, as customers marry, otherwise change their stations in life, and/or undergo other changes in their needs and interests. Thus you must run to remain in the same place; while you must do everything possible to keep your established customers, you must accept the reality of customer turnover and constantly cultivate new customers to compensate for the loss of old customers. Taking old customers for granted is a common cause of business failures. The pursuit of new customers must be one of your major and *permanent* marketing objectives. How often businesses are in trouble because they did not seek to gain new customers until they found themselves in trouble for lack of established customers. You must never get so busy making sales that you don't have the time to make customers.

Some of these new customers may prove to be one-time or occasional buyers only, while others may become the steady, repeat customers that are the core of businesses based on the repeat business of satisfied customers. It does depend in large part on the nature of your business, of course: Most customers buy groceries every week, some even shop for groceries every day; most customers for automobiles buy them occasionally, every few years, although a few buy new automobiles every year or every two years; and most home buyers buy houses only once or twice, at most. Some repeat customers will stick with one supplier or one brand through thick and thin, while others never develop any sense of brand or dealer loyalty. The first-time buyer is an unknown quantity, in this and other respects, of course. Only time and history reveal enough to begin classifying him or her.

There is no way that you can know with any certainty which customer aligns with which of the preceding characteristics, although you can be reasonably sure that you cannot count on the buyer of a house to become a steady or repeat customer. Still, the satisfaction or dissatisfaction of a home buyer can be responsible for winning or losing house sales to friends and relatives of the original buyer. Good will is still a specific business asset.

How Much Should a Customer Cost?

When a marketer runs a sales campaign, especially in a direct marketing environment, one of the factors that enters into the calculations is the cost of each order. That helps the seller determine how well the campaign did in the short term, on the basis of number of orders, size of orders, direct profitability, and other such measures. There is a long-term aspect to most campaigns, however, that marketers do not always take into account. It is the acquisition of new customers, whose value and cost of have little to do with the value and cost of each order and must be calculated on an entirely different basis.

It costs money to create customers. If you spend $10,000 on a campaign and get 1,000 orders, you may consider that you paid $10 each for those customers. That may or may not have been a profitable investment in terms of immediate return, depending on what your gross profit (or loss) on each order was. On the other hand, suppose you lost $2 on each order. Did you really lose money here? Or did you, in fact, buy 1,000 customers at $2 each? The answer is not as simple as it may seem at first. There are variables to consider here. The ROI (return on investment) is not easy to calculate, for there is a short-term ROI and a long-term ROI.

Is Every Buyer a Customer?

There is some conventional wisdom that says no buyer can be counted as a customer until and unless he or she orders something from you for a second time. If only 800 of those first-time buyers return to buy a second time, by this reasoning you have bought 800 new customers at $2.50 each.

What Is a Customer Worth to You?

Not all customers are created equal: Some customers are going to be worth more to you than are others. That depends on the customer, to some extent—what and how he or she buys—but it also depends on you, on the kind of business you are in.

If you are in a business where you can look to building a central core of customers to whom you sell regularly or, at least, frequently, you probably got a bargain in buying new customers, even if they came at far higher cost than hypothesized in our example. In the end, you will profit, even if you did not turn a direct profit on the initial transaction. If you have enough experience to have developed reliable models, you will be able to assign to each of these new customers a "lifetime value" (LTV, in DM jargon), which is what the customer is probably going to be worth to you in sales until he or she becomes a former customer (i.e., during his or her lifetime as your steady customer). That is why many kinds of companies can afford to acquire new customers at a loss on the first order received or even the first few orders. In fact, many deliberately offer items below cost—loss leaders—to attract and acquire new customers.

Whether you do LTV and other kinds of marketing calculations regularly on a formal basis or fly your market planning and operations informally, by the seat of your pants, this is essentially what you are doing. You are buying customers if you are in the kind of business that depends on having steady customers buying from you regularly. Databased marketing is then most appropriate to your marketing needs, helping you build customer relationships, especially a sensitivity to your customers' wants and needs. If you sell a widely diverse line of products and/or services, you probably need to build a number of marketing databases, as you identify different customers for different products and services, and thus pinpoint your niche markets.

Yours may be another kind of business, one that is based on one-time sales; there are many such businesses. Here, the fit of the marketing database may be questionable as in the following possibilities.

There is the case of the single-item promoter, the entrepreneur who engages in selling only one item at a time. Joe Cossman is one such entrepreneur. As he has himself explained it, the approach is to search for some single item that appears to be viable for the single-item approach and test it. If it still appears viable, the next step is to launch an all-out direct marketing campaign by any or all methods—mail, print advertising, radio and TV promotions (e.g., those late-night "infomercials"), and any PR the promoter can think up. Such ventures may last a year or more, until the profitably of the venture—the ROI—begins to lag badly. The entrepreneur then winds the campaign down and turns attention to finding a new item to promote.

One of the best known of the products Cossman promoted was the ant farm of a few years ago. The late Joe Karbo, another such entrepreneur, sold 600,000+ copies of his little paperback book, *The Lazy Man's Way to Riches,* at $10 apiece. Ken Hakuta, promoter of the highly successful "Wall Walker" toy, is still another example, as are many who sell kitchen gadgets, record and tape albums, and sundry other items through direct mail and late-night TV promotions. Flip through your TV channels, especially those of the smaller stations, any night after the 11 o'clock news to see such promotions in action, often as half-hour commercials disguised as shows. (They are called, euphemistically, "infomercials.")

The orders received by such promoters as these are not necessarily strictly one-time sales events. Some of the customers may buy the item again to use as gifts for others or may otherwise have use for more than one of the item. Multiple and repeat sales are the exceptions, however, in these kinds of special promotions, and they are not usually a significant factor in marketing success or the lack of it. In some cases the mailing list is useful to help promote the next item to the same customers. That is usually a long time later, however, when the customer list is badly aged and of limited value. (Mailing lists do age rapidly if they are not maintained.) In general such promoters are likely to seek new one-time buyers, as their accustomed way of doing business, and do not worry especially about customer loyalty and repeat sales. Repeat business is the rare exception much more than it is the rule and is therefore not an objective.

There is therefore little question that this must be classed as a one-time-buyer-based kind of business, and both costs and profits must be derived from that one sale, rather than any future sales and presumed LTV. It thus argues against the expensive development of a marketing database, at least nominally. Presumably, the cost of developing the marketing database is too great to be a viable proposition here, at least at this time. It is not impossible that the future will bring a sharp decline in the costs of building marketing databases, in which case these analyses may not be at all valid. But for the present, it is probably more practical to accept the relative inefficiency of traditional mass marketing for these kinds of ventures.

Suppose, on the other hand, that your business consists of such one-time sales as million-dollar homes, yachts, major plant equipment, and other such truly big-tag items that call for a major investments by customers able and willing to make large expenditures. Such sales are not easily made. They require extensive, multiple marketing efforts, even written proposals and "dog and pony show" formal presentations, to develop sales leads. They require extensive follow-up qualification of prospects and follow-up sales presentations, often elaborate and expensive ones. They do, however, usually involve quite substantial markups. Expensive although it is to build marketing databases, the size of such sales and the margins of profit in them thus justify the expense.

Suppose, on the other hand, that the bulk of your transactions are one-time sales on a much more modest scale, such as home improvement repairs, big-screen television sets, or replacement engines for automobiles. These are also one-time sales of fairly large size, with all the marketing needs that are typical of such businesses, but the dollar volume involved in the markup or gross profit is much smaller than in the prior case. Does the margin here justify the costs of developing marketing databases for one-time sales?

Here, we are in something of a middle ground: The viability of an investment in databased marketing here may be highly questionable. It will require some kind of trade-off analysis to determine whether the cost of developing the marketing database is excessive compared with the LTV of customers, when that LTV is equal only to the value of a single sale.

THE PROSPECTING DATABASE

The Common Characteristics

What these big—either big-big-tag or medium-big-tag—sales have in common is that the market for these sales is a relatively small portion of the public. In general, they are none of them one-call businesses. Each sale in these businesses represents a great deal of marketing effort. It generally requires more than one presentation, often an entire series of presentations including mass mailings, radio and TV appeals, free seminars, street-corner interviews, contests, "free" offers, trade show booths, and other programs for interfacing with the public at large, with general, unqualified prospects. But that is the rub: They are only general prospects, about whom you know nothing. The probability of selling your major big-tag item to any prospect chosen at random is minuscule. You must better those odds, if you are to have a successful (i.e., profitable) campaign. Thus the entire purpose of any special event is to sift through and screen the sea of general prospects to find the special or qualified prospects, those worth pursuing with follow-up sales presentations that have a reasonable mathematical probability of producing the desired results—sales. (Where a series of presentations is involved, it is necessary to discriminate between the sales presentation and the prospecting presentation, that presentation designed to generate sales leads.)

At the same time, it takes a relatively large number of initial presentations to develop leads. By far, the majority of initial presentations do not result in sales or even justify follow-ups, and so it is important to do the prospecting as efficiently as possible. In a large sense, initial presentations in this kind of marketing arena represent a screening process, one in which the "impossibles" are screened out so as to identify the "possibles." It is from this set of "possibles," then, that real effort stems to develop good sales leads.

Thus you develop a database even here, perhaps not the completely matured database that has been described earlier, but one that falls somewhere between the mailing list of raw, unqualified prospects and the mature database of exceptionally well-qualified prospects. It is the database of those who responded to your initial prospecting initiatives and screenings and thus provides you with at least a first-level prospecting database of those who have shown a qualifying interest and a capability to buy what you are selling.

Factors of Qualification

Two major factors must be resolved in qualifying a prospect as worthy of additional marketing effort beyond the initial probe—interest and capability. Both are important, but all too often the latter one is neglected when the prospect exhibits what appears to be great interest. I saw evidence of this when a young salesman appeared at my door one day offering me a presentation of a grand opportunity to become the proud owner of the marvelous, new encyclopedia he was entrusted with representing.

I explained to this eager and sincere young man that my children were out of school, fully grown, flown from the nest and raising their own families; I therefore had no use for a new encyclopedia.

He pressed on and I explained further that I had nothing important to do that evening, and I would listen to his presentation, if he needed the practice, but he ought to know up front that I had no use for a new encyclopedia and certainly would not buy one.

He came in and made his lengthy presentation, which I did find interesting enough. I listened attentively and thanked him, showing him the door politely. He could not believe that I did not give him an order, since I appeared to be interested enough. That was obviously because he wanted so badly to interpret my apparent interest as indicative of my being a good prospect. It was an unfortunate example of the wishful thinking that can so easily get in the way of objective analysis. A good marketing database is a help here too, as a safeguard against wishful thinking.

You must, of course, be able to discriminate between curiosity and genuine interest in buying. Many individuals may become interested in or curious about things they could not possibly afford or can't use. That does not necessarily refer only to individual consumers as prospects; it is equally valid in dealing with organizations. When I was cast in the role of marketer to the federal government agencies in Washington, DC, I often encountered young executives with their own offices (sometimes rather elaborate ones in the newest of government office buildings) and shiny clean desks. Sometimes they had rather light duties and little responsibility, and were delighted to have the diversion of someone calling on them, and many were eager to "get a project" of their own. They might very well encourage follow-up marketing, including written proposals and formal presentations. As so many others before had been forced to do, I soon learned to eliminate a great deal of wasted effort and expense by asking a few tactful questions, such as these:

- Is there a written requirement in existence for this project? (Are we talking about a real project or just ruminating here?)
- Are funds currently available for this? (Do you/your organization have any money to spend?)
- Who must approve this program (purchase)? (Who has the authority to award this project?)

Answers to these and similar euphemistically phrased questions soon let me know whether the individual had any authority or budget to let a contract, and whether he or she could be a conduit to or an indirect means of pursuing a contract. Procedures and instruments for qualifying prospects (e.g., separating the curiosity seeker from the serious prospect) must be instituted in the process somehow.

Finding Prequalified Databases

In practice, you don't necessarily have to start with completely unqualified prospects. Depending on the item you are selling, you can often prequalify at least some of the prospects from available information. You can set up a few known requirements in advance, such as that of income level, occupation, education, and other factors, even prior purchases. These data can tell you a great deal about the prospect's probable ability to use the item in question, as well as the ability to afford it and perhaps even the likelihood of interest in whatever you wish to sell.

Qualifying means screening out those obviously unsuited, as well as identifying those who appear to be well suited: seriously interested and in a position to make the purchase. For example, only a computer owner would be a good prospect for a new kind of disk drive or advanced software, and only a licensed pilot is likely to be a prospect for a new private airplane or most items related to owning and flying private aircraft. Thus the prospecting database may begin with a mailing list chosen for its accompanying data that represent prequalifying factors.

The problem with using the typical rented list is that you rent it for one-time use only, and you may very well need it for several, repetitive uses, for follow-up. You therefore need a list you can use more than once. Using the list one time only would probably not be more than marginally helpful: The cost of a marketing effort to sell highly specialized and expensive one-time items is a large one, and further qualification makes a great deal of sense, whether the contemplated follow-up is a mass mailing, a telephone campaign, or a house-call campaign. If you are using rented lists you may therefore wish to rent the list more than once, an expensive solution, or make special arrangements to use the list on some other basis than one-time rental. (List brokers appear to be more and more oriented to making such special arrangements, as clients begin to build their own marketing databases.)

Other Uses for Prospecting Databases

The development of databases for prospecting is appropriate to but not confined to markets for big-tag and one-time sales. The need for improved prospecting is being increasingly recognized, as the steadily rising costs of marketing erode the profitability of the traditional mass marketing by DM methods. Authors Gerald Reisberg and Samuel Gilbert addressed this issue in an article, "Finding Quality Prospects," (*Target Marketing,* February 1991). They cited the case of "a well-known industry leader" who was changing her mailing strategy and building databases of prospects. Where she had formerly focused her company's direct mail campaigns almost entirely on their customers, she was beginning to build databases of prospects that appear to match closely the company's best-known customers and targeting those databases for aggressive mailing campaigns. That, of course, calls for a great deal of qualifying of prospects. In general and as a commentary, the authors cite the greatly increased costs of mailing and the resulting increase in the risk factor as requiring more precise qualifying of prospects.

Segmentation by Profitability

Prospects should be linked to markets and market segments, classified by order of profitability as a priority scheme, to make the most efficient use of this idea. It is inevitable that some niches or segments are going to be more profitable than others. That can come about in several ways. It may be because you have segmented your market by customer "quality": poor, good, and best customer (e.g., least, better, and most profitable customers), in terms of frequency and dollar volume of sales. It may be because you have segmented your market by customer LTV (lifetime value) setting levels in either poor-good-best designations or in levels of estimated total dollar values. However, it may also be a function of how deeply you have been able to penetrate the given segment: A segment that you have penetrated to a depth of 4 or 5 percent is presumably far more profitable than one where you can claim only a 2 percent penetration (although that does not always follow).

Even these are not the only factors that can affect probability. Some products and services are inherently more profitable than others. As one example of this, I suspect that my automobile dealer has made far more profit from servicing my automobile than he did from selling it to me originally. I may well have been a far more profitable customer than someone who buys much more expensive models than I do or who buys new cars more frequently than I do, but who go elsewhere to have their cars serviced. In that simple statement, I have pointed out four segments of that dealer's market:

1. The buyer of bottom- and mid-grade automobiles.
2. The buyer of top-of-the-line models.
3. The every-year or every-other-year car buyer.
4. The regular-service customer.

Actually, there are more than four segments identified here because there is a segment that combines (1) and (3), (1), (3), and (4), or other combinations, so you can identify as many as eight other segments represented by combinations of the items in the list.

There is also the consideration that some segments are easier and less costly to market to, and are more profitable for this reason. Thus 3 percent of one segment may be more profitable than 4 percent of another for such reasons as these.

The "Smart" Prospecting Database

In the computer field, a great many hardware and software items become "smart" items in new incarnations. That adjective implies the addition of some new or enhanced capability resembling an ability to make choices or otherwise think. Thus early modems, the devices that enable one computer to "talk" to another computer via a telephone line, were soon succeeded by "smart" modems that could do much more than simply convert silent digital pulses to audible signals that could be transferred over an ordinary telephone. The program "SmartKey" enables the user to program a single key to act as another key or produce an entire series of keystrokes—even an entire file— with one keystroke. Thus, a "smart" database used for prospecting may have any of a number of special attributes or capabilities built into it. Author Max Bartko introduces this idea in his article, "How to Build a 'Smart' Prospecting Database" (*DM News,* June 24, 1991). In it, he explains that many mailers are now using database technology to modify and enhance the older method of renting lists and subjecting them to typical merge/purge processing. To do what he suggests requires that you depart from the typical list-rental arrangements and find an alternate source or make some special agreements. There are, of course, the compiled lists, such as those discussed in Chapters 3 and 4, which are yours to use as often as you like, once you have bought them. (Your ownership is limited to free use of the lists, not to resale of them, however.) However, by far the bulk of the list business lies in list rentals, usually for one-time use or, at least, for a specified number of uses, each of which must be paid for. One requirement, therefore, if you are using rented lists, is that you must have made a deal with the list owner and/or broker entitling you to use the list repeatedly over some period, with regular updates, as you build your special marketing databases. Here are some of the characteristics and capabilities of such special, smart databases:

- A special form of merge/purge when calling up a list, automatically suppressing names that are already on your house lists.
- Advance development and tailoring of lists for individual offers or of several related offers and reservation of each list for that/ those offers only.
- Sundry other capabilities (e.g., make and report various counts and select only names qualifying for postal discounts, such as zip + 4 and presorts).
- Net-net arrangements (paying only for names actually mailed).

These are all special arrangements, outside the traditional methods and practices for renting lists, and will require some negotiations with list owners and list brokers. Nevertheless, they or something like them may well become a standard arrangement of tomorrow, for business realities may compel it: If mailing lists must give way to marketing databases, and each direct marketer must develop his and her own unique marketing databases, serious changes in the list business must come about.

Chapter 9

The Computer in Databased Marketing

Databased marketing is computer dependent, but for databased marketing to become universally practiced, it must graduate to the desktop computer: the PC. We have much to learn yet about using the PC in databased marketing, but imaginative marketers and computer experts have made great strides already, and the versatility of the PC as a databased marketing asset is providing its own collection of surprises.

THE HARDWARE CONSIDERATION

The computer is itself not new, but the computer that is on everyone's desktop is new. That is, the computer that required a large room of its own is not new, but the desktop computer is; it is as new as the concept of what started as the personal computer (still known as the "PC" although it has long outgrown the restriction of that term). The meaning of the word *computer* has changed drastically in the image it invokes. Where once relatively few people even knew what a computer looked like, except for those shown on TV, every schoolchild now knows that a computer is a TV-like screen, with a flat cabinet and a keyboard, about the size of a TV set. In less than a decade, this device that was originally little more than a hobby for young people with sharp minds and basement workshops has placed full computer power in just about everyone's office, from the spare-bedroom offices of home-based small businesses to the thousands of executive offices and secretaries' desks in the high-rise office buildings of the world's supercorporations. Desktop computers are counted today in the millions. There has been, for several years, discussion in the industry about the likelihood that the PC, in the constant and rapid expansion of its capabilities and capacities, will soon render the mainframe computer an obsolescent relic.

The swiftness of PC development has been far greater than anyone anticipated. The difference today between the capabilities of the large, mainframe computer and the advanced PC is shrinking, especially as multicomputer establishments install networks interconnecting their many desktop computers and providing all of them with access to large central storage, printing, and other peripheral facilities. All of that is simple fact, despite the loyalty of many to the mainframe computers of earlier decades, for there are those who demur, reluctant to surrender their attachment to the behemoth computers that belong to the past.

Databased marketing is most definitely computer dependent. However, if it is to become the universal or near-universal strategy for marketing—at least for direct marketing, where it is so apparently a good fit—it cannot depend on the mainframe computer, but must be amenable to functioning with smaller systems. Thus, the examination of how the desktop computer functions or can be induced in databased marketing is critically important. The examination reveals an amazing diversity that is still growing.

One important difference is that the basic or most common mode of operation is far different with the desktop computer than with the mainframe. Most applications were run in "batch" or "offline" mode with mainframes, and they were relatively slow, with their large tape servos, the big reels of magnetic tape spinning for many minutes to find the data bits and bytes required. Relatively little computer operation was done in "real time" or spontaneously, as data became available for input. With the PC, the opposite is true: For one thing, instead of the lengthy periods required to find information buried somewhere on one of the nine-track tape reels used by mainframe tape servos, the file can be found on a hard disk and presented on-screen in milliseconds, often even in microseconds, with a PC. That makes it possible to do such things as scanning the record of a customer or even making corrections to or adding information to the record while talking to the customer over the telephone or across the counter. You see this every day, even in the smallest retail establishments.

There is the matter of complexity of operation, too. The individual employed as the computer operator of a mainframe, although probably the least skilled of all computer technicians, still had to have some special training, so mainframes had and still have full-time computer operators. On the other hand, just about anyone can learn to operate a PC with little and usually informal training. There is some change in this situation now because mainframes can use disk storage too. There is also some crossover because in many cases the PC is used today as a terminal of the mainframe (i.e., anyone using the PC in such arrangements can view or retrieve information from and send information to the mainframe). Still, the mainframe computer continues to trend to the lumbering giant with its many big tape servos spinning endlessly, while the PC trends more to being the fleet-footed sprinter.

Databased marketing executive and author Arthur M. Hughes has written a book, *The Complete Database Marketer* (Probus Publishing

Co., Chicago, 1991), that I consider to be among the best of the several books I have read on the subject. He is, for my taste, perhaps a bit too much the purist: He is almost puritanical in what he insists are the necessary minimum qualifications of databased marketing. I believe that he is slightly out of step with the computer professionals and possibly confused about some rather fine distinctions, such as the difference between memory and disk storage, but those terms are in the murky realm of technical jargon and his meanings are plain enough in a well-written book that furnishes a great many valuable insights. (I confess that he did broaden my views in several respects.) Still, I find some of his assertions too dogmatic. He insists, for example, that only a mainframe computer can do the job or even meet his definition of databased marketing, according to the following rationale: A marketing database begins life as a customer database, and it must be constantly growing in its accumulation of data about those listed, with the data arising from dialogue with the customers. He believes this factor makes it inevitable that telemarketing must accompany the development of marketing databases, serving as the means of continuing dialogue with customers and the source of the data to be added to the database records. (He appears not to admit of other means for dialogue with customers.) Further, for a database to qualify by his definition, it must be accessible to and actively used by a number of people concurrently, at least some of whom will be the telemarketers passing on new information gleaned from the dialogue with customers, and used to swell the obligatory increase of data in each customer record. This requires such a large memory, storage capacity, and great processing speed (Hughes specifies 8,000 megabytes of disk storage and processing speed of seven million instructions per second as required minimums) that a mainframe computer is required, and the PC is admissible only as a means for communicating with the mainframe computer or to run marketing support systems that only resemble but are not true databased marketing systems.

I freely concede the author's right to define in his own terms this admittedly rather new discipline that many experienced marketers profess to know little or nothing about. It must also be conceded, however, that other definitions are possible and that this new wave of marketing methodology is not a black/white, go/no-go, is/is-not proposition, but may exist somewhere along a spectrum where it may fall short of the ideal and yet deliver the major benefits of the method. In short, it makes sense to consider databased marketing to be a scalable quantity, as we do direct marketing; for example, is the mailer of 5,000 pieces not a direct marketer because he/she mails fewer than 500,000 pieces? Ergo, is the possessor/user of a database of 5,000 names less a database marketer because he or she maintains a database of fewer than 500,000 customers and leads or communicates indirectly, rather than directly, with customers?

Hughes is apparently not entirely alone in his views. In *The New Direct Marketing* (introduced in Chapter 6), the authors also strongly imply the belief, albeit less dogmatically expressed, that the memory and storage requirements of databased marketing are so great as to all but mandate the need for a mainframe computer. One rationale for their position is the extensive memory and storage space needed by typical programs that provide the inexpert user the help he or she needs to run the programs effectively without special consultants. Implied, at least, is an admission that the modern microcomputer (the older term for the PC) may have an important role to play in databased marketing. Yet, there appears to be a reluctance to go beyond this grudging concession.

If we confine ourselves to the orientation that only with a mainframe computer can databased marketing be a reality, we make it impossibly difficult for the small businesses even to aspire to building marketing databases, much less employ databased marketing on a grand scale. We are saying, in effect, that only the larger marketing operations—the larger companies—can use databased marketing. We know that that is an unacceptable precondition, totally foreign to our free-enterprise philosophy. We must study databased marketing as a marketing system/ strategy/methodology that may exist in almost any size, for that is a reality. A definition that excludes the small business from participation will be rejected by a large portion of the direct marketing industry, as well as by a great many marketers in other industries. Let us therefore consider what a user *can* do with a modern PC or fully capable desktop computer.

A FEW STARTLING STATISTICS

Anyone today can collect, record, organize, sort, search, find, compare, maintain, manipulate, evaluate, and retrieve information in vast quantities and at electronic speeds while seated at a desk, using equipment resting entirely on the desk, that is, desktop computers and their necessary peripheral devices. Those speeds run commonly today to millions of data bits per second: 33 megahertz computers, processing bits of data at "clock speeds" of 33 million bits a second are sold every day across the counter in routine transactions: There is nothing startling any more in desktop equipment that operates at such speeds. Entire files are processed in split seconds. In some applications, pages flash across the monitor screen too fast to be seen, much less read. Some of us are so conditioned to these speeds that we are impatient with the wait of a quarter second; we have come to expect near-instantaneous results when ordering even the most complex transactions.

A 3.5-inch plastic square of the type known as a *high-density* disk can hold 1.44 million *bytes* of data. A byte is equal to one alphabetic character or 8 bits of data, and there are about 4,000 bytes—32,000+ bits, because control signals and printer commands are also required—to a single-spaced typed page, so we are talking about storing the equivalent of approximately 360 pages of information on a disk that fits comfortably in a person's shirt pocket. A 60-megabyte (60 million byte) tape cassette, smaller than a package of cigarettes, can hold about 15,000 pages of information. The information can be compressed electronically, if desired, which would about double the capacity of the disk and/or the tape cassette, permitting you to store about 30,000 pages of information. (I have more than 20 book manuscripts stored on one 40-megabyte tape, and it is not more than about one-half full. I will probably not live long enough to fill it, much less fill the 60-megabyte disk whose physical dimensions are no greater.) The typical desktop computers of today are equipped with fixed disks of 80, 120, 200, and 300+ megabytes (20,000, 30,000, 50,000, and 75,000+ pages, respectively), which can be about doubled by electronic compression. If that is translated into records, it can easily represent a capacity for 200,000 to 400,000 or more individual records, depending on how the database is structured. Even then, the number can be virtually doubled by compression, and even larger fixed disks are available as large as 160 *gigabytes* or 160 billion bytes. And they can be compressed too, so that a desktop computer today may be able to store well over 300 billion bytes or alphanumeric characters. Moreover, all that power inheres in a single, commercially produced desktop computer selling today in the range of $1,500 to $4,500, depending on various options you may choose. Obviously, you can have more than one such computer—a great many offices do—and you can easily link them to each other, combining their capacities. That is done commonly today when you have a number of desktop computers in one suite of offices and workspaces: You can link them in a LAN (local area network) so that you do not need to provide each computer with a printer, a hard drive, a modem, and other peripheral devices. Instead, you establish server devices—hard disk storage, printers, and other peripheral units that all may access via the linking networks.

These are some of the quantitative capabilities of today's desktop computers. Although we still refer to them by the term "PC," for personal computer, they have long since outgrown the implied restrictions of that adjective "personal." Most of today's more advanced desktop computers rival the capabilities of yesterday's mainframe computers and even of many of today's mainframes, and are used increasingly in offices as general business computers as well as personal computers on individual desks. You can see, therefore, that you do not have to be dependent on a computer service bureau if you do not wish to be, and you do not have to be big enough to afford a mainframe computer of your own: It is not difficult today to be completely self-sufficient in computer capabilities that approach those of mainframes, if they do not fully match them.

The connection with databased marketing is, of course, obvious: Databased marketing depends on the capabilities of computers to build and maintain the databases, and to put them to whatever uses are necessary to exploit them in the several ways we have mentioned here. But beyond that we need to use computers for such corollary functions as those mentioned and discussed briefly in Chapter 7. There, we discussed such functions as merge/purge, mail/merge, and some of the marketing economics that have been changed by the easy availability of desktop computing at low costs. What we did not delve into was the subject of desktop publishing—"DTP," in today's jargon.

THE PROBLEM OF MANIFOLD MARKETING MATERIALS

Presumably, when you market to niches, the marketing strategy and the appeal are going to be different in each case. Logically, each niche market is therefore going to require its own, unique presentation package. Thus, one of the problems of niche marketing, especially if you have a large number of small or relatively small niche markets, is the cost of developing and printing a correspondingly large number of individual presentation packages, each tailored to its niche. In fact, for many marketers that cost is a key issue in deciding on how large a niche must be to be a viable marketing target. The probable cost of penetrating any market is an issue, weighed against the estimated sales volume and profit potential. The cost of penetrating a large number of small markets can be a much greater problem, calling for an entire complex of estimates.

This therefore requires careful planning. You must divide your presentation or promotional package into two parts, the front end or introductory materials, and the backup or reinforcement materials. The front end must be tailored to the prospects of the niche being addressed. The backup materials are fixed and standard for all prospects, regardless of the niche.

The need for careful planning should be obvious: The backup materials must be suitable for all, so that you can produce them in quantity and gain the economies of scale that are so typical of printing. That isn't as difficult as it may sound, if you consider the marketing presentation as having two phases, the "front end" and the "back end" referred to here, which I like to think of as "the promise" and "the proof."

THE ESSENTIAL DIFFERENCE BETWEEN NICHES

Market niches are groups or classes of individuals, identified or determined by different individuals' needs, interests, and desires, such as low costs, fast results, convenience, confidentiality, easy financing terms, small quantity purchases, large quantity purchases, immediate shipment, extended credit, special imprinting, drop shipping, or any of many other possible factors that are important enough to influence the prospect's buying decision. Thus "the offer" is really a promise—a promise to drop ship, to extend credit, to surprint a product with the customer's name, to ship by special express means, to produce fast results, to sell at most competitive price, to offer special discounts or special package deals, to include bonuses and free gifts, or otherwise to promise that which is the most important feature in motivating the prospect to submit an order.

It is wise to also be aware that a prospect's buying decision is always based on a competition of some kind: It may be a competition with another supplier of what the customer wishes to buy. It may be a brand competition. Or it may be a competition with whatever else the customer is considering spending his or her money for. When you pursue the customer with a limited number of dollars to spend (a rather typical customer), you are inevitably competing for that customer's dollars. Sometimes you are faced with a customer who wants the kind of product you sell but is uncertain about brand name, so you are in competition with another brand or another dealer who sells the same item. You should have a realistic fix on this part of the marketing problem if you are to create an effective appeal.

The Front End or Unique Element

It is self-defeating to offer all the possible promises to everyone and hope that each prospect will read the all-encompassing package of claimed benefits and sell him- or herself; it just does not happen. The promise that will influence the prospect to buy must be *the* promise, the sole, main, leading promise that eclipses everything else or it will not do the job. And in a great many cases the sale is won or lost with the headline or lead of your copy. You must concentrate on making that as powerful as possible.

Thus each niche must have a front-end package that makes the main promise quite clear: It will be a direct promise to satisfy the main need or desire of that customer, and it should not be diluted by other promises that divert the prospect's attention from the main motivator. Unity of appeal is essential, and multiple appeals often cause confusion and destroy the sale.

The essential difference between niches and the seminal factor of each niche is, then, that promise. It must distinguish the niche by being absolutely distinctive, unequivocal, and clear. And it must be made with marketing materials that are unique and apply to only that single niche. It must, for example, promise the price or cost advantage to the niche customer most concerned with price, the promise of fast results to the customer so concerned, and the promise of an ironclad guarantee to that customer so concerned. Featuring the guarantee of fast results to the customer worried about cost simply reduces your response rate and wastes your postage. Perhaps above all, databased marketing means not making this kind of strategic mistake. Thus, where you may have mailed the same package to 50,000 prospects and won a 2 percent return, you will be mailing a dozen or more packages to those 50,000 prospects and earning an 8 or 10 percent, or perhaps even greater return.

The Back End or Common Element

Having made the promise to deliver the benefit that the prospects in a given niche most want, you must prove your case, prove that you can and will deliver what you promised. You have made the promise and you have been quite clear about it. But the prospect is an intelligent human being. He or she wants *proof* of both your sincerity and your ability to deliver what you promise. He or she wants proof that the product or service you are hawking is what you claim for it, that it will be what you say it is and that it will *do* what you say it will do. But he or she also wants proof that you are representing a reliable and respectable business firm that can be trusted, unlike some earlier marketer who delivered a product falling far short of the promises made.

That is why you need the clearly stated guarantees, the testimonials, the logical arguments, the photos of people in white laboratory coats, the certificates reproduced, and all the other evidences of dependability and trustworthiness. Those are part of the back end of the marketing materials package, and they can be a uniform element of your presentation, equally effective for all the niches. This part of the package, unlike the front end, can be the same for all 50,000 addressees if you design the entire package carefully enough.

Planning and Strategies

To ensure that uniform and universal suitability of the back end materials for all 50,000 names in your marketing database, you must consider the strategies you will use for all the front-end packages and take care that the backup materials are not incompatible with any of those strategies.

You must also take care that the most expensive parts of the package (e.g., those with process color, broadsides, and other expensive pieces) are those of the second, backup part: You would want those printed in long runs: they would be prohibitively expensive in multiple short runs.

Obviously, then, the front end materials, tailored carefully for each individual niche, should be those which are by design least costly to create and produce: They are going to be, perhaps, the introductory sales letters, the simple brochures, the lift letters, and, possibly, order forms and leaflets offering bonus deals, special discounts, and other inducements, if they are peculiarly part of offerings to niches, rather than to everyone. That may even include testimonials, in some cases. However, the basic philosophy is to segregate that which must be tailored for each niche and is thus a short-run item that can be designed and produced at modest unit cost, from that which will be common to the package and will also be, perhaps, the glitz in the package that is designed to support the front-end promises, whatever they are.

It takes careful planning and creative imagination to bring this off in this manner, but it can be done. The DTP capabilities of your desktop computer can be an asset here, with careful planning. They represent a capability for creating and producing those multiple front-end portions of your sales presentations.

Desktop publishing, at its full capabilities, requires a good-quality laser printer and the right software, as well as a computer with ample capabilities. Properly equipped, the system can turn out materials close enough to formally typeset quality (i.e., that set by commercial typographers) that only an expert could tell the difference, and the customer is neither discriminating enough nor even the least bit interested in whether the copy was created by a commercial artist/typographer or on your own, in-house system. The example shown in Figure 9–1, for example, was set on my own little system, using a modern word processor, which is far below the maximum capabilities of larger systems and DTP. It illustrates how easy it is to create a polished and professional newsletter with a simple system. The capabilities go far beyond this simple example, of course. They extend to a wide variety of typefaces and graphics, even to reasonably good halftone reproduction. Actually, the example is not truly a DTP product; it is a product of the DTP-like capability of the WordStar word processing software I use. Most modern word processors offer such capabilities, overlapping DTP functions. It is incredibly easy to do such things today with modern software and even easier with true DTP software, complex as the product may seem.

The capability for desktop publishing is not entirely that of the computer. The quality of the printed product is dependent on the printer and what the computer uses to send detailed instructions to the printer. (Computer programs usually come with a variety of printer drivers, and you select the one that is appropriate for your own printer.) The driver for a laser printer will thus include instructions that only a laser printer can carry out. Hence, you do need a laser printer to get a product of top quality.

You can use the laser-printer output as camera-ready copy that can be sent to the print shop, where it will be made into a plate and installed on a press to run copies in whatever quantity you request. For a great many purposes, that is entirely adequate quality for plating an offset press.

WRITER'S INTELLIGENCE NETWORK

"No man but a blockhead ever wrote except for money."
--Samuel Johnson, 1776

No. 101   Editor/Publisher Herman Holtz

SPECIAL ANNOUNCEMENT
Writer's Intelligence Network is reinstituted.

The *Writer's Intelligence Network*, a monthly compendium of useful information for independent writers, was a great success a dozen years ago, when it was first introduced. As its author, I was forced, most reluctantly, to discontinue its publication when the requirements of my many book contracts compelled me to choose. Now, 48 books and hundreds of articles, proposals, and columns later, and for the first time in all those years, I am able to once again offer to help other struggling writers to success. *Writer's Intelligence Network* exists again!

It will be again an 8-page report every month, with tips, ideas, and guidance for all those striving to succeed as freelance, independent writers. Now, a dozen years later, it will be *more* in more than one way: It will be *more* in that it will now be geared to the modern technology that writers use--computers and word processing, with spell checkers, desktop publishing, and the sundry other miracles of technology. But it will be even more than that, much more. It will be also a free consulting service from the author of all those books, articles, proposals, and columns! (Read on, to learn about that special feature.)

Following are just a few of the kinds of information you will normally get from the monthly *Writer's Intelligence Network*.

- Tips for enhancing acceptance probability.
- Using computer aids most effectively.
- Most promising markets today and how to crack them.
- How to find your own market niche.
- New market requirements.
- Marketing ideas and insider tips.

- Special markets--e.g., governments.
- Prime contracts.
- Subcontracts.
- The advantages of "quick response"
- Proposal writing.
- The consumer market.
- Newslettering.
- Special ideas for winning acceptance.

Figure 9–1. Newsletter format prepared with ordinary DTP facilities.

You have an option here: If your run is not excessively large (e.g., you need only a few hundred or perhaps only a few thousand copies) you may find it feasible to do the entire print run on the laser printer. Heavy-duty laser printers can be used for such relatively short runs.

Either way, you will probably cut costs and certainly save time in launching tests of the niches you have identified.

INDIVIDUALIZING MAILINGS WITH MAIL/MERGE

You will recall the brief discussions of mail/merge (Chapter 7), with the explanation that mail/merge is a capability for merging each name and address on a list with a form letter, so that each letter is addressed to an individual. I mentioned further that this capability goes beyond merely addressing each copy of the form letter to an individual: It can be and is used to individualize mailings in many ways. Figure 9–2 is an example of this kind of mailing.

Note how this advertising of a relational database is personalized with my own name and address. The figure shows the order form, which was attached to the flap of the return envelope and perforated for easy removal. My name appears somewhere on all elements of the material, even as a return address on the return envelope.

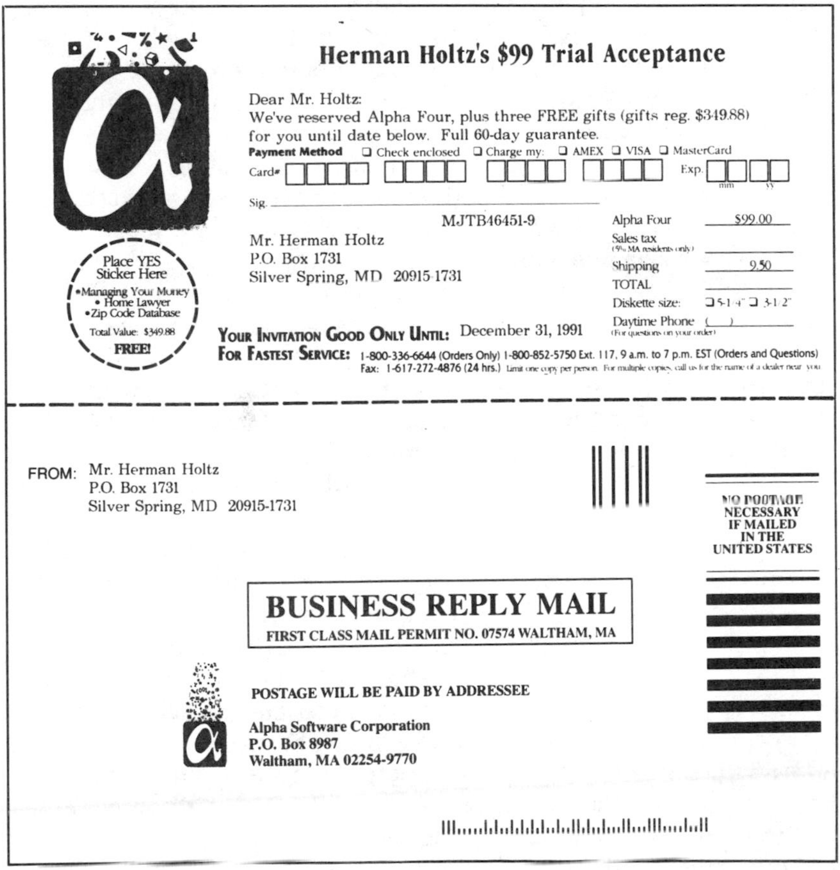

Figure 9–2. A truly individualized response device.

NICHE MARKETS OF OPPORTUNITY

Marketing, in the simplest terms possible, is matching something to sell with someone who wants to buy. In a few cases, the beginning entrepreneur starts a venture on the basis of access to some market—perhaps he or she knows most of the major hotel purchasing agents and managers in the United States and Canada and is experienced in selling to them or enjoys acquaintanceship and cordial relationships with hundreds of buyers in electronic manufacturing companies. He or she thus seeks a product or service suitable for that market as a basis on which to launch his or her venture. That is the exception or at least the less frequent case. Far more often the entrepreneur starts with some product or service and goes in quest of a market for it.

Identifying and selling to niche markets is no exception to this pattern: Many ventures are launched on the basis of an entrepreneur's knowledge of and/or access to some niche market. More commonly, the entrepreneur starts with a product or service to sell and seeks a niche market as a better means to launch a new venture than tackling the entire possible market. Selling to a niche market is less costly because it involves a much smaller target population of prospects and, if the niche is well chosen, the response rate is much greater than may be expected of the general market.

The computer has changed and is changing marketing in many more ways than we have yet considered, including databased marketing generally and marketing with respect to niche markets especially. We need to open our minds to many alternatives to the traditional ways and to traditional thinking. The power of the computer to build huge databases of detailed customer and prospect data—individual profiles—opens many new doors. We have spent a great deal of time together exploring and discussing market niches and niche markets. We have even found that in a strict technical sense, each individual customer prospect is a niche in the market, if profiled in such detail as to be identified as a unique individual with individually defined buying motivations.

In any case, we have or should have found, as have others before us, that any group of customers sharing a common major interest or need (i.e., a main motivation) is a niche, but it may or may not qualify as a niche market. The niche is not a market unless it has enough prospects in it to make a marketing attack viable economically. The euphemism means, in plain language, having enough prospective sales volume to be worth the gamble of trying to sell to it. The specialized marketing effort will cost money, and the precomputer costs of launching a marketing attack may not have been worthwhile. The desktop computer has changed that, however, by making it far easier, faster, and less costly to launch a direct-mail effort, and so even rather small market segments are often worth pursuing.

What the computer and its databases can do for you is thus show you how to not only *discover* niche markets but also *create* these markets, where you may not have even suspect their existence.

Finding Niche Markets by Discovery

The conventional uncovering of niche markets is a discovery process of seeking out the niches that exist in a given database for some given service, product, or line of services or products. The discovery or identification of niches as niche markets depends on the confluence of their (the individuals' or organizations') motivations with the attributes of whatever you sell: When some characteristic or potential benefit of what you sell can be shown to coincide with an interest or need of that group of individuals, you can prepare and deliver a marketing presentation and sales argument tailored to that group as a niche market. And that applies, of course, to additional niche markets, for there are usually several or even many segments in any market that can be addressed as niche markets. The imaginative marketer is always alert to discover new markets, which are usually niches. However, for the creative marketer, that is not enough to take full advantage of ongoing and continuous market study. Suppose, for example, that you encounter a niche for which you do not already have a recognizable matching product or service. Must you pass by that niche regretfully? Or can you take advantage of the discovery by *creating* a service or product that exploits the niche and thus *creates* a market? Yes, you may be assured that this can be and is being done by those enterprising people who do not wait for the mountain to come to them.

An Example

At one point I made a business of providing services to companies whose main marketing activity was the pursuit of federal government contracts. One important marketing research tool of such companies is the government's daily periodical, the *Commerce Business Daily,* which would-be contractors must study carefully every day to find opportunities for submitting bids and proposals to the federal agencies. It is an indispensable tool in that field.

I soon learned that many small business owners shrank from studying this periodical every day. They lacked the time and also the expertise to do it as well as the will to work at becoming experts; they were, in fact, intimidated by the periodical. Yet, they were interested in pursuing government contracts if there was a way they could do so that was compatible with these conflicting desires and fears.

It was certainly a niche, and it was surprisingly easy to make it a niche market by designing a plan to do the daily study for these small businesses and steer them to suitable opportunities for a suitable fee. I found the response to an offer to do this task quite enthusiastic and gratifying.

There are other possible alternatives to trying to force-fit what you normally offer to the market opportunities you see, and we shall get to them shortly. But let's look further at marketing opportunities connected with niches and niche markets.

Niche Markets Depend on Matching Characteristics

The twofold basis for each of these niche markets, then, is the variable of individuals and their characteristics, and the fixed factors of what you sell and its features and characteristics: The two must match and complement each other. Or, to put it another way, if you are the typical entrepreneur and marketer, you approach the search for niches and niche markets in terms of the products or services you sell. The identification of the niches is dependent on those factors because they are segments or niches in terms of what you can sell them, and you typically restrict that to what you "carry." A niche for something you do not carry or deal in is not a niche market, as far as you are concerned.

Creating Niche Markets or Turning the Proposition Around

Let's open our minds to other possibilities. Classically, you approach marketing possibilities always in terms of what you have to sell; what you have to sell is the fixed item. Try turning that around: What if what you sell is not fixed? What if it, too, is a variable that you can perhaps vary to suit the market, rather than the reverse? What if, that is, instead of searching your database to see if you can find niches for what you sell, you consider handling items, goods and services, that are right for some of the niches in your database? Instead of choosing markets for the items you sell, you choose items to sell to the markets you have in your database.

To put this another way and so, perhaps, make the strategy clearer, instead of dealing in some line of products and services, you deal in a line of markets—niche markets. You "own" these markets because they are part of and are selected from your own databases. You know all about the wants of these markets. You need merely to satisfy those wants.

If you sell a broad line of goods or services, you may be doing some of that now, considering the possibility of niche markets for various items in your line. Possibly you make special searches for niche markets suitable for the slower-moving items. But that is restricting your activity to whatever you now carry, and probably foreclosing some lucrative possibilities. Suppose you have occasion to consider selling something you do not carry at present. As a typical businessperson, you are likely to be confronted quite often with special opportunities to buy merchandise, often at a fraction of the original cost. The late Joe Karbo, for example, acquired a warehouseful of surplus "spy in the door" gadgets (that device in apartment-house doors that enables residents to see who is at the door before opening it) for a tiny fraction of their original cost. He was quite a masterful marketer and promoter, and was therefore successful in identifying a market for these and disposing of them at a substantial profit.

There are many examples of this. The offers are tempting, but no matter how attractive the deal, its worth to you depends on whether you have a market for it. For example, you are offered a lot of generic brand (unknown brand name) cosmetics at extremely favorable prices. Your immediate reaction is a question: Can you sell them—do you have some kind of identifiable niche(s) for which these would be right?

You can search your database, after you have determined the characteristics that would define a niche for this line of products. You will want to retrieve the names of women, perhaps, although men may buy cosmetics as presents for wives and sweethearts. (You will have to decide how suitable the line is for use as presents.) You will certainly want the names of known cosmetics buyers. You may want also the names of those who buy frequently by mail, and who spend as much as $50 or $100 by mail.

On the other hand, if the lot you are contemplating is big enough and cheap enough, and if you have the means to single out the prospects who constitute a viable market segment for it, you may want to wholesale the product to distributors and dealers, selling only in case lots. That means seeking out an entirely different kind of customer, the business firm who is a suitable prospect.

You may want both, or you may even be able to think of a half-dozen suitable kinds or classes of prospects (niche markets) for the item. Then you would wish to study your database or databases to seek out those markets.

In short, in this case your database and the individuals who populate it are the independent variables, and the potential items to be sold are the dependent variables. Their viability as a product line depends on whether they match any of the niche markets you can project from your database.

The Analytical Process

This requires that you be familiar enough with the profiles of those who populate your database to judge whether you are likely to have suitable niche markets embedded therein for any given product you wish to consider. It requires also that you have a reasonably good idea of what kinds of prospects you would need for the items. Dealing practicably with the offer of something to trade in, under these circumstances, requires a few steps to analyze the problem (i.e., the marketability of the item) and reach a decision:

1. What is the product/service used for?
2. What are the normal or typical characteristics of the item?
3. What, if any, are the special characteristics of this lot?
4. Who are the principal users?
5. How/where do they usually buy it?
6. What does it usually cost?
7. What are the characteristics that define the typical buyers?
8. Into how many classes (niches) can we divide the above?

Still Another Twist

There is still a third way to put the marvelous powers of the computer and its databases to work to find—actually *create*—new niche markets. We have considered finding niche markets for what you normally sell, and we have considered finding niche markets to take advantage of special opportunities (e.g., getting great bargains on large lots of merchandise you do not normally carry or deal in). But suppose you study your databases to discover niches representing unsatisfied markets for goods or services that you do not carry and that have not been offered you. In a deliberate quest to create markets, you discover marketing opportunities by the less common method of matching markets with items to sell. That is, you already have access to markets that exist, potentially at least, as niches in your databases. When you uncover them, you can go in search of something to sell them.

For example, you may discover that your database includes a large number of young retirees who are interested in pursuing second careers. That is a large niche, but it is not yet a market, as far as you are concerned, because you are not now selling to or prepared to sell to that market. The market exists, however, and there is a potential there for sales and profit, a serendipitous opportunity. How can you put that opportunity to work for you?

If it appears to be a market reasonably close to what you are selling, you might go in quest of products or services suitable for the market and add them to your line or spin off a special department. Or if the idea is compatible with your existing business, you might wish to consider offering dealerships or franchises to these individuals. Or, at the least, you might rent the names as a premium mailing list. Whatever the specifics of the individual case, if you have learned of a want and you have the market in your grasp, surely you can find some item to fill the need and furnish you a profit.

Problems versus Opportunities

Positive-thinking workers who wish to advance themselves follow the maxim that there are no problems but only opportunities, or that every problem is an opportunity. When they are able to solve problems for management, they have paved the way for their own promotions. They thus welcome problems, understandably. For the marketer, the maxim is equally true, although in a somewhat different fashion.

Every marketing problem challenges the marketer to find a better way to market, or satisfy the desire of customers for, the goods and/or services he or she offers. The study of databases to uncover niches thus often leads to uncovering problems, and their solution then leads to more effective marketing. The quest for viable market niches can easily lead you to improvements in your product or service in the following manner.

You may very well find a large segment of your market that is unhappy with some particular of your product or your line of products. The problem may be with the product (e.g., some customers may want more, less, other, or no scent in your laundry detergent, and some may prefer a dry version to a liquid version), but complaints are not necessarily with the product itself: It can easily be with packaging (e.g., maybe some customers would prefer smaller sizes, unbreakable containers, dispenser packages, or even refillable packaging); it may be with labeling (e.g., some customers might want better instructions, or more information about calories and fat content); it may be with distribution (e.g., perhaps those in rural areas have difficulty finding your product in the local supermarkets); and it may even be with aspects of the customer service you provide (e.g., some may have found it difficult to get answers to their questions when they called or they may object to paying tolls to call and believe that you ought to provide a toll-free number), or other areas of your marketing program and related services.

Thus judicious use of your computer to implement databased marketing can and should go well beyond merely discovering individual wants and niche markets for what you normally offer. Databased marketing is—can and should be—highly creative marketing in its basic orientation to the customer. That itself has two major aspects, of which only one is the tremendous research benefit that results from continuing dialogue with the customer to find niche markets and improve your marketing strategies and copy in other ways. The other major benefit is the good will that results from the kind of customer relationship once common in the neighborhood mom-and-pop store and now made possible by a real-time computer system that can be made to present any customer's file on screen in milliseconds, so that when she calls or visits the store she hears something like, "Good morning, Mrs. Maxwell; I hope that you are enjoying the dinner service you bought in our store recently. How can I help you today?"

Among the arguments made for the computer requirements of the idealized databased marketing system is that of a need for a 1-microsecond response time and an absolute limit of 5 microseconds for the system to produce the information called for. That appears to me not only unnecessarily restrictive, but in itself much more an argument for the PC than it is for the mainframe.

Still another technical argument I have encountered maintains that the customer database file must be online at all times (even at 3:00 A.M.?). The reason for that, too, is not clear to me. Why does anyone need a customer file online outside normal business hours? If the customer data must be manipulated in some manner outside business hours, that is normally done by batch or offline operations. It seems hardly necessary to support the cost of around-the-clock operations, at least for a mainframe. A personal computer operation around the clock is easily handled in a BBS style (i.e., unattended by anyone).

Too, why do these requirements apply to only customer files? Are not database files of prospects and, especially, of leads equally important and deserving of the same requirements?

Finally, the argument is made that those "running the hardware" (mainframe computer operators?) "really understand database marketing." I am quite sure that I do not know what this means. Does it refer to the problem I raised much earlier about relinquishing responsibility for marketing decisions to computer technologists? Or does it mean that the marketers do not and should not be expected to understand databased marketing? If so, they are not likely to have a great deal of success with it, are they? That hardly seems the best position to assume, for all the reasons stated earlier, as well as the obvious one of the un-wisdom of abandoning responsibility for making strategic and tactical marketing decisions. In fact, as a marketing executive you can never truly escape that responsibility; it is yours always, whether you like it or not.

It is not, in my opinion, enough to know these things only philosophically and to entrust all implementation to computer technicians and other non-marketing experts. You will be a far better marketer if you know something of computer capabilities yourself, and it is not that difficult to learn these things. But we will discuss these problems in another chapter.

Chapter 10

Computer Literacy

At the heart of databased marketing is, of course, the computer and the software necessary to build and use the necessary databases. There is also the need for appropriate skills and knowledge. Even if you are the marketer with computer experts on staff or on retainer to help you, you need to have some personal understanding of desktop computers and modern software.

MUST WE HAVE A COMPUTER PRIMER?

One assumption made by too many about the use of computers in databased marketing, even by those writing about databased marketing, is that we will all hire computer experts as staff members or as special consultants and that they will handle all technical needs, so we need not worry about that end of building and using marketing databases. However, as author John Gessford pointed out wisely in his book *How to Build Business-Wide Databases* (see Bibliography), the marketer cannot afford to allow the technician to trespass unrestricted in the marketing domain and make marketing decisions.

You, the marketer, must make the important basic decisions about your marketing database, and there are more than a few that must be made. There is the matter of formats and content, which are closely related: The format of your records determines, to a large extent, what the content will be. Obviously, you must be the decision maker on what information belongs in the database and what does not belong there. You must also decide what you will need (i.e., how you will retrieve data) from your databases: That means what fields will be included in the record and which will be key fields, for sorting, organizing, and retrieving records. That isn't all of it, either: There are other matters that you, as the marketer, must decide, such as how many kinds of reports and other database-derived documents will be needed on a regular basis and how they should be designed, what special reports may be needed, and what kinds of labels will be needed. To make those decisions and have them properly implemented, you must be able to converse easily with computer experts and not be "snowed" with computer jargon by technicians who often simply do not know how to explain technical matters in lay language to the uninitiated or, all too often, how to translate your needs accurately into the technical decisions and actions needed to produce the results you require. (You may have already sensed this problem in reading some earlier chapters, despite the pains I took to try to avoid computer shock and use lay language as much as possible.) Hence this chapter is needed, not to try to make you into anything resembling a technical computer expert, but to (1) teach you a handful of basics with some of the relevant language of computers generally and databases especially, (2) give you an adequate appreciation of what is possible and reasonable to expect of your computer system, and (3) make you reasonably independent of the computer specialists who so often befuddle and intimidate us laypeople with their computer-technical jargon. You are not going to be so intimidated in this chapter. (It is more likely that I may offend you by being overly simplistic, but please bear with me if that proves to be the case.) More than that, you are going to be furnished with armor against that kind of intimidation by others. We laypeople all need that armor, if we have not previously provided it for ourselves.

There is at least one other important objective in providing some basic computer literacy here. If you own or plan to own your own desktop computer, you may prefer to do your own computer work, as an increasing number of people do. (It grows constantly easier for the average individual to do so.) There is a great deal to be said for gaining complete independence in your marketing activity, and it becomes more and more practicable to do so every day. I, for one, would encourage you in that, and I thus hope that the information in this chapter will help you become your own expert, able to communicate clearly with technical experts and/or set up and run your own system, a not unlikely prospect or unusual activity today.

Aside from that, we must also deal further with the problem touched on in the previous chapter of being the prisoners of the past by confining our thinking to the older, established ways of doing things with the mainframe computer and the handicaps imposed by those considerations. (So tradition-bound are some that they refer to keyboarding data onto magnetic tape and disks as "keypunching," a term that belongs with the obsolete 80-column punch cards and punched tape.)

TRADITIONAL DIRECT MAIL PRACTICES

Perhaps it is a bit of an anachronism to use the word *traditional* to refer to or describe something as recent as practices of less than a decade ago, but we live in fast-changing times. That is especially true of technology, and the direct-mail industry is very much concerned with and dependent on technology, especially computers.

Traditional direct mail relied on press-on labels and manual handling for small direct-mail shops and Cheshire labels for the large shops, those who used machines to automate the process of mailing out large quantities of direct mail. List brokers soon made lists available on 9-track tapes, too, as large mailing houses turned to computers of their own to further automate mailing. What has been the most significant development that compels us to regard the practices of less than a decade ago as obsolescent and meritorious of the term *traditional* is the speed with which the desktop computer developed, both technologically and in terms of its rapid acceptance and appearance everywhere. Every major list broker today still offers lists on 9-track tapes and on sheets of Cheshire labels, but most also offer lists on disks for desktop computers, on "stickyback" or "press on" labels, and an increasing number will supply lists via telephone/modem connections directly to your own computer, as reported in Chapter 4.

Before the computer made today's data-handling flexibility easily possible and abundantly available, the list industry was cast in somewhat the philosophy of Henry Ford, who, as I mentioned earlier in this book, was alleged to have said, with reference to his Model T Ford automobiles, that his customers could have the automobiles in any color they liked, as long as it was black. You could thus rent the available lists in whatever form the broker had available or you could do without them. The computer changed that in at least two ways:

- The lists were more and more qualified in many ways, as computerized information and data banks made it possible to acquire information from the U.S. Census Bureau (a truly prime source), motor vehicle administrations, credit-reporting agencies, associations, banks, printed directories, and numerous other sources. Much of the information had resided in some of these repositories for a long time, but it was prohibitively expensive to copy and reproduce it in some useful form by manual means. However, when the data was entered into computers and could be transferred easily (via ordinary dial-up telephone lines) to other computers, that was another story: It then became practicable technically and viable economically to begin "overlaying" ordinary name-and-address lists with this demographic and other data. Direct mail then began to become "targeted" at prospects carefully selected on the basis of qualifications per the demographic and other ancillary data.
- You could specify the lists you wanted, and they could be assembled for you from the list broker's database. That is, lists could be at least semicustomized or tailored to your individual needs and desires. In fact, the more progressive list brokers would actually counsel you on what they could offer, tailored to your needs.

Even this was relatively recent and was dependent on available hardware. Until the desktop computer came along and began to mature, only mainframe computers could be relied on to handle the monumental tasks of gathering, sorting, combining, merging, and purging the lists that resulted. (That it is still less than perfect is attested by the increasing incidence of problems visited on individuals by errors in credit reports and other records.) That is changing rather swiftly, as the capabilities of desktop computers continue to expand and threaten to overtake those of mainframes, while they also put computer power in your hands and mine. Computers are no longer the sole domain of the technical experts. But the change goes even beyond that simple truth.

TODAY'S COMPUTER WORLD

The computer world has expanded and diversified to the extent that no one, not even the most highly educated and most experienced technicians, are expert in all areas. In fact, to be an expert at all, it is necessary to specialize at least to some degree. Note the title of Gessford's book, just referred to, for example: Not only is this a book of more than 400 pages about databases, it is even further specialized as being about how to *build* databases further qualified as "business-wide" databases. Even in my limited discussions of relevant computer technology, I will restrict coverage to only that relating directly and indirectly to your probable usage, which is only a fraction of what I sometimes refer to as "computerology" today.

One reason for this is, as mentioned, to enable you to discuss your needs with your computer experts without being at a total disadvantage. Even if they are your employees, permanent or temporary (e.g., consultants), your computer experts can easily become adversaries, albeit unwittingly, when they are guided by their own conscious or unconscious biases on computer hardware, software, and operation. They mean to be helpful, but they are not, after all, marketers and especially not database marketers. They are interested in what runs most efficiently and effectively on the computer, not on what is the most effective marketing tool. You must specify most clearly to them, not how to get the results you want, but what those desired results are. Then listen to what they propose to do and judge for yourself if that makes sense. If they are talking over your head, insist on explanations in language you can understand, and accept nothing unless and until you are sure that you do understand it. To do that successfully you must be yourself at least minimally expert in computerdom. Ergo, the need to become literate in the field.

Aside from that rationale just expressed, this chapter is based also on the full recognition that you may be one of those "small-time operators" who can and does do it all (or nearly all) him- or herself.

That is increasingly the case in this era of home offices, home-based small businesses, and computer systems (hardware and software) designed to be used by the layperson, or one who is nearly so. Today, if you wish to devote the necessary time and energy, it is easily possible with modern hardware and software to do it all yourself, and you will probably want to go far beyond the rudimentary computer knowledge offered here. In either case, even this scant computer lore will be useful to you as a launch pad, its primary value being to help you overcome any fears you may have had. (Computerphobia is not unknown.)

"POWER USERS" AND "FRIENDLY" SOFTWARE

Those who use computers regularly and with such ease that they carry out complex computer operations routinely and with little cogitation, are often referred to as *power users.* That distinguishes them from the rest of us, who plod along uncertainly, groping through the many strange (to us) fields of modern digital domains. The term *power user,* however, is an inexact one, of course. It describes a condition in a league with *computer literate* and other descriptive terms that sound vaguely like condescending epithets with a broad overtone of elitism. There is no borderline or threshold across which a person steps to become, suddenly, computer literate or a power user, nor is there any precise characteristic that marks an individual as a power user or as computer literate. I believe that I am computer literate, but I do not, for example, count myself a power user by any means, although those with less computer experience than I might think me one.

The intelligentsia of the computer world also refer sometimes to the "power" of a computer, referring to its qualities of speed, responsiveness, and other characteristics of its capabilities. The more a computer has of any of these, especially speed and its related characteristic of responsiveness to commands, the greater its power is reputed to be. Again, it is a quality judged only in relative terms, without a true standard of any kind.

Earlier (Chapter 7), I described computer capabilities in general as being much more the function of the software than of the hardware. That might also be said of computer power and of user power: The software programs must take advantage of the hardware capabilities and also help the inexpert user take fullest advantage of what the machine can do.

The realization came early in the development of the PC that success in selling computers and software for them required that they must be easy to use: They had to be so designed that anyone could learn to use them without extensive special training. The achievement of this idyllic state was dramatized in the earlier times of less than a decade ago by the then common practice of software developers describing their products as "user friendly." The term was intended to assure buyers that little special skill or training was required to run those programs; they all but ran themselves.

That "friendliness" feature, the capability for running in an almost completely automatic or at least semiautomatic mode, became an obligatory characteristic of software designed to be used on a PC: All software programs became increasingly "friendly," in the sense that less and less knowledge of computer operation was required to run the programs successfully. A rough analogy can be made with the development of first the self-starter motor and then the automatic transmission for automobiles: Ransome Olds hired Charles Kettering to design a self-starter for his Oldsmobile because, he said, he knew that few women would drive any automobile that had to be cranked by hand. Millions of men and women also found it discouragingly difficult to master manual gear shifting, and the invention of the automatic transmission was a tremendous boost to sales of automobiles. In the same way, simplifying of computer operation, with both hardware and software improvements and improvisations, was needed to boost sales of computers to the general public.

Features that simplified computer operation soon became the *sine qua non* of software to the extent that the term "user friendly" simply disappeared as a superfluous and unnecessary adjective. Today, virtually all software, from the simplest to the most complex, is designed to help the less experienced PC user by being largely self-actuating and by including various aids to eliminate the need for memorizing a lengthy list of commands and procedures. The efforts to simplify extend even to the hardware, with many users today employing a "mouse," an electromechanical device that moves an arrow about the screen to do things that otherwise require fairly complex series of commands.

THE RANGE OF COMPLEXITY

Computer software varies in complexity over a quite wide range, and the more complex programs tend to be the larger ones. Size is measured in *kilobytes,* abbreviated *kb*. A *kilobyte* is 1,000 *bytes,* and a *byte* is eight *bits* or eight electrical pulses. A software program may vary from as few as several hundred kb to as many as several thousand kb or a few *mb* (megabytes or million bytes). Although the large programs do tend to be far more complex than the small ones, even this is not always so: It is possible for some kinds of programs to be lengthy without being overly complex.

Database management programs tend to the larger sizes because even the simplest such program is complex when compared with many other kinds of programs. Too, databases, by their nature, tend to be large. But it also depends on the type of database manager: A rather small flat-file database system that I use as the vehicle for my own small mailing lists currently occupies only a little more then one million bytes of my fixed disk, for example, although that grows as I add names to the files. More sophisticated flat-file database programs run to several times that size. The even more sophisticated and versatile relational databases, such as those you should use for databased marketing, are usually even more complex and much larger. Still another factor affects complexity, which we shall discuss shortly.

THE TOOLS OF FRIENDLINESS

The development of the desktop computer and its software has been more revolutionary than evolutionary: It has proceeded spasmodically by frequent great leaps—quantum jumps—rather than by the gradual process typical of evolution. It has often been a chicken-and-egg situation: Has the hardware influenced the software development or vice versa? Greater memory and storage capacities in the hardware have inspired software developers to more complex and sophisticated programs, but the need for more memory and storage capacities to accommodate more sophisticated software has inspired engineers to develop improved hardware systems, especially in memory and storage devices.

Regardless of which is cause and which is effect, the simplification of operating software programs is largely the result of the inventiveness of the software developers: the programmers. Before exploring the ingenious devices of the programmers, however, we will look briefly at a few fundamentals of computers.

Computer Language

Computers have multitudes of highly complex communication channels in their operating systems. As in the case of humans and communication among humans, languages are required to carry out the communication. You really do not need to know anything at all of computer languages, and even the rudiments presented here are greatly abridged and simplified, even oversimplified, accounts. However, basic knowledge of the subject, even at that level, helps in understanding some things you should know about.

The computer has a primary language all its own, known as "machine language," that it uses for its internal communications. It is a relatively primitive language, referred to sometimes as a "low level" language, and is difficult to learn and use. (Early computers were programmed most laboriously by specialists who had learned this language. They issued "instructions" or "commands" to the computer in this language. Those instructions were represented by various combinations of two electrical pulses, which cause certain actions in the machine.) Fortunately, it is not necessary now to know this primitive and difficult set of machine codes:

There are "higher-level" languages that act as interpreters between the programmer and the machine, and are much easier to learn and use. Programmers use these higher-level languages to write their programs, which are actually each a complex set of commands to the computer. Special software then translates the commands into machine language. At the same time, a set of simpler commands are available to the user, usually represented by a key press or two. These are prescribed by the software program and tell you what commands to issue to the software program to do whatever you want to do. The software then issues appropriate instructions or signals to the computer circuits. Thus, pressing certain keys might order the program to erase a line or two or mark a block of text to be moved or printed.

Opening Menus and Pull-Down Menus

That process was relatively simple, but it still meant that the user had to learn—memorize—a lengthy list of commands for each program. WordStar alone has several hundred such commands in its main, word-processing program, plus many more in its auxiliary programs. WordStar, and soon many others, offered a "menu" on the screen to help the user remember the commands. That is still a current practice, with many programs offering an "opening menu," but today most of the menus are the "pull down" variety: You may "pull" them down like a window shade when you need to refresh your memory or have the menu issue the commands for you, and then send them out of sight when you are finished so they don't clutter up your working space on the screen. In many cases, the menus are of the window variety: They come down superimposed on whatever is on the screen, and they can be at more than one level. Figure 10–1 illustrates the WordStar opening menu and two subsequent help menus, with a second menu as a window over the first one, and still another type of pull-down menu in common use.

Key Redefiners and Macroinstructions

Next the "key redefiner" software came along. These were special programs that could "redefine" the keys on your keyboard, while still permitting you the normal use of the keys. For example, I can redefine the "h" key to type out "Herman Holtz" when I wish it to. (In fact, I use that key to print out my complete letterhead when I wish to write a letter, and I have other keys programmed to print out the names and addresses of people I write to often.) These kinds of key redefinitions are known also as "macros," an abbreviation of macroinstruction. Soon, as these kinds of programs proved to be popular in providing shortcuts and simplifications, other programs, such as word processors, communications

WordStar

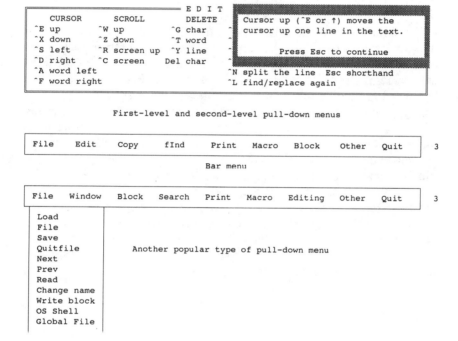

Figure 10-1. Typical menu systems.

software, database managers, and spreadsheet programs adopted the idea and began to incorporate macro or key redefinition capabilities in their own programs.

The menus illustrated in Figure 10–1 are of significantly different types. The first one is passive and merely lists commands, e.g., "D" to open a document, "E" to rename a file, and so on. The next one also merely lists commands with an explanation of what each does, but if the user next presses "^E" (the CONTROL key and the "E" key simultaneously or the "E" key while the CONTROL key is held down), the superimposed next-level menu comes down as a "window" with additional information. (Invoking "help" may bring down a fairly large block of text instruction, even an example, to assist the user.)

Next shown is a bar menu that appears across the top or bottom of a screen, listing the commands available to the user. It may be an interactive one, in which the user need only type the first letter of the command or function called for. However, if two of the functions have the same initial letter, as in the case of "File" and "Find," another letter in the term is capitalized as the letter needed to invoke the command.

Menus of this type also often serve as reminders of other things, such as identifying (by number) the line and column where the cursor is at the moment, naming the file or function currently in use, giving the date and time, and other such notations.

The last-shown menu is an interactive one that uses pull-down or pop-up menus, as shown. Such a menu can be invoked to appear under each of the terms listed in the bar by typing the initial letter of the term or by placing the cursor on the term and pressing ENTER or an arrow key. The top line, "load" would be highlighted when the menu appears. The user may use an arrow key to move that highlighting bar over any of the terms and press the ENTER or RETURN key (two names used for the same key). The indicated command will then be issued to the computer and the operation will be carried out. However, with this kind of menu, the user usually need not move the light bar at all, but only press the first letter of the operation wanted, regardless of where the light bar is. The light bar will then move to that line and the operation will be performed. Usually, such menus are optional aids, both for doing and for learning: They can be abandoned, as the user becomes more familiar with the program and can issue the commands without using the menu, which is much faster.

Tutorials

Many of the larger programs come with complete training programs, usually "tutorial" files and even "documentation" files, which are virtual manuals that can be read on the screen.

Tutorials can take two forms, and in some cases it takes both: It can be a complete subprogram, passive or interactive, that the user may run and/or it may be an extensive "help" program that is a supplement to the formal tutorials.

Help Files

Help files are related to pull-down and pop-up menus, although they tend to be brief textual passages. Whenever the user is puzzled or at a loss as to what to do, he or she may invoke the help files, using whatever distress signal the software designer has prescribed (often function key F1 or the letter H). This will bring a menu or block of text on-screen as a window superimposed over whatever is on the screen at the time. (In some cases it may bring an entire screen as the window.) Help may exist at more than one level, as menus do, so that the distress signal brings down a menu from which to choose a more precise indication of the information you need or even lead you through a full tutorial relevant to your immediate need.

Function Keys

The hardware developers were not left behind in this trend to maximizing the ease of use either: Computer keyboards soon began to sport a double row of ten *function keys* (and many today have 12 such keys). These were keys that could be programmed to furnish macros built into them by the software design. In one of my programs, I use the function keys to report my name and password when I log on to a bulletin board, to center my copy, to save a file, and for sundry other functions. Many programs use the first function key, "F1," to invoke the help file. It has become almost, but not quite, a de facto standard. (The keys are usually programmed by the software, so they may mean different things—execute different commands—in different programs. Thus F1, although popular as a convenient means for invoking help of one sort or another, may be used in other programs to exit the file, order something printed, or for another purpose.) In my case, I have programmed my function keys, using my SmartKey redefiner program to do many labor-saving and time-saving chores for me.

All of these changes have now made most software so friendly that the term ("user friendly") is superfluous and rarely heard today: Most buyers of software expect it to be replete with such aids as pull-down menus, help files, and macro command capabilities, and the software developers know that they must provide these aids if they are to com pete successfully in the marketplace. (I would probably have never acquired my first copy of SmartKey or felt a need for it had all these other aids been built into the hardware and software when I bought my first computer.) The term itself has thus disappeared from view, but the concept of "user friendliness" (i.e., the addition of a variety of aids) has progressed remarkably, probably far beyond what was contemplated in the beginning. (That, of course, has been the history of modern technology generally and of computer technology especially.)

Macroprograms

Incorporating key redefiners into other, larger programs proved to be the harbinger of a trend. It soon gathered speed and began to proliferate by adding many other satellite programs and subprograms to every main program. Many software programs today are thus what I refer to as "macroprograms." For example, my own current word processor program, the latest of its genre and the fifth version of the program that I have owned, includes a spelling checker, a thesaurus, a key redefiner (referred to by the vendors of this system as "shorthand"), an outlining program, a word counter, a communications program, a mail/merge program, a "shell" program, a database manager, a calculator, and several other special utilities for making the chores easier (copying files, moving them, searching for them, erasing them, translating the text of one word processor into the text of another, and sundry other chores). This not a special or unusual arrangement; quite the contráry, it is quite typical. Most good word processors are similarly loaded with ancillary programs that would have been each a separate program only a few years ago. However, the trend was not and has not been confined to word processing programs by any means: All kinds of major programs, including communications, spreadsheet, database management, and others, have tended increasingly to include ancillary or subprograms. And those inclusions have tended to be the inclusion of word processors, key redefiners, editors, and sundry other kinds of directly and indirectly related software. Thus, as word processors may have database managers as subprograms, the reverse is true: many major database programs also offer word processors or editors, key redefiners, and sundry other subprograms.

Database management systems were no exception. In early days, many of the flat-file database programs were easy to use but had few features other than the most basic ones associated with databases and their management. They had to be especially programmed to carry out any but the simplest operations of database management. The more sophisticated relational database managers had many more features, especially the ability to combine data from and facilities of a number of files, even using a large number of separate files as though they were a single entity. However, to take advantage of those features effectively required special skills because they too had to be programmed in a suitable "high-level" programming language. You could use the database manager to draw information from other databases and assemble a list, make labels, write a report, or do many other things relational database managers are designed to do, but you had to first write a program for most of these functions. You had to be truly a power user, able to write programs that would instruct and guide such DBM software to do all the things of which it was capable.

That has changed too: There are relational database management programs now that you can operate without writing a special program or being an expert user. In fact, while some still have provision for operation with special programs, they can be used to carry out highly complex and sophisticated operations without such special programming, usually with menus. (On the other hand, you need not be intimidated by the notion of writing a program: In many cases today, the programming is truly quite simple, as with dBASE dot prompt statements and DOS batch files. The experienced dBASE user, although not generally a computer expert at all, may very well be able to write at least some of the simpler programs.)

Software Still Tries to Be Friendly

There is a newer and probably better term than "user friendly" that is sometimes used today to convey this idea: Producers of software with such "friendliness" often use the word *intuitive* to describe the ease with which the program can be used. The term *menu driven* is also often used to describe programs in which the user can resort to the help of menus for all steps, although in most cases the use of the menus is optional: As the user gains experience with the program, he or she can abandon the menus and operate more rapidly without them. But they do enable the novice computer user to run newly acquired programs at once, before he or she has really learned the new program.

THE SIGNIFICANCE OF "RELATIONAL"

We have used the term *relational* as an adjective for *database* and yet been a bit vague as to what it means. We cannot abandon the subject or the idea, for it is central to the key issues here. In fact, it is an essential for databased marketing, which demands a wealth of information. Nominally, the term means that a relational database manager can relate one database to another or actually *link* them as a single entity. The databases can be widely separated geographically or in terms of their nature or content; that has no bearing on their relationship for our purposes. The linkage, is strictly based on how the data to be derived from the various databases relates to or can be used in conjunction with the data from the other databases for building marketing databases. They can be totally diverse in kind and distinctive from each other, such as in the case of the following few kinds of files and records commonly documented as databases in typical business organizations:

Invoices or receivables	Employee files
Payables	Sales records
Inventory	Call reports
Purchasing	Sales forecasts
Customers	Tax records
Inquirers	Advertising records

Such separate databases can be linked in a variety of relationships: e.g., one to one, one to many, or many to one. It may also bind all the databases so closely as to form a set and operate as if all the databases were one, under central control, transferring information back and forth and using any and all files to generate routine and special reports, answer queries, build lists, print labels, create custom menus, and provide password security, among many other possible applications.

TYPICAL DBM PROGRAMS

dBASE, the product of Ashton-Tate Corporation is probably the best known program of its kind, although there are many others of equal stature. A sophisticated relational database manager of relatively recent vintage is Alpha Four, a product of the Alpha Software Corporation. It, too, has been extremely well received and lauded by a great many expert reviewers of database software, and although by no means unique, Alpha Four quite possibly is the most advanced program of its kind. For purpose of illustration, I will refer to these two programs in discussing what such programs offer you in implementing databased marketing. (That does not represent advocacy or endorsement one way or another; there are many excellent programs.) That raises another point that must be clarified here.

A Caveat: Keeping Our Eye on the Ball

Databases and database managers can be and are employed to carry out a quite enormous array of business functions, as suggested by the short list of possible databases just presented. Quite obviously, many of these have direct relationships with marketing, the subject to which we are here dedicated. Some have limited or indirect relationship to marketing, such as being sources of data that may relate to marketing strategies and customer modeling. And some have no relationship to marketing at all. Thus, although these and other database management programs are widely used for purchasing, production, shipping, accounting, and many other business functions, we are interested in and shall discuss only those functions that relate to or, more specifically, contribute to data-based marketing in some manner. Remember, in this connection, that we turned to relational database managers, after considering flat-file database managers, out of necessity: The flat-file system is fine—even superior—for the simple purposes, such as reservation systems, ordering systems, or uncomplicated lists. These need only to keep track of supply and demand, keyed to dates and times and updated frequently. (They are necessarily real-time systems and must be kept as up to date as possible.) Databased marketing has quite different requirements, as we have seen, including a diverse input of many kinds of data from many sources, with a multiplicity of manipulations and analyses from which to draw conclusions and create models. It is possible, too, that while the relational database system is used to create individual prospect lists of one sort or another (e.g., mailing lists), some of these lists may be transferred to simple flat-file database systems for convenience, rather than used directly to print reports, mailing labels, or other output.

A FEW OUTSTANDING CHARACTERISTICS

All database management systems offer you a variety of useful tools. There are the usual sorting and indexing functions, and sorts can be made in alphabetical order, in chronological order, in order of size, or in almost any order and on the basis of just about any or almost any field. Over and above these basic functions is a report-writing function that is equally versatile and flexible. Even the simplest flat-file database managers afford some report writing. Figure 10–2 shows a report generated by such a system. The edit file of one of the items is shown as Figure 10–3. Had I chosen to, I could have included all the information of the edit files in the report, but I chose not to. The report, by the way, is one I designed for my own purposes. All the systems encourage great flexibility—your own choices—for report design. This system, simple though it may be, is no different: It invites me to design my own reports, furnishing me the tools to do so. This database is very simple, since it is only a list of certain kinds of periodicals, with the most basic of information about each one. In building a database for marketing, you face a different situation entirely, requiring many times the volume of data shown in Figure 10–2.

Normally, you construct records in the edit mode in any database system. Here, you build each individual record, with its many fields. Each one occupies at least one screen or, quite often, one or more pages. (Remember that here we are talking about a relational database system that can draw data from as many as 10 other databases. That can make for a huge volume of data for each record, of course, and thus for extensive records and extensive reports of all kinds.)

There may be many occasions when you want to study the files, especially to make comparisons, look for trends, or even to search out a record when you don't have a firm individual ID or name in mind, or even when you really do want just to browse, looking for ideas. It isn't very easy to do if you depend on flipping through screen after screen of records, hoping to spot trends or significant sequences of any kind by pure chance and mental agility. That would require a mental agility of which few of us are capable. Fortunately, the problem has been anticipated, and its remedy lies in the "browse" feature of the better relational database managers. It is the alternative presentation to that

Periodicals List

New Business Opportunities
Attn: Rieva Lesonsky, Editor
2392 Morse Avenue
Irvine, CA 92713-6234

Business Today
Attn: Melody Haakenson, Editor
P.O. Box 10010
Ogden, UT 84409

Across the Board
Attn: Sarasue French, Asst Ed.
845 Third Avenue
New York, NY 10022

Business View
Attn: Eleanor K. Somer, Publ'r
P.O. Box 9859
Naples, FL 33941

American Salesman, The
Attn: Barbara Boeding, Editor
424 N. Third Street
Burlington, IA 52601-5224

Byte Magazine
Attn: Frederic Langa, Editor
One Phoenix Mill Lane
Peterborough, NH 03458

Barrons
Attn: Alan Abelson, Ed.
200 Liberty Street
New York, NY 10028

Common Sense
Attn: David Durgin, Editor
Upstart Publishing Co.
Dover, NH 03820

Better Business
Attn: John FR. Robinson, Publ'r
235 E. 42nd Street
New York, NY 10017

Communications Briefings
Attn: Frank Grazian, Editor
Encoders, Inc.
Blackwood, NJ 08012

Business Age Magazine
Attn: Claire Bremer, Editor
135 W. Wells Street, 7th Flr
Milwaukee, WI 53203-1800

Compute!
Attn: Gregg Keizer, Editor
324 West Wendover Avenue
Greensboro, NC 27408

Business Marketing
Bob Donath, Ed/Assoc Publ'r
220 E. 42nd Street
New York, NY 10017

Computer Product Selling
Attn: Karen Paxton, Exec. Ed.
425 Park Avenue
New York, NY 10022

Figure 10–2. First page of a simple report generated by a flat-file database system.

edit mode of single record after single record display, in which you normally build the record, field by field. Essentially, it is a tabular alternative to the presentation of individual records and was shown in its most basic form earlier, in Chapter 2.

In the browse presentation, the data of many records are summarized in a tabular display that includes so many columns that it usually requires a span of several screens to view all the columns. (Essentially,

Pub'n	Common Sense
Name	Attn: David Durgin, Editor
Address 1	Upstart Publishing Co.
Address 2	12 Portland Street
City St Zip	Dover, NY 03820
Tel-voice	603 749-5071
FAX	
Notes	NL, biz, how-to; 100–500 wds, $10–50; on accept.
Notes	Preg. Prp - 3/6/91

Figure 10–3. One of the records (edit mode) shown in Figure 10–2.

INV	DATE	SHIP VIA	TERMS	PART NO.
103	01-12-1989	First-class mail	Pre-Paid	C103 S008
104	02-28-1989	UPS—Blue	C.O.D.	C103 S011
105	02-28-1989	Federal Express	90 days	C103 S015
106	02-29-1989	UPS—Red	60 days	C103 S032
107	03-01-1989	First-class mail	30 days	C105 H012
108	03-12-1989	First-class mail	Pre-Paid	C123 S019
109	03-15-1989	UPS—Blue	C.O.D.	C103 S008
110	03-18-1989	UPS—Blue	60 days	C103 S008

ITEM	AMOUNT	QTY	TOTAL
Electric Desk	225.00	1	225.00
Keyworks Advanced	99.00	2	198.00
Typefaces	69.95	1	69.95
Greenworks	236.50	3	709.50
CGA Vid Board	298.99	4	1,195.96
Zip code database	999.90	3	2,999.70
Electric Desk	225.00	1	225.00
Electric Desk	225.00	1	225.00

Figure 10–4. Browse list of invoices.

INV	DATE	SHIP VIA	ITEM	AMOUNT	QTY	TOTAL
103	01-12-1989	First-class mail	Electric Desk	225.00	1	225.00
104	02-28-1989	UPS—Blue	Keyworks Advanced	99.00	2	198.00
105	02-28-1989	Federal Express	Typefaces	69.95	1	69.95
106	02-29-1989	UPS—Red	Greenworks	236.50	3	709.50
107	03-01-1989	First-class mail	CGA Vid Board	298.99	4	1,195.96
108	03-12-1989	First-class mail	Zip code database	999.90	3	2,999.70
109	03-15-1989	UPS—Blue	Electric Desk	225.00	1	225.00
110	03-18-1989	UPS—Blue	Electirc Desk	225.00	1	225.00

Figure 10–5. Browse list split.

the typical vertical orientation of individual records in the edit mode is now transferred to a typical horizontal presentation of the records, in a line-by-line display.)

A brief example is shown in Figure 10–4. In practice, browse lists can be and are usually much larger (i.e., wider, with more columns) depending on the number of fields in the database. It can require many screens to traverse the entire file in surveying and studying it. That is itself a problem, but most systems offer a great deal of flexibility, such as permitting you to split the displays, as shown in Figure 10–5, where two columns were cut out to facilitate side-by-side study of the items. This, however, is an exaggeratedly simplified example: In practice, you can manipulate the data in many ways, using the browse feature together with file-splitting, sorting, indexing, and other functions available to you in these highly sophisticated systems. It is almost a literal truth that the possibilities are limited only by your own imagination.

Chapter 11

The Economics of
Databased Marketing

*Databased marketing is still too new to have much of a history and/or
models for determining what sales cost in that mode of marketing, but
we can use the experience of other marketing methods as a guide to at
least some extent.*

EARLY DIFFICULTIES IN FINDING
ECONOMIC PRINCIPLES

There are several great difficulties in studying the economics of databased marketing. One is that we do not yet know what databased
marketing is. We have no widely accepted definition of databased marketing, as yet, and perhaps we never shall. To many direct marketing
experts, the term is all but synonymous with targeted marketing, direct marketing, and niche marketing. Some consider any database with
ancillary data, demographic or other, to be a marketing database. A
great many others simply confess quite freely that they do not know
what it is, but they tend to the simpler definition.

We also have some direct marketing experts who insist on including
a variety of qualifiers as important parts of any definition. To them, a
marketing database includes only existing customers, which excludes
prospect lists, of course. Some of them also insist that the data in a
marketing database must emanate from dialogue with the customers,
and even that the dialogue must be on-going and have some degree of
permanency. Further, their definitions require that the marketing
database must be implemented in a large enough computer system to
accept many concurrent inputs (mandating a mainframe computer).
Altogether, they would impose conditions that would exclude the small
direct marketer.

Two things bearing on the definition are apparent at this point:
(1) Databased marketing is an outgrowth of, or at least a close relative

of, direct marketing. The majority of those interested or involved in databased marketing are direct marketers; (2) databased marketing is concerned with the customer and building information about each individual customer.

This problem of definition has its anomalies, even its paradoxes. One is the conflict between the notion that a marketing database must be confined to existing customers, while one of its purposes is to model the archetypical customer so as to identify the best prospects for inclusion in the database.

A major complicating factor concerning the economics of the method is a direct consequence of the widely disparate definitions: The simpler definitions place marketing databases in a class somewhat above that of mailing lists suitable for targeted marketing, and thus within the reach of all in direct marketing. The definitions at the opposite extreme would require such a great investment that a great many currently successful direct marketers could not afford to get seriously involved in building their own marketing databases. This would have a rather obvious and great effect on the economics of databased marketing, and so I believe we must adopt a middle course here in defining databased marketing for purposes of studying the basic economic factors of this new concept.

MARKETING ECONOMICS IN GENERAL

It is hard to imagine any function of a business—of *your* business—that is more important or closer to the heart of your business than is marketing. Marketing, or creating customers, is what business is about: All businesses exist to sell something, services or products. They may be services or products created by you or they may be services or products created by someone else and distributed by you at retail or at wholesale, but that has nothing to do with the essential nature of business, the trade of services or products for dollars.

It is certainly no revelation to note that business success is based on somehow getting more dollars coming into the enterprise than going out of it. Every business sells products or services for more than they cost, the difference being known as *markup* or *gross profit*. Even the nonprofit enterprise that does not look for net profit needs to have enough gross profit to meet all expenses. That is not true profit, however. That gross profit must cover all the costs of running the business, with enough left over to represent a *net profit,* however small. For most businesses, that net profit (i.e., the after-taxes figure) is small enough—a single-digit figure near the lower end of the single-digit range—to allow for rather little error. A deviation of only a percentage point or two all too often makes the difference between success and failure. Almost all business is fragile in that sense.

Those costs are both fixed and variable. Rent or mortgage payments are costs you are committed to in advance and so are fixed costs, for example, while you are not bound to any fixed postage and advertising expenses, and so they are variable costs. They are also a part of the marketing cost, and that cost of marketing, that effort necessary to win the sales, is what concerns us here. Among all the variable costs, it is the cost most closely associated with the overall objective of the enterprise. In most cases, it is also one of the most controllable costs. Unfortunately, in a great many cases it is also the cost most difficult to equate with results. That is, while you can usually determine precisely what most costs buy you, quite often you cannot be sure just what marketing costs have bought you.

One reason for this problem is that marketing, in general, has so many imponderables. Marketing is much more than merely advertising: It includes location, good will, special promotions, publicity, sales, word of mouth, and even more subtle and indirect factors. If, for example, you operate a retail establishment open to the general public, your location is itself part of your marketing. You would have chosen a location most suitable for walk-in trade, within whatever budget limits you have set, and so its cost is at least partially a marketing cost. You pay much higher rent for a location in a busy mall or on a busy shopping avenue than you would in a "neighborhood" location. Presumably, the greater amount of "traffic" in a busy location means more customers and more "business" or sales. How much more you have almost no way of knowing. Even if you have a chain-store operation, which permits you to make a few comparisons, you can come up with only approximations, at best.

Much the same problem applies to various other marketing efforts and costs: Cause (advertising, promotion, etc.) and effect (sales) cannot be linked and correlated with anything even approaching precision, unless you are dealing with very large numbers. Then, mathematical disciplines can help establish averages that are usually much more accurate than averages derived from relatively small numbers. For most of us in small and mid-size businesses, it is, over and over again, the story of the executive who laments that he knows he is wasting half of every dollar he spends on advertising, but he doesn't know which half it is. In fact, it is often far more than half the dollar that is wasted, and it is not only the advertising dollar that is not returning anything approaching full value. In any case, we are going to confine ourselves here to the everyday, mundane approaches that are more suitable for the average small and mid-size enterprise trying to measure results in terms of expenditures.

The difficulties of evaluation and measurement are not overstated for many, and perhaps most kinds of business ventures, but the case of direct marketing is quite different. Here, too, there are some subtle and indirect influences that have an effect on sales and are thus part of marketing, but for the most part the direct marketing effort is quite visible, and it is relatively easy to correlate cause (costs) with effects (sales). In short, marketing as a cause and sales as an effect can be linked quantitatively, with reasonably good accuracy so that you can determine what the sales cost you on a gross basis and even on a unitized basis in marketing via direct mail. That, unfortunately, is far less true for most other marketing methods.

MAIL ORDER AND DIRECT MARKETING ECONOMICS

I established much earlier that there are reasons to link databased marketing with traditional mail order and, especially, direct marketing as the closest relative to or, at least, the most applicable marketing experience. In fact, I found that many experienced marketers regard databased marketing as synonymous or nearly so with targeted marketing, and I find that a reasonable conclusion: It would be easy to make a good case for databased marketing as targeted marketing in an advanced stage of development. This is not to say that marketing databases and the principles of their use are not equally applicable to and useful in other methods and arenas of marketing than direct mail; they are. However, when it comes to studying the economics of marketing with databases, we can almost surely learn most from study of mail order and direct marketing economics, the methods that databased marketing most closely resembles and with which it is or should be most closely associated.

We must understand, in studying these marketing methods and their economics that there are classic or traditional mail order and direct marketers—those who market in those fields exclusively—and there are other marketers who use mail order and/or direct marketing only occasionally or as only one of their many marketing methods or efforts. We may thus expect some divergence of attitudes and opinions: The dedicated, full-time direct marketing professional is likely to hew closely to the mark, concerned with fractions of a point, and many other fine details, while the occasional user of direct marketing is likely to adopt a somewhat cavalier attitude in assessing the economics of the more general and much more indirect marketing methods he or she must use most of the time.

The two terms, *direct mail* and *mail order,* are used interchangeably by a great many people, especially those in the smaller businesses based on or using these closely related, although not identical, methods of marketing. Those involved in direct mail full time tend to protect the identity of what they do; others tend to refer to all of it as "mail order." The reason lies at least partially in modern developments that have changed the nature of direct marketing, direct mail, and mail order; the enormous proliferation of communication and fulfillment channels have erased many of the original distinctions of each. In fact, my own frequent references in these pages to mail order and direct marketing/ direct mail may have added to confusion on the subject, for the marketing divisions and subdivisions of both are increasingly difficult to separate. Let's review it all briefly and try to establish a few basic truths, not for pedantic reasons, but so that we can make sense of the economics in trying to correlate costs with results.

Philosophically, direct marketing is marketing by any method that makes a marketing appeal or sales presentation directly to each individual prospect, rather than to the world at large, to some selected group at large, and/or through some middle person (e.g., a broker or dealer). Therefore, knocking on doors or selling at flea markets, trade shows, exhibits, auctions, and similar events are activities that are, technically, direct marketing. Reaching buyers indirectly through some kind of distributor is not direct marketing, which may take various forms but is traditionally associated most closely with the companion marketing industry of direct mail. The problem, however, is still more complex.

There are three major elements of each sale in direct mail and in mail order that are logically sequential and the same philosophically:

1. Soliciting the order
2. Winning and receiving the order
3. Filling the order

Probably mail order came first, as a new idea, when Montgomery Ward and, soon enough, others began to advertise their wares and offered to both receive and fill orders by mail. That was in a day when the U.S. mail was the principal source of long-distance communication and transport of small parcels.

That offer was attractive to rural residents who could not get to the towns and stores conveniently; They welcomed the opportunity to shop through catalogs and order by mail, and the Sears, Roebuck catalog soon became, probably, the best known and most treasured of them all. It has, in fact, entered into history as part of "Americana."

Advertisements appeared in "Mail Order" sections of newspapers and other periodicals (and still do today, to at least some extent). Before long, however, it occurred to someone to compile lists of names and addresses of individuals and mail them catalogs and other direct solicitations at the then modest cost of the postal service. So, although the need for a distinction was then not yet either made or recognized as necessary, there was a difference between using the mails solely to receive and fill orders ("mail order") and using the mails to solicit the orders, as well as to receive and fill them ("direct mail").

In the minds of many, especially direct mail experts, that distinction between mail order and direct mail survives to this day, although conditions have changed and the rationale for the distinction seems less justified than before: We no longer rely on the postal service to the extent we did in the early days. Today, mail order merchants advertise by means of print, billboards, and radio and TV broadcasts, and they receive orders by telephone and fax, as well as by mail, filling orders via a number of shipping and express services, as well as by mail. Although they still identify themselves as direct-mail marketers, they sometimes also turn to broadcasts, telephone, and other means—the latest, solicitation by fax messages—to solicit orders, even though some of those means are technically no longer direct marketing. They also usually offer now to accept orders by telephone and fax, as well as by mail, and to accept charges to credit cards, the numbers of which are furnished by customers via mail, telephone, and/or fax. Too, many who market principally by direct mail use mail order methods—advertising in mail order sections of periodicals—to solicit inquiries and thus build their own mailing lists for direct mail follow-up. One large direct mail company, for example, offers personal mailing labels as a loss leader, and sends its catalog out to everyone who orders the mailing labels. The idea is to get the "bounce-back" orders and create new customers.

Any distinction among the marketing methods known as *mail order, direct marketing,* and *direct mail* is further blurred because many marketers use all the methods: A number of direct marketers have opened traditional retail outlets, as have Montgomery Ward and Sears, Roebuck, for example. (Interestingly enough, I read recently on an electronic bulletin board of the great excitement attending the opening of a Sears store in Fairbanks, Alaska.)

At the same time, many traditional retailers have added direct marketing divisions; many large department store chains, for example, have catalog and mail order or direct mail departments. Thus many in mail order are also in direct mail, further vitiating definitions attempting to distinguish one marketing method from another. The use of the mails for one of the functions is thus significant, but it is not of itself definitive, nor will it matter greatly in discussing the problems, changes, influences, and opportunities that are common to this entire family of marketing industries and subindustries.

Direct marketing thus includes solicitations by telephone, fax, and broadcasts (those late-night TV offers of music tapes, records, and discs), but these are relatively minor elements of direct marketing: Direct marketing has grown to a multibillion-dollar industry, but it is still predominantly a mail-oriented business in its solicitation of orders.

If there is, therefore, truly a significant distinction between "mail order" and "direct mail," it is simply that of soliciting orders through print advertising in the media—periodicals—versus solicitation by mailing packets of literature to prospects.

COST OF ORDERS

Earlier, in Chapter 1, I discussed "cost of sales" versus "selling costs." I explained there that selling costs are those incurred directly and exclusively to get the sale—e.g., advertising cost—whereas cost of sales is an accountant's term that includes selling costs, along with many other costs for activities necessary to the sale, including fulfillment costs. "Cost of orders" is yet another term, identical in meaning with selling costs, except that it is a bit more specific in that it implies the unitized cost (i.e., the cost of each order). That is the cost we wish to try to establish here. It is useful to devise a means or mode for determining the cost of orders for each individual campaign, so that we can compare one marketing method, strategy, or program with another. That, in fact, enables us to address the main objective of databased marketing, maximizing the sales result of each dollar invested in marketing in these inflationary times when rising costs are an ever-increasing threat to direct mail.

Bear in mind, now, the basic defect in most other kinds of marketing programs: It is usually so difficult as to be almost impossible, in those other kinds of advertising and sales campaigns, to determine just what sales resulted from any given advertising or promotion, although some suggestions for improving the process were given earlier. Advertising will normally produce some sales, but some sales will result from other causes, making it a practical impossibility to ascertain, with any certainty, how many orders resulted from the advertising alone.

Some of the devices suggested earlier, such as special inducements and coupons printed in the advertising, help to measure the results of advertising and sales promotions, but even they do not fully solve the problem. Customers learn of the specials through other means, such as tips from sales clerks, in-store signs, and alternative advertising: Many marketers run concurrent print advertisements, radio and TV commercials, contests, in-store displays, and sundry other parallel promotions in a multimedia spread. That may produce good results, but it makes it all but impossible to determine the effectiveness of each promotion: The customer may have learned of the promotion through any or all of the presentations, but unfortunately, you will have no way of relating results to marketing effort. It may well be best explained by another concept, often known as the Pareto Principle: Applied here, it says that 80 percent of sales success results from 20 percent of the marketing and vice versa, the other 80 percent of the marketing expense and effort produces the remaining 20 percent of the sales results. How can you distinguish the profitable 80/20 percent ratio from the unprofitable 20/80 percent ratio?

In mail order, it is possible to key or code the advertising so as to identify every order that comes in as a direct result of the mail order advertisement. Like the brands on cattle, the key or code furnishes an absolute identification for every order

Keying Advertising and Orders

Perhaps you have noticed in many advertisements inviting you to order by mail or telephone to an address that includes a "department number," such as W. C. Jones & Co., 1234 Fifth Street, Dept. 3HOC91, Mishegas, Ohio 45555. "Dept. 3HOC91" is a code. Every order that arrives addressed to Dept. 3HOC91 can be credited to an advertisement placed in the March 1991 issue of *Home Office Computing* magazine. (If the advertisement runs in the April issue, it will carry the address "Dept. 4HOC91.")

Of course, the key can be entirely arbitrary, but it makes sense to design a key that contains its own identification of the advertising to which it refers. But a "Dept." designation is only one way to establish a key. It can be done by adding a meaningless item to an address—an A can be added to a street or box number (1234 Fifth Street may become 1234-A Fifth Street), W. C. Jones & Co. can become W. A. Jones & Co. or simply Jones & Co., and so on. Any such device can be used for the purpose of linking each order to its source.

Gathering Data in Mail Order Sales

You must, of course, keep records along the lines of Figure 11–1. This kind of record gives you a comparative accounting of alternative media, assuming you ran the same advertising copy in each medium. These are comparative figures in a sense. It would normally be far better, however, if the records were for the same month, since seasonal fluctuations in response may distort the figures. Still, you can get a good idea of how each medium produces, at least for the campaign in question. There

DOLLAR A DAY promotion thru 12/31/91

KEY	PUBLICATION	ISSUE	NET COST	SALES	NO. ORDERS	COST/ ORDER
3HOC91	Home Office Computing	Mar 91	$645.50	$1150	37	$17.45
HH223A	Cosmo	Apr 91	875.75	2237	44	19.90
J34EXC	Popular Mechanics	Apr 91	756.65	1935	62	12.20
435XX	Income Opportunities	Feb 91	635.00	856	22	28.86
TREX	Success	Jun 91	476.25	998	27	17.64
NN–21	Wall Street Journal	Jul 91	285.00	375	12	23.75
ZBT11	Money	Aug 91	654.55	856	28	23.38

Figure 11–1. Recording one month's advertising results.

are, however, other considerations. Even if the advertising copy ran for only one month, orders may continue to come in for some time after the advertisement has run—they usually do—and so the figures shown here would not be final figures, but only interim ones. It could be several months before you have final figures. (I have gotten orders as late as two years after a promotion, and just yesterday I received an order from a classified advertisement that ran nearly a year ago.)

As figures accumulate over the long haul, you might very well find that the cost per order might change from the figures derived from the early results. They might decrease considerably, as time goes on and additional orders come in. (Note that the chart of Figure 11–1 is as of the end of that year.) On the other hand, if you run your advertising for many months, you may very well perceive a drastic change in cost per order: Typically, advertising has a cumulative effect and tends to become more productive of results, as time goes on, to some point where it finally peaks. In fact, the first appearance of your advertising may not produce enough result to turn a profit: It is not unusual for a mail order campaign to require several months to become even profitable, much less reach a peak.

We must recognize that a print advertisement is rarely as productive in a single appearance as it is after appearing in a series of at least three times. Assuming that you would run print advertisements in that manner, a much better way of keeping a record and studying the result is to make a month-by-month comparison, as in Figure 11–2. Here you can see the cumulative effects of continuous advertising and get a more extensive view of its effects on the cost of getting orders, and perhaps decide which advertisements to continue and which to end. You can watch the trend with repeated appearances of copy in any single medium, you can compare media for results, and, if you run the copy long enough, you can identify seasonal fluctuations.

DOLLAR A DAY promotion thru 12/31/91

KEY	PUBLICATION	ISSUE	NET COST	SALES	NO. ORDERS	COST/ ORDER
3HOC91	Home Office	Mar 91	$645.50	$1150	37	$17.45
	Computing	Apr 91	645.50	1252	39	16.55
		May 91	645.50	1654	46	14.03
HH223A	Cosmo	Apr 91	875.75	2237	44	19.90
		May 91	875.75	2789	59	14.84
		Jun 91	875.75	2607	55	14.03
J34EXC	Popular	Apr 91	756.65	1935	62	12.20
	Mechanics	May 91	756.65	1979	63	12.01
		Jun 91	756.65	2358	71	10.66

Figure 11–2. Recording three months' advertising results.

You can easily use variants of this approach to measure and compare results from different kinds of copy: different headlines, different body copy, different prices, or other differences. Figure 11–3 suggests a method for doing that. Three keys identify three different versions of the copy—perhaps three different headlines or three different prices (change only one thing at a time when testing copy in this manner, if you want to be sure that you can relate effect and cause accurately) to see what the differences in result are.

This is not exactly easy to do with complete accuracy, either. If the different versions are run in different months, other factors—seasonal ones, perhaps—may interfere with getting an accurate correlation of each version of the copy with the results that version produces. If you run the three versions of the copy in the same month but in different media, you have to hope that you have selected media that are at least roughly equivalent to each other, reaching the same audience of readers. That, however, is another imponderable over which you have no control. Thus, while you can get some idea of how to correlate mail order sales with the cost of getting each sale, it is still far from a precision process. In fact, there are several disadvantages:

■ It takes a long time to gauge results because for most media, the advertising runs a long time after the space has been bought, so it is at least a few (and often many) months before there are enough results to get even reasonably complete figures and to make adjustments necessary to make the campaign a viable proposition.

■ It is a costly way to test and measure, unless you are running small and inexpensive advertisements.

■ It is difficult to get any results approaching precision in accuracy.

■ You have only partial control, surrendering a good bit of your control and options (e.g., timing) to the media and their publishers. They dictate to you when you can run your copy, how much advance notice they require, and even where, in the publication, your copy will appear. Even when you pay premium prices for choice locations you are limited in how specific your choice may be, except for broad measures, such as "above the fold," one of the covers, or other such extra-cost option.

DOLLAR A DAY promotion thru 12/31/91

KEY	PUBLICATION	ISSUE	NET COST	SALES	NO. ORDERS	COST/ ORDER
3HOC91	Home Office	Mar 91	$645.50	$1150	37	$17.45
4HOC91	Computing	Apr 91	645.50	1252	39	16.55
5HOC91		May 91	645.50	1654	46	14.03

Figure 11–3. Comparing different copy for results.

- You may or may not be able to get a "split run" (one half of the periodical's run carrying one version of your advertisement, the other one half of the run carrying another verison of your advertisement, both versions keyed) in any given medium; not all publishers and media offer this highly desirable feature for testing.

Direct mail, in contrast, has an almost opposite set of characteristics, offering advantages precisely where mail order offers only disadvantages.

Gathering Data in Direct Mail Sales

As far as testing and monitoring results to correlate them with then cost, direct mail presents a much different proposition in several ways that become apparent immediately, as we examine how to measure these results. The major advantage, overall, is that testing by direct mail puts you in the driver's seat: You have almost absolute control over all factors of when and how: testing your proposition, your copy, your price, your mailing lists, and any other factor in a direct mail campaign.

- You can mail to any list and to any part of any list whenever you wish.
- You make your own "split run" tests, splitting them into as many pieces as you wish.
- You can run a test whenever you wish because you are not at the mercy of any publisher's deadlines and other rules.
- You can get results and gauge the rightness of your copy, your mailing list, your price, or whatever you are testing in a few weeks, rather than over many months.
- You can do follow-up testing because you control the schedules and can get results in a few weeks. (Long lead times for most print advertising make follow-up testing difficult to do on a practical basis.)
- You control the costs because you decide how large the test mailings are to be.

It is as true in direct mail as in mail order, and perhaps even more true in direct mail, that a sales campaign may take some time to become profitable. Because you run a first limited-size mailing to test the waters (i.e., to test your proposition, your copy, and your mailing list) you should consider that part of your marketing to be research, an investment cost. Even then, a first mailing may not produce significant profit or even any profit. What matters is whether you get a *substantial* enough result to justify continuing the campaign.

Response Rate

A great many people in direct mail are concerned with *response rate,* the percentage of pieces mailed that result in orders received, as discussed in Chapter 1. There are even those who pontificate about response rates required for effective results, as though there are universal rules or principles controlling the industry.

The fact is that a response rate has only a most limited significance, which is confined to a given campaign and is significant only if and when a single product or service is involved. (If you are selling a line of goods, rather than a single product, there are orders of almost infinitely varying size, so that the size of the average order is another factor to consider.) Depending on the markup (in dollars, not in percentage rates) and on the cost of the mailing, a 1 percent response rate in one case may be highly profitable, while a 4 percent response rate in another case may be disastrous. What is significant is return on investment, and that involves such matters as the "allowable cost" for each order and the breakeven points.

Breakeven is the critical point. Figures above it represent profit, and figures below it represent loss. "Allowable cost" is, therefore, that cost which represents breakeven or recovery of all costs.

Allowable Cost per Order

In the examples shown earlier of a hypothetical mail order campaign you saw only gross figures, culminating in a cost-per-order figure. That gave you no idea of whether that C/O (cost per order) figure represented a profit or a loss because you didn't know the markup—the net or even the gross profit/loss represented by that C/O figure. If it costs you $17.45 to get an order for a $59 item on which your markup is 40 percent—i.e., $23.60—you have a gross profit of $6.15, but that is not net profit. You must pack and ship the order, you must accept returns, some inventory shrinkage, and some bad checks and other losses. If they amount to about 25 percent, a not unreasonable expectation, your per-order cost rises to $21.81, which brings your profit margin down to less than $2 per order. In fact, your allowable cost per order is $23.60, the breakeven point.

The Significant Variables

A number of variables can make the difference between profit and loss. If you are on the cusp between profit and loss (i.e., at or near the breakeven point) any of several possible actions on your part may make the difference and enable you to turn a profit on the program. However, you cannot simply do as you please; you must deal with market realities. Even for a given case, the response rate is not the only variable that can make the difference between earning a return on investment—profit—and not earning a return on investment— loss. If you sell a line of goods by direct mail, you have orders of varying size, and so anything you can do to increase the average-order size will have the same effect as increasing the rate of response. But consider all the possible things you can do and the pros and cons of each possible action:

■ Raise the price of the product. (Can you do so without a loss of business nullifying the advantage of greater markup?)

■ Require customers to pay "handling and shipping" costs, over and above the price. (Many mail order and direct mail dealers do so today.)

■ Bargain harder to reduce costs for list rental, printing, shipping, and other such expenses. (You probably won't get large reductions, but you may be able to get costs down a few points.)

■ Pay close attention to the costs of your mailing package. There are many options here to cut costs (e.g., using self-mailers, taking advantage of bulk mail and other U.S. Postal Service bargain rates, and using lightweight paper to reduce weight of the package.

■ Find ways to raise the response rate.

FACTORS AFFECTING THE RESPONSE RATE

One way of addressing the latter item and the one preceding it as well is to consider the literature package, specially the sales letter it contains. By conventional wisdom, the sales letter is the *sine qua non* of direct mail literature. It sets the tone for the entire presentation, and everything else in the package is nominally in its support. Often, however, there are few other elements and in some cases, even no others. In any case, the question is, How long should a sales letter be?

Not surprisingly, there are different schools of thought on this. There are those who state flatly that a long letter produces better results, while others are equally vehement in advocating a short letter. The consensus, nevertheless, appears to be in favor of the longer letter as the more effective one. It apparently follows the direct mail dogma, "The more you tell, the more you sell."

First of all, there ought to be an "it all depends" here. The lengthy letter may work well in one place, whereas the short letter may work best in another application. It depends on several factors, at least these three broad ones.

- What you are selling.
- What else is in your package.
- What kind of buyers you are addressing.
- How well written the letter is.

If the longer letter is the more effective for your purposes, you ought logically to require less of a grab bag of other materials—brochures, badges, novelties, and so on—in the package. Certainly, the typical package will be less costly if greater reliance can be placed on the letter, since the letter is almost always less costly than most other elements of the package, Testing is certainly in order here to determine which works best for you.

Another concern relates to mailing lists. There is a strong tendency in the direct mail business to assign the mailing lists prime importance as a controlling factor in the response rate and therefore deem the lists responsible for the success or failure of a mail campaign. Those who have such an abiding faith in the "right" mailing lists as being critical to success tend to minimize the importance of other factors in contributing to poor response rates. At least, the first suspicion, when a campaign produces disappointing results, is that the mailing list was inadequate, rather than that the copy, the price, or some other aspect of the program is the culprit. Other possible causes are then assigned a much lower probability.

If this appraisal is correct, the marketer must, presumably, be somehow able to choose the "right" mailing list—if it exists. But that raises the "$64 question." What *is* the right list? How/where can we even identify it in theory, much less actually find it and use it?

THE MARKETING DATABASE AS THE RIGHT LIST

All of this raises another question regarding the definition of databased marketing, especially as it relates to conventional mailing lists. That the definition of databased marketing is by no means established universally is readily apparent now. There are many definitions and interpretations, with the single agreement that it is definitely customer oriented and is highly targeted. Some even seem to regard it as a supermailing list. Among the commonly accepted premises are that it has, as the overall goal, the building of exhaustive files recording the personal attributes of each individual that are relevant to marketing to that individual, which might support the latter idea of being a supermailing list. However, imagine a supermarket where you insert your special credit card or check-cashing card into a slot to release a shopping cart. An audiotape in a special miniplayer (or a videotape using a miniscreen) addresses you: "Hello, Mrs. O'Reilly. Last week you bought [a list of several purchases of last week]. We have these items on special sales this week, as well as the following items [more items identified]. You can find them in aisles. . . ."

This notion was recently voiced on an electronic bulletin board by a marketing specialist who divined the concept as a modern application of expanded marketing information and technology. He did not refer to databased marketing and presumably was not familiar with the term. Still, he understood the current marketing trend, under the influence of the capabilities now being made possible by modern technology. He understood the goal of using technology so as to create a special relationship with a customer by addressing him or her as a unique individual, whether that is called databased marketing, targeted marketing, segmentation, or niche marketing.

This has an economic value, of course. Being able to address each customer with an individual, highly personalized greeting will undoubtedly improve response. But the new economics of direct marketing/databased marketing are a bit more sophisticated than that.

OTHER ECONOMIC FACTORS

So far, the marketing economics we have discussed have been based on direct and immediate returns on your investment. Even if some of the returns are not realized for a number of months after the campaign has ended, you must count them as direct returns on investment. However, there is another return that must not be overlooked: The long-term return of having a loyal customer, who buys from you again and again. This is an economic factor abbreviated as "LTV," for "lifetime value." It refers to the value of a customer over the lifetime of the customer. That does not refer to the actual lifetime of the individual who happens to be your customer: You have no assurance at all that the individual will remain your customer for as long as he or she lives, and it would be unreasonably optimistic to assume this. Lifetime value must thus refer to the lifetime of the relationship or the length of time the individual remains your customer.

This concept requires a different kind of thinking about the economics of your marketing and a different kind of accounting to track the costs of acquiring customers as a long-term investment. In fact, some consider this to be peculiarly suited as a basic value and accounting system for use in conjunction with databased marketing since it is a factor or function of a continuing relationship with customers.

Customer lifetimes vary widely, not surprisingly, because people vary widely in their characteristics. There are those who become comfortable with a relationship and stubbornly resist change. Short of suffering excessive neglect or even actual abuse at your hands, they will stick with you through thick and thin. At the other extreme are those who like to experiment and try new and different experiences. Even with kid-glove treatment and abundant TLC (tender loving care) you will have trouble keeping these customers. But they are the two extremes. The vast majority of your customers will fall into some middle ground: Treated well, they will tend to remain customers longer; treated indifferently, they will have shorter lives as your customers. American automobile manufacturers have lost forever many customers who will never forgive them for their refusal to make good on the "lemons" they sold years ago, before foreign competition and some modern laws compelled them to modify their attitudes. In general, as many businesspeople have learned only slowly and at great cost (and some have never learned), it costs money to acquire a customer and it is usually much less costly to keep the customer than to find a new one.

PURSUING SALES VERSUS PURSUING CUSTOMERS

To a great degree the value of any sale depends on whether your primary goal is making the sale or making a customer. Deliberately overcharging, selling poor-quality merchandise, misrepresenting, giving poor service, and/or treating a buyer rudely clearly mean that you are more interested in the sale itself than in establishing a relationship. Loosely speaking, everyone who buys from you is a customer, at least for that one sale. However, there is some conventional wisdom that says the buyer does not become a customer unless he or she returns for a second purchase. The lifetime value of a customer is thus largely dependent on how you treat a customer. Most of us have visited stores we will never patronize again, and we have visited others that we return to with pleasant anticipation of a friendly greeting from someone who is almost a friend.

That is not the only factor. As I pointed out earlier, there are those entrepreneurs whose entire approach is to sales per se because they promote and sell only one item. For them, databased marketing and LTV have little meaning. However, they represent a tiny fragment of business and industry, with little significance overall.

There are others whose approach to selling is the appeal of low prices. Their reasoning is that if they discount enough, find enough bargains to pass on to customers, and advertise enough, they need not worry about how well or how poorly they treat their customers.

Chapter 12

Individualizing Appeals

Is it possible to have the cake and the penny too? There is great hope that it is possible, with the right kind of advance planning and a clear understanding of the problems.

THE PARADOX OF TARGETED MARKETING VERSUS MASS MARKETING

In databased marketing we are faced with the apparent paradox of a system that proposes to use mass-market merchandising methods to target individual customers. On its face, this appears to be the antithesis of mass marketing: The often-stated long-term goal of databased marketing is to make customized sales appeals, tailored to the characteristic expressed wants, buying habits, life style, and other clues relevant to each individual's behavior and customer profile. In apparent direct opposition to this, however, is the way most direct marketers, traditionally mass marketers, embrace databased marketing as their own creation, an outgrowth of direct marketing and its increasing use of the computer to automate DM systems. Thus, while the validity of databased marketing for applications in all marketing arenas is recognized, it has been applied initially in the direct marketing field as its closest natural fit. It does, in fact, probably adapt more easily to DM (where it has been aimed at creating more effective and more efficient models in direct marketing) than to any other field of marketing, although it is undergoing development elsewhere too.

There are logical difficulties: Adapting custom marketing to a traditional mass-marketing milieu is not the only paradox. There is also the difficulty of trying to develop a most expensive marketing tool, the marketing database, to a use that traditionally has been the domain of the small business, especially the neighborhood mom-and-pop stores. These vanishing retailers knew all or nearly all their customers personally and could customize sales suggestions for each customer, but such entrepreneurs could never afford to build even customer databases, much less marketing databases. Even today's larger businesses must consider the costs seriously, for there are not a great many economies of scale here. The cost per entry in a large marketing database is not appreciably smaller than it is in the smaller marketing database.

The practical problem therefore poses a rather obvious question: Is it practicable to design and present a customized and individual sales presentation to thousands, and even tens of thousands, of customers and prospective customers who are listed in your database? This is a question I have touched on earlier, with the observation that it may be feasible to design and produce individualized presentations to a few dozen or even to a few hundred prospects, if the item is a truly big-tag one. It is an especially impracticable idea, however, when the item is a small one, such as a bottle of aspirin tablets or a line of canned soups. It is impracticable to market such products individually to the consumer. By their nature, these items represent small order sizes, which is certainly a factor in the allowable cost of getting each order. Are we then to consider databased marketing as suitable only for individualizing marketing to customers for major items, that is, for big-tag sales? The introductory position offered was that theoretically, at least, full development and use of databased marketing (i.e., truly individual, custom marketing presentations) could be made to pursue only major sales. The use of databased marketing for other sales, those of lesser average order size, would have to be made through only partial realization of the databased marketing ideal, the discovery and pursuit of niche markets.

It was an accurate position to take, on the basis of the assumptions made. However, it was based on a relatively shallow analysis: It did not consider all the possibilities; rather it considered only sales of small items directly to the ultimate consumer, the retail distribution. But aspirin tablets and soup are not sold directly from manufacturer or distributor to the individual customer: There are other sales situations and other kinds of customers, as well as some other considerations that we did not take into account. Thus the question did not properly address the whole problem, especially not that of the applications of databased marketing to business-to-business transactions. Average order size is not the only consideration, but let's examine it first.

THE AVERAGE ORDER SIZE

It is not always the customer or the nature of the merchandise that determines whether the average order size will be large or small, vis-à-vis the marketing costs. "Large" and "small" are relative terms, and even the values they reflect are not always measurable in dollars. Marketing is a mix of many variables and you must consider all of them. Here, for example, we go astray if we restrict our marketing imagination by visualizing the ultimate consumer as our only customer for any commodity, especially inexpensive ones.

Business is conducted at several levels, and small commodities are almost invariably marketed via at least two intermediate levels of distribution before reaching the consumer. But the real distinction here is between business-to-consumer sales and business-to-business sales. There is usually a wide difference in terms of both the size of the marketing databases (i.e., number of customers and customer prospects) and the average order size. But that is far from a complete profile of all the considerations entering into the data you want in your marketing database.

Consumer versus Business-to-Business Sales

Although it may be impracticable to build databases of any kind to market aspirin, soup, toothpaste, or screwdrivers on a custom basis to individuals, it is not impracticable to build marketing databases to market such items to retailers buying for inventory and resale or to institutions, both of whom will buy in quantity. The practicality of databased marketing is not dependent on any single factor, such as the goods or type of customer. As only one example, many databased marketing ideas that do not work well in marketing directly to the consumer may be far more practicable approaches in business-to-business marketing, where the average order size is a far different proposition. Typically, too, if you are selling at wholesale to large institutions and retailers, you are working with a far smaller database. That also helps to make the matter of individualizing and customizing your sales appeals a far different one, and presumably more easily achieved.

Customer Acquisition

Another and most important variable is the value to you of the customer. What is a given customer worth to you? How much effort and money are you willing to invest in pursuit of a given customer? Does IBM or GM represent a customer of greater value than does Harry's Diner? Would you invest more heavily in pursuing a first sale to IBM or GM than you would in winning a first order from Harry's Diner? Or, to put the question into another logical framework, is it necessary that each sale produce an immediate profit?

This is a double-edged question. There is, first, the potential size of any order from an IBM or GM versus the potential size of any order from a Harry's Diner. But there is also the question of whether you are in pursuit of sales or of customers. I recall a time when, as the manager of a branch office of a corporation with many branch offices, I was in pursuit of a first order from a major division of IBM that happened to be located in the same area. My consideration was gaining IBM as a customer, not the value of any first order I might be able to win. I happened to know some of the characteristics of the organization, one of which was that it was not easy to win as a customer but that it had great loyalty to dependable suppliers and did not change them often. That made it a particularly desirable account to have, and I expended great effort to win it.

This does not mean that the same consideration may not apply to individual consumers as customers. If you sell costly jewelry or designer gowns, many individual consumers may be worth any reasonable effort, even individual, customized sales appeals, to win as customers.

WHO IS YOUR CUSTOMER?

Despite the arguments just presented in the preceding pages, there remains an important unanswered question: Who is your customer? If you have a retail business, whether it is a hamburger stand, a department store, or a plumbing service, you will surely answer that with great confidence by identifying those who place cash in your hand in exchange for the goods or services you sell. But suppose you are a manufacturer, a wholesale distributor, or a franchiser: How will you then answer that question? Is your customer the organization who buys and resells your goods, the one who buys directly from you? Or is your customer the consumer who buys from your dealers, retailers, franchisees, and others who distribute what you manufacture, sell wholesale, or franchise?

The short answer is that both are your customers, although your marketing database is directed primarily to closing sales with those who actually pay you directly, such as the retailers. The more information you can get about individual consumers, the more you can tailor your product and all related activities—packaging, promotions, prices, sizes—to the consumer's taste and thus help those who sell for you at the retail level. (A little later, I will further discuss this and some related matters.)

WHAT IS A CUSTOM SALES APPEAL?

The foregoing arguments, pro and con, are based on the premise that the stated goal of databased marketing to reach customers individually means that customized sales appeals must be customized 100 percent—designed for the individual customer from the ground up. That is not the case, however: "Custom" does not mean that the entire package of literature must be tailored to the individual. Even in marketing directly to the individual consumer, rather than through some kind of distribution network or franchise, a compromise between the extremes is usually possible with just a little imagination. Let us take, first, a compromise between inexpensive commodities and big-tag items, such as medium-cost jewelry—rings, watches, fountain pens, bracelets, and other such items. A compromise between an impracticably expensive, customized sales presentation and a typically ineffective form letter means using the computer's mail merge capabilities to produce something along the lines of the "personal" message you get from Ed McMahon exhorting you to enter the National Clearinghouse contest. Your own name is inserted freely and frequently in the standard, mass-oriented message. Each piece of paper bearing your name and personal salutation is formatted and printed out individually by a laser printer. It is rather obvious that your name is a force-fit, and you would probably have to be relatively ingenuous to be deceived as to how personal the message really is: It is not necessary to be a computer expert to recognize the computer's role in this. Yet, the frequent insertion of the individual's own name has a positive effect on the overall persuasiveness of the literature package.

Despite this benefit, this is not a true example of databased marketing because it is a mass appeal and a mass approach, using a standardized form presentation: Millions of addressees get exactly the same literature, except for the insertion of their names. To qualify as databased marketing, the appeal would have to be truly customized to the individual customer to at least some extent. The sales appeal, that is, would have to be oriented to some of the personal characteristics and/or interests of the customer. The National Clearinghouse promotion is based on the broad appeal of the possibility of winning a great deal of money, but that is an appeal to everyone or nearly everyone, even if there are a few exceptions. However, if databased marketing were applied to that National Clearinghouse promotion, the literature that reaches me would have a message in it pointing out the periodicals of special interest to me as a writer and/or any other of my professional and personal characteristics. If I were a suburban homeowner, the message would point to the home-improvement magazines, perhaps. I might be urged to consider the advantages of subscribing to such periodicals as *Popular Mechanics,* if the database revealed that I had a home workshop of some kind or to such investor periodicals as *Money* magazine if I were shown to be an investor of some kind.

Would that expense be justified by a profitable increase in orders? Logically, yes, although it would be necessary to test it and see if there was, indeed, that benefit. However, the added expense should not be great, especially not as a percentage of the cost of the promotion overall. Customizing the content of the letter that is the centerpiece of a DM package would mean breaking the mailings down into lists sorted and retrieved by the respondents' personal interests. It should not add greatly to the labor required and certainly not much to the format and printing bill. Probably the greatest expense would be the advance planning to study the databases, the periodicals, and matching periodicals and groups of periodicals with the interests of those listed in the databases. In my opinion, the National Clearinghouse promotion overall focuses almost exclusively on the grand prize and makes far too little effort to sell the magazines on their own merits. And, ironically enough, this is an almost ideal situation for establishing a dialogue: The literature could include a questionnaire that the respondent would complete, probably as a subordinate contest for an additional prize, furnishing information for the follow-up mailings that the promoter makes anyway. In my opinion, it is a missed opportunity.

The question then becomes, How much customization can you afford—justify, that is—for each given situation? Customizing sales appeals so that they are not prohibitively difficult or expensive, relative to the value of the potential sale, is possible far more often than you might conclude from a casual appraisal. Practical compromises make it possible. Of course, we are not talking about true, individual customization; we are talking about customizing your sales appeals to segments of your market, niche markets consisting of relatively small groups of people with similar characteristics and interests. It is possible to create a form letter and possibly other form literature that can be easily customized in the manner that databased marketing requires, using the capabilities of the modern computer. Let us suppose, for example, that June is approaching and your database reveals a number of people with children of an age typical of those graduating from high school. Mail merge makes it possible to address a form sales letter to each such parent, but modern technology offers capabilities beyond that: You can easily refer to the addressee's son, sons, daughter, and/or daughters about to graduate and invite the addressee to visit your store or scan the enclosed catalog to find suitable graduation gifts. You might enclose a special discount coupon or promise a gift from yourself for the graduating son or daughter. (Such a promotional item is especially powerful as an inducement under these circumstances.)

Figure 12–1 illustrates one simple approach to this. It is customized to the extent that it reveals knowledge of the customer's son's name and the fact that he is about to graduate from high school. Only two blanks need to be filled in here: The addressee's name and the child's first name. The remainder of the literature—the catalog, with a bound-in order form, and any other circulars, cards, and brochures—are standardized and are the same in each envelope mailed out to an individual addressee. Each envelope, however, includes this brief letter, in which the software can automatically fill in the addressee's name and the child's first name from the database.

This simple example is used here only to illustrate the base idea of how the information in the marketing database can inspire promotional ideas

BREWER'S DEPARTMENT STORE

12th & Market Streets   Potatoland, Idaho 65321

Dear M_____ :

It is that time of year again, and you are undoubtedly looking forward to the graduation of your son, _____, and wondering what to buy him as a graduation gift.

We are enclosing our special Graduation Gift catalog for your convenience. It is full of items suitable for the high school graduate, especially one planning to go on to college, as your son is planning to do. You will also find many items suitable as gifts for the children of your friends and relatives who are also looking forward to graduation this year.

We will be happy to handle your order by telephone or mail, and ship or deliver your order, suitably gift wrapped and with cards for you to inscribe with your own message of congratulations.

We look forward to helping you make this an auspicious occasion.

Cordially,

Joseph T. Macke
Marketing Director

Figure 12–1.   Customized sales letter.

and generate sales appeals with the special pulling power of directly addressing personal concerns of the customer. We will look at far more sophisticated examples that are easily achievable by extension of the method described here.

Not all market niches are fixed or permanent. Figure 12–1 shows a special example of a niche market that includes those who happen to have a son, daughter, or someone else quite close in a graduating class. It is a temporary niche that arises each year as June approaches, but many niche markets do come and go in this manner, as a result of a transitory condition. To benefit from this, you must anticipate the occurrence, if it is a predictable and recurring one, but also be alert for the unexpected and unpredictable condition that creates opportunities for niche markets, even if transitory ones. An important national or world event that arouses special interests you can turn to advantage, for example, furnishes such opportunities. When it was revealed that President Ronald Reagan was fond of jelly beans, candy manufacturers who were manufacturing jelly beans or had the means to do so quickly took advantage of a niche market that opened for them, as did candy retailers, gift stores, and others. The Gulf War stimulated sales of U.S. flags and the manufacture of many related "patriotic" items. The heavy publicity attending the taking of hostages by terrorists, along with the Gulf War, created a transitory, but strong, market for yellow ribbons, sending some manufacturers into 24-hour work shifts. The jelly bean niche market was long lasting and still exists, albeit much smaller than originally; the Gulf war "patriotic" market and the yellow-ribbon market had much shorter lives and are now quiescent. But back to our original example for a fuller discussion.

Question: How do you know which of those listed in your database has a child ready to graduate? *That,* getting, recording, and retrieving such information for use in marketing, is what databased marketing is really all about: Your database qualifies as a marketing database and enables databased marketing only when it contains personal information of this kind, allowing you to appeal personally to the customer. That requirement is one of the reasons that databased marketing focuses so intently on your original *customer* database as the *sine qua non,* the basis, of databased marketing. The premise is that your customer database will include such information and that you will add to it continually. However, the inclusion of this kind of information in your customer database is not an inevitable or automatic event. You may gain some of it by chance, but you can't depend on serendipity. The data come to you regularly and dependably only when you take positive steps to gain such information and add it to your database— when you get a continuing dialogue going with your customers. That is the first question to be addressed here, while we seek answers: How can you get that dialogue going to gather the information that will transform that customer database (which is often not much more than a simple mailing list of customers) into a marketing database (or, more likely, into a set of marketing databases)? Bear in mind the important qualification that a proper marketing database enables you to do at least four important things in connection with your marketing:

1. Make a reasoned (fact-based) judgment of those goods/services for which each individual is a good prospect.
2. Select the best prospects for whatever it is you wish to sell or to use as a special promotion.
3. Make reasoned judgments on what merchandise/services you should and should not offer your clientele generally, and also make such judgments on new items you are considering adding to your line.
4. Enable you to model your best customer(s) by type or characteristics so that you can prequalify prospects and have a picture, in advance, to guide you in seeking new prospects.

This is true for *each* marketing database you create, and unless your business is such that your customers are a uniform set, you will have more than one database. If yours is a printing business, for example, your customers, classed by the kind of printing services they normally require, might be characterized by any of the following kinds of needs:

- Long-run printing and binding of manuals.
- Short-run printing of proposals and reports.
- Typesetting of copy.
- Printing of a variety of multipart forms.
- Long-run printing of brochures.
- Short-run printing of memos and other unbound documents.
- Extensive cutting, folding, binding.
- Printing of all black and white copy.
- Printing process color on calendared stock

Of course, some of your customers may have frequent requirements for a mix of such services. The point is, however, that each customer is characterized in terms of his or her most frequent needs. That affects how you sort, classify, and index each customer in your marketing database. If you have overbought some expensive, glossy stock and want to run a special to get rid of it, you have to pick the likely customer, who would be that one at the end of the list shown here. It is unlikely that any of the others shown would be likely candidates.

IN THE BEGINNING: STARTING THE DATABASE

Customers come to you in a variety of ways, and in some cases you have a good deal of initial information about them, while in others you have little information and are starting from scratch. If a given customer came to you as one of a rented list of names, you probably have at least some demographic data to enter into the customer's database record. If the customer initiated relations with you by applying for a charge plate or your own in-house credit card, you have the information from the credit application. On the other hand, if the customer came to you by chance (e.g., as a casual walk-in or respondent to an advertisement) you have only the record of the customer's purchase as starter information. It is now up to you to get more information that will help you build that marketing database and make it the valuable marketing asset it can be.

WHAT INFORMATION DO YOU NEED?

Before addressing the matter of how to start a dialogue with your customers to gather more information (and the right information), there is the question of just what information you want or need. That is a first consideration here calling for a great deal of introspection and planning. It is one of the reasons that you can't get on the telephone and order marketing databases. Because they must be tailored to your needs, which are almost surely unique in some respects, you must build your own marketing databases. One reason for this specificity is that your marketing database (i.e., the information it contains) must be appropriate to what you sell. The simple example of Figure 12-1 is geared to the business that sells items suitable as gifts for June graduates. It would not be helpful to the firm selling plumbing supplies or kitchen appliances to know which of those listed in their marketing databases had children ready to graduate. The hypothetical example of the National Clearinghouse promotion would require information concerning career interests and such personal interests as hobbies and reading preferences. Another business might mandate a need for information on respondents' state of health; interest in health issues; weight problems, if any; eating habits; or other clues qualifying them as customers for whatever the concern wishes to offer.

Obviously, the kind of information you want in your marketing databases is that which is directly useful for marketing generally and sales appeals especially. To decide what kinds of information that would include, you must contemplate who your ideal customers are and why they will buy what you sell. If you sell gift items as such, you need to draw up a list of who normally buys gift items, on what occasions, and for whom. You can approach this by developing lists, as in the following example listing gift items:

Weddings	Retirements
Engagements	Promotions
Baby showers	Holidays
New babies	Special occasions
Birthdays	Deaths
Anniversaries	

Each of these considerations suggests information to be sought after and added to the marketing databases. It also suggests the need to keep the databases up to date. Where the head of a family has died recently, a personal solicitation to shop for a Mother's Day or Father's Day gift would be in bad taste and should be avoided. On the other hand, it is a good idea to send a message of condolence to anyone listed in your databases who has suffered a recent family tragedy or, for that matter, any grave misfortune.

The preceding list indicates at once some of the kinds of information you want. As I have already revealed by the example of Figure 12-1, you want information here of any school-age children in the customer's family that will tell you in what year(s) the graduation(s) are to be expected (i.e., children's names and birthdates). Any other dates ought to be sought out too, however, as leads to others' birthdays and anniversaries. But you want to know also about other occasions that normally inspire gift buying. And the knowledge of deaths in the family serves as a precaution against suggesting a gift for a father or mother who is no longer alive, as well as inspiring condolences when the tragedy is quite recent.

Question: How can you get information on all the gift-giving occasions for each customer listed in your database? Obviously, the answer to this question can come to you only from the customer, and you must find some tactful and discreet way to ask for this information. Here is an idea you are welcome to use: Offer, as a free gift to each customer, a neatly printed reminder list of all their "occasions." The list could be in the form of a nicely printed sheet, a booklet, an annotated calendar, or something other than a simple list. Most are easy enough to manufacture. The announcement you send the customers includes a draft form for the customer to fill out, with your suggestions, such as shown in Figure 12–2.

A great many customers will respond, especially if you include a prepaid return envelope. (This kind of solicitation brings a high level of response if you repeat the mailing several times to all who did not respond on the original mailing.) When you transcribe the information from the draft form to your database, you also print it out, via your laser printer, on whatever form you have chosen to send the customer as the promised gift item.

Some of the same data is useful for other businesses. A travel agency may benefit from sending congratulations and a sales appeal to someone who has announced a wedding, retirement, or other occasion that might inspire a honeymoon, vacation, or other travel—even a trip as a graduation present. People getting married are usually reasonably good prospects for furniture and/or other household goods. Engagements and weddings call for diamond rings and wedding bands, and weddings call for catering services, photography, and other items associated with such occasions. Honeymoons and other travel call for luggage and suitable clothing for travel and other climates.

These are obvious needs that inspire the lists of information you want. Here are a few of the questions you might seek to answer:

- Who normally buys what you sell (men, women, students, housewives, engineers, lawyers, etc)?
- For what purpose (to satisfy what goals/wants/needs) do people buy your items?
- On what occasions do they buy these items?
- How often do they buy such items?
- In what quantities do they buy such items?

BIRTHDAYS:

Husband: _____

Wife: _____

Children:

_____

_____

_____

_____

Brother: _____

_____

Sister: _____

_____

Mother: _____

Father: _____

ANNIVERSARY: _____

GRADUATION: _____

OTHER OCCASIONS:

_____

_____

_____

_____

NOTES:

Figure 12-2. Suggested draft form for gathering information.

- Do they characteristically seek brand names when they buy such items?
- Do many buy such items by mail or telephone, or do they customarily buy in person and inspect before buying?
- Do they look for guarantees when buying such items?

You thus want to collect the information that identifies those people in terms of appropriate wants, needs, occasions, and any other factors defining them as customers and furnishing insights as to their typical buying practices. Obviously, you will find a great deal of variance, and you will have to study enough customers to establish what appears to be the norm—what is true for the majority of customers and may thus be accepted as an indicator of the typical customer.

That doesn't mean that all or even most of your customers are going to fit a mold. They may well do so for one product or one service, but if you handle a diverse line of goods or services, you will probably need a marketing database for each. Those customers who want me to help them write proposals are not the same customers who want me to present training seminars or who want to buy my monographs. I need to understand the difference among these various types and classes of customers if I am going to market to them effectively.

WHERE/HOW TO START IDENTIFYING THE NEEDED DATA

When you collect information for a marketing database, you need specific information, but that does not mean the same thing in all cases. You need names, dates, places, definitions, and so on, for those to whom you would sell gift items, as hypothesized here earlier. You could attempt to determine whether a given individual is by nature a gift-giver, but that is not easy to determine, unless you have already had a good bit of experience selling to that customer. It is more practical to learn whether the individual has occasions calling for gifts and, if so, what they are and when they occur. Too, you want such information to be as definite as you can make it—not only when, but to whom, as in the case of children graduating or family and friends getting engaged, married, and having babies.

Where do you start? We started here with a business selling gifts and occasions calling for gifts. We soon discovered that many businesses overlap each other. Luggage and travel services are not normally perceived as gifts, but often they are given as gifts, as are many kinds of household goods and other items short of the plumbing supplies mentioned earlier. That suggests another place to start analyzing the kinds of data you want in your databases: You can start by first listing what you sell, as a preliminary to who buys that merchandise and service, and why they buy it.

If you are a cataloger or general store of some kind, you probably have a rather diverse list, but you don't have to list each individual item, at least not at first; you can start by listing classes of items.

Suppose that you sell a line of office supplies and some office equipment. It can hardly be helpful to list the individual items—pencils, paper clips, and so on. Start by listing items in groups, perhaps as follows:

- General office supplies: pens, pencils, paper, stationery, inks, toner . . .
- Computers and related supplies: tractor paper, disks, labels . . .
- Printers.
- Word processors.
- Calculators.
- Modems.
- Computer software.
- Fax machines and fax paper.

If you start with the things you sell and your existing customer list, the first step, after establishing the basic database design, is to seek the common characteristics to see which ones predominate. Why do they buy from you? What motivates them? Is it favorable prices that you offer? Fast service? Your courtesy? The completeness of your line? Treating the humblest customer as though he were GE or IBM? The easy credit you extend?

There may be other common characteristics that do not appear to be linked to anything you do or are: Perhaps a great many of your regular customers are independent, home-based entrepreneurs. Or perhaps they are heavily computer oriented. Or they buy frequently in small quantities. Or the reverse: They buy infrequently in large quantities. Perhaps they tend to certain types of businesses. Or they have any of many other possible characteristics. It is important to establish the general nature of your customers—private individuals, retailers, professionals in private practice, nonprofit organizations, or others. Obviously, you must define these in terms of your own business, and without regard to others. It may well be that your own business operation is not typical of your industry, but that does not matter: Your marketing databases must reflect your customers, not others.

THE ATYPICAL CASE

The underlying premise of databased marketing is that you start with your established customer database as the first step in building your marketing databases. That, of course, assumes that you have been established in business long enough to develop a customer database. It is not of much help, if you are an entrepreneur who has just started or is just planning to launch a new business. In those circumstances, you obviously do not have a customer database as yet, although you may have a substantial prospect database. You may or may not have much information about the individuals on your list, probably depending on where and how you got the list. That makes things a bit more difficult, but it doesn't change the nature of what you must do: You must still build the marketing database, starting with whatever you do have. In such case, your initial approach should be a bit different, in that it should be directed to whatever you believe is logically your best market, but you should make a concerted effort to gather maximum data on all customers as soon as you acquire them.

WHAT DOES "DIALOGUE" MEAN?

Dialogue is generally interpreted to mean conversational exchanges. Strictly speaking, dialogue is any exchange of information, but as used in connection with the building of marketing databases, it refers to *feedback* from customers and prospective customers. You want to know what your customers think—especially about you and your business—and what they want. How you get that information is not nearly as important as ensuring that the information is reasonably complete and accurate.

That is one thing wrong immediately with questionnaires, surveys, and other methods for asking people what they think and want. A great many people are most reluctant to tell you want they really think and feel; they tend strongly to tell you what they believe to be acceptable, what reflects favorably on their own judgment, and what you want to hear. And even those who believe that they are being entirely honest and objective often deceive themselves and unknowingly offer fiction, rather than fact, in responding.

Feedback on Purchases

One kind of feedback is unflinchingly frank and accurate: the feedback of purchasing patterns and history. A clear message can be read in the history of a customer's purchases. The individual who buys skirts and blouses regularly, rather than dresses and gowns, leaves a clear enough message about her clothing preferences and what she is most likely to buy in the future, especially, to what kinds of sales she is most likely to respond enthusiastically. The feedback of purchasing history is in itself a form of dialogue, since the customer is telling you what his or her preferences are and what he or she likes about you.

CUSTOMIZING BUSINESS-TO-BUSINESS SALES APPEALS

The problem of customizing appeals and materials for business-to-business marketing is a bit different from that of doing so for business-to-consumer marketing. And yet, philosophically it is the same: Everyone is motivated by self-interest, and business owners have wants and needs that are distinct and different from each other, just as consumers do. Selling to Sam Walton (Wal-Mart stores) is not the same as selling to Sears or Montgomery Ward. A difference you may note immediately is that Wal-Mart stores are not located in, or in the suburbs of, the country's largest cities, but rather are found in rural and small-town areas. (Wal-Mart has recently expanded into Maryland, but in locations 50 or more miles from the metropolises of Baltimore, Maryland, and Washington, D.C.) Wal-Mart buys in huge quantities, sells most items at maximum discounts, and operates at a far lower overhead than any of its competitors. To do business with Wal-Mart (i.e., to sell to the chain) you must have a very sharp pencil. Another important consideration to retailers is marketing support by manufacturers of the goods they sell. You therefore should seek to determine in each case how important that is to the individual customer and what kind of marketing support is most important to that customer: cooperative advertising, free promotional materials, backup advertising, public relations programs, contests, or other.

At the same time, you must remember that the ultimate consumer is your ultimate customer, and you want to include in your marketing databases whatever feedback information you can get from consumers to increase their loyalty to (read "fondness for") your product. Here, too, you want to search out all the possible niche markets, and pass all this data on to your dealers. That is an important kind of marketing support.

You must also include in your database the kinds of products sold by each chain. Although Wal-Mart's direct competitors are Sears, Montgomery Ward, and K-Mart, Wal-Mart does not handle all the lines sold by their competitors. It is not likely that Wal-Mart would be responsive to even the best prices on computers, automobile tires, and lathes.

These are not by any means the only large mass buyers in the country, of course. There are many other store chains in various businesses—clothing, hardware, shoes, restaurants, and other lines. There are large organizations other than retailers: the many corporations and supercorporations, the governments and their agencies, the hospitals and other institutions. There are airlines, hotel chains, manufacturers, processors, importers, banks, and publishers. Each of these is a volume buyer of some things and probably justifies—even requires—highly individualized, customized marketing approaches if you are to succeed in winning their business.

Chapter 13

The Many Uses of Databased Marketing

Prediction: The versatility of databased marketing will ultimately astonish its most enthusiastic supporters. It may prove to be the absolutely indispensable marketing weapon.

THE SWISS ARMY KNIFE OF MARKETING

The more we explore databased marketing, the more we discover potentials the existence of which we had not even suspected. The principal uses and benefits projected by most of the early aficionados were clear and distinct but few in number, consisting of these three major functions or objectives:

- Increase response from the customer database.
- Identify niche markets.
- Clone existing customers from prospects.

Had any of these items been the sole benefit, it would have been enough. It would have been enough to double, triple, and even quadruple response from an existing customer base. It would have been enough to uncover a number of profitable niche markets. It would have been enough to model customers so as to identify the ideal prospects to add to the customer database. But the versatility of databased marketing does not stop here; there is more. Other uses and benefits have been mentioned in earlier pages, but only in passing and not in the detailed discussions they merit.

PRODUCT LINE CHANGE AND DEVELOPMENT

It has often been pointed out that the company still selling what it was selling 5 years ago is on the verge of obsolescence and needs to look to what is happening in its industry if it is to survive. Presumably, then, the company that is still selling what it sold 10 years ago is already moribund or has really expired already, and needs only to discover that fact and then lie down and draw its last breath.

Dinosaurs Are Still with Us

The evidence for these beliefs is not hard to find: Dinosaurs exist in all industries. American automobile manufacturers were rapidly becoming dinosaurs or perhaps already were when the Japanese automakers drenched them with the cold shower of truth: The surviving big three have been busily trying to make appropriate, but belated, changes since. Few video-rental stores try to charge annual membership fees today; competition has driven the practice out, and few patrons would pay such fees. Banks can no longer get away with delaying the clearance of checks long enough to give themselves weeks of interest-free use of money that is not morally theirs to use. (In this case, they were so stubborn about giving up this practice that a resultant public outcry forced Congress to limit this abuse by legislation.) Mom-and-pop stores have been replaced everywhere by convenience stores, patterned frequently on the 7-11 model, as fast-food restaurants are modeled after McDonald's (which is itself changing rapidly in many ways and adding new items continually). Because more and more wives work at full-time jobs today and "TV dinners" have become a subject of derision, the food industries have devised many new kinds of prepackaged meals. At the same time, ironically, many supermarkets today offer foods in bulk—commodities such as breakfast cereals, nuts, flavorings, dried fruit, and condiments—in old-fashioned, help yourself, "cracker barrel" style. More and more, companies are diversifying into other lines, especially when their original line represents a declining or threatened industry, such as cigarette sales. (This diversification into conglomerates has made it increasingly difficult to know what company you are really dealing with today.) The rate of change appears to be increasing steadily. Many new products, even highly successful ones, have short lives, at least in their original forms. The Beta type of videocassette recorder dominated its market for a time, was threatened by a newer model, the VHS type, and was finally vanquished completely by the latter. Transistors attacked the market formerly dominated by electronic tubes and were themselves succeeded by the chips that dominate electronics today. And, although you can easily find vehement arguments to the contrary, the PC is today threatening the future existence of the mainframe computer and the minicomputer. Even mighty IBM has been forced to give ground here.

The Inevitability of Change

In short, change is just as inevitable as the proverbial death and taxes. We cannot predict with any accuracy what the changes will be, but we can predict with certainty that changes will come, almost continuously. What this means to you as a businessperson is that it is hazardous in the extreme to rest on your laurels, to persist in pushing a product line of which the public appears to have grown a bit weary, or to delay too long in making needed changes. There comes a time when change is a must, and those who do not change must perish, as have many companies, some of them rather large and for years highly successful. But when is the time? What does the market want? How will the market react to whatever new products or services you contemplate offering? George Morrow, a pioneering manufacturer of personal computers less than a decade ago, succeeded brilliantly at first with his highly functional and efficient economy model of the then popular "CP/M" (generally represented to be an abbreviation for "Control Program/Microcomputer," although others insist that it really stood for "Control Program/ Monitor") class of personal computer. The IBM "DOS" (Disk Operating System) model soon came along and was wildly successful in ousting the CP/M model, replacing it everywhere in a surprisingly short time. George Morrow was soon out of business, unfortunately, by his own admission a victim of being too slow to change over to DOS-class computers. (By the time he recognized the need to make the change, it was too late.)

The need to change comes about as a result of many possible conditions and circumstances, including these few:

■ Technology and/or other influence has made what you sell relatively inefficient, unattractive, or otherwise obsolescent, and thus it has declined in popularity. Public reaction compels you to change or perish.

■ The markets have long been saturated with what you sell, as a result of growing competition, and your market share has therefore shrunk rather badly.

■ The public is weary generally of the product/service, which was, in fact, a fad (e.g., hula hoops, mood rings, and Pet Rocks).

■ The product/service was never more than a modest success, and you have come to the belief that it is not possible to make more than that of it.

■ New products are coming onto the market, still with little history, but clearly competing with the older products, such as those you handle; you cannot ignore them.

■ You have been offered a new product line related closely to what you now sell; it appears to be attractive in many ways, but it is a completely unknown quantity in terms of probable market acceptance.
■ You have been offered a new product line unrelated to anything you now sell, but it appears to be a reasonable idea for diversification and expansion. You are uncertain about its general marketability and fit to your current market and following of customers.

It is probably never easy to know when a slowdown means something is dated and fading or the market is only in a lull. It is thus difficult to determine whether it is time for a change. Even without the question of time for a change it is always hard to judge whether a contemplated new product or service is likely to succeed, no matter how attractive it may appear to be. You can guess, and you probably have in the past. You can ask friendly competitors, fellow members of your trade association, visiting salesrepresentatives, and friends and relatives what they think, and you probably have. You will probably get little data or helpful evidence of any kind, but you will get all kinds of opinions, many conflicting with each other, and you probably have experienced that too. The result is confusion. In the end, you are back to Square 1. You may as well have settled for your own visceral reactions. But wait: There is one resource you have not turned to—the customer. Who is better qualified to tell you what the market is and is likely to be in the near future?

If loss of market share, whether as a result of greatly increased competition or for other reason, is your problem, changing your lines or adding new ones is only one of the possible changes that may provide a solution. There is also the possibility that more intensive marketing or a different approach to marketing may make the difference and restore your market share to what it was earlier. But, again, there is the question of what changes in marketing to make. Different media? Discount program? Major sales program? Big PR campaign? Again, you have the usual alternatives of where to turn for facts and opinions, and you can anticipate the same results. And, again, there is always the most reliable source of guidance, those who have been buying from you.

Going to "the Horse's Mouth" for Your Information

There certainly is no greater authority for marketing information than the customer, who *is* the market, after all. That is why we test: When we test, we are asking the customer what he or she wants, how he or she reacts to our offers, our promises, our products, and our way of doing business. Unfortunately, we can never do all the testing we would like to do because the cost of doing so is prohibitive. We therefore settle for a small-scale test of a key item or two, with results that are better than rolling out blind, but sometimes not a great deal better.

There is a better way. If you have a marketing database, you have the line of communication you need. If your marketing database has been in existence a while and you have been adding to it steadily, you may already have all the information you need. If what you have is a true marketing database, it has been developed through dialogue with (i.e., feedback from) the customer. The data you have should represent the customer saying to you, "This is what I like and dislike. This is what I want. This is what I will buy. This is what I think of what you sell and how you sell it. This is how I will respond to your offers." That information is the essence of databased marketing. In fact, anticipation of the need to make fact-based estimates of what your customers want and how they are likely to react to changes, should be one of the concerns driving your original database design. The information items in your database will depend in large part on what business you are in—what you sell—of course. Thus you may or may not want to know about your customers' hobbies, preferences in entertainment, chief worries, clothing preferences, and other product- or service-related interests than those linked directly with what you sell. You will in all cases, however, find it useful and even necessary to know about your customers' fears, aspirations, prejudices, families, and purchasing history, as it relates to what you sell. You will certainly want to know about your customers' exposure to the media you use for advertising: Do they read newspapers? (Which sections?) Listen to radio? (What kinds of programs?) Watch TV? (What programs?) Open all mail, even if it is obviously advertising? Take advantage of rebate offers? Usually order free information? Attend trade shows? (What kind?) Go to conventions? (What kind?) Attend hobby shows?

None of this is to suggest that you can rely entirely on what your customers *say.* We all learn, long before we are gray, that what people say is often at great variance with what they really think. Even more to the point, what they do often directly contradicts what they say. So it is unwise to gamble your marketing (and your business future) entirely on what customers say. You must be guided, or at least temper what customers say, by studying what they do.

Thus you must gather some of the data from other sources than the customer records in your marketing database. If you conduct periodic sales analyses—for example, a monthly report on sales, stratified in some ways (by item, by zip code, by type or class of customer)—you get highly specific and reliable information there on customer *behavior.* A slowdown or general decline in sales of a given item or line of items may have special significance, although it may not be conclusive in itself. But it is enough of a clue to send you back to the customer records in your marketing database to see how the data there correlates with "the facts on the ground," with what your customers are actually doing. If you are using a good relational database system for your marketing database, the invoice files, files of sales reports and analyses, and other relevant databases provide those facts about what your customers are actually doing. The data in these other databases are also part of your marketing database by reference: You can import all or any part of their data into your marketing database for direct analysis, such as correlation with other records (i.e., regression analysis), a most important kind of analysis. If sales of index cards have been declining, you may wish to search your database to see which customers have been regular purchasers of index cards in the past, which have slowed down or stopped buying index cards, and whether this information appears to correlate with anything about those customers. Or has everyone slowed down in buying index cards? Has it happened before? Is there some seasonal cause? Is there something else they buy and use in place of index cards? If so, what is it and where do they buy it?

Changes fall generally into two classes, although it is not always easy to distinguish one class from the other: There is the kind of changes we have been discussing here for the most part, changes in your present operations, your product line, your marketing methods, your services, or other elements of your business; and there are also changes by adding new elements to what you sell and do—products, services, and/or marketing programs. The first category of change is evolutionary and primarily the "keeping up" or survival-necessity kind of changes, (i.e., fighting obsolescence and meeting the competition). The second category is expansion marketing, inspired by aggressive development, which often adds new income centers to the business.

HOW THE DATABASE FITS INTO EXPANSION MARKETING

It has been repeated again and again by the most prestigious philosophers of business that no business can stand still: It must grow or it will perish. Growth, however, does not mean swelling—not merely growing larger—but changing as necessary, the subject of these past few pages. Most of what we have been discussing as one area of marketing database use was aimed at accommodating to inevitable change and threatened obsolescence, as it comes about or as you anticipate it.

Reactive and Proactive Marketing

That marketing we have been discussing is defensive marketing, reacting to and fighting threats to business survival. That it is defensive does not make it less important than other marketing: It is critical to continued business success, but it is, nevertheless, primarily reactive marketing. It is your response to what is happening or what you anticipate will be soon happening to your business if you do not take measures. I also touched briefly on adding new products or services, but again in the sense of reacting to offers and apparent opportunities that happen to come your way, as distinct from offers and apparent opportunities that you have deliberately sought out as a hedge against potential business problems, whether imminent or not.

In many and probably most businesses, the early years are devoted to building a firm business base founded on the original concept. In the successful enterprise, with aggressive, proactive marketing, the customer base grows steadily. Eventually, a plateau is reached, in which the customer base is stabilized, growth is slow at best, and the conduct of the business has become more or less a fixed routine. This is the stage at which the marketing tends to become reactive and defensive in many cases: The successful entrepreneur has built a valuable asset and, anxious to preserve it, may grow much more conservative in marketing. In other cases, however, having reached this stage of stability, the aggressive entrepreneur casts about for opportunities to expand.

The Two Routes to Expansion

There are two possible routes for expansion, other than that of the normal slow and steady growth of the successful business: One is through a great expansion in marketing to gain greatly increased sales of whatever it is that you sell. The other is in a great expansion in marketing by adding products or services—diversifying and enlarging the line you sell to create new and added income producers. Both call for aggressive, proactive marketing. Instead of reacting to chance opportunities for increased sales or adding new products and services, you are in active pursuit of such opportunities. More than one entrepreneur has created a free newsletter to use as a marketing tool, for example, and found it so popular that he or she was able to initiate subscription fees for it and create an additional center of substantial income thereby. Consultants lecture free of charge as a marketing device and then discover that they can command respectable fees for lecturing. And soon they also learn that they can write books and make audiotapes that their audiences will buy in "back of the room sales," providing still another source of income. (In many cases, the newer activities overshadow the original business, which then shrivels and is replaced by the newer venture.)

In all cases you can use your marketing database to test your customers' probable reactions to specific, predetermined changes in methods of marketing and/or new products and services. Often, the most effective way to do this is to offer several alternatives, trying to gauge which evokes the most favorable reaction.

There are many ways you may use your marketing database to help with this task. However, because it involves a relatively large universe of possibilities, it is somewhat difficult to do. Here are just a few ideas, to illustrate the wide range of possibilities:

- Choose highly selective samples for testing each new idea.
- Test your regular products/services via new and different media or offers to closely matched customers.
- Test your regular products/services via a single new medium on sets of customers carefully chosen for their diversity.
- Test several products on a sample of your most responsive customers.

The purchasing history of your customers is probably the most valuable input you can get from your marketing database, as it was in the applications discussed earlier in this chapter. The behavior of your customers in the past is a good indicator of their probable behavior in the future, not surprisingly. The customer who has habitually been among the first to buy every new home electronics gadget (as a brother-in-law of mine has been) is certainly a good prospect for the most recent one on the market. The woman who tries virtually every new style is certainly someone who you will want to invite to see the newest fashions. The inveterate TV watcher is an argument for advertising on TV, if you have enough of those addicted TV watchers in your database.

The Marketing Database as a Test Bed

Notice that in the various cases just discussed, testing is an important use of the marketing database. Testing is classical in direct mail, a *sine qua non* of the industry, but it has been done traditionally on list samples selected largely by educated guesses, and for characteristics chosen by the same method of introspective analysis of what appears to be probability. That is, to mail a package to 100,000 prospects you might decide to test 5 percent of a list you judge to be the right one for your purposes. You would choose names, perhaps 5,000 or 10,000, taken at random from that list. You might, that is, mail the test package to every 20th name on the list. You might decide to test the price. You would then mail out two or three test packages of names chosen from the list, testing two or three different prices. (It doesn't make a great deal of sense to test only one price.) You could also test your copy, the list itself (i.e., to judge its appropriateness to whatever you are selling), the package, or any of several different factors. Testing is generally done on two or more samples of whatever you are testing to get comparative results. But you would, of course, be limited in how many different tests you could run, as a practical matter.

The marketing database is a great aid in testing, as long as you are mailing only to your own customer lists. Used for that, you should presumably have no need to test the list, since they are your own customers, and you have direct knowledge of what they buy. What you test when mailing to your own database are the other factors—price, copy, offer, and so on. You also get an additional payoff when you test your own database: You gather new and additional information that you can add to your marketing database, strengthening it further.

When you are using rented lists for a campaign or part of a campaign, probably by far the more typical situation, you are limited in what you know about the list, since it is not part of your marketing database. All you know about it is whatever the list broker furnished in the way of information, principally demographic data, geographic data, and possibly some psychographic data. However, you may be able to make good use of your own marketing database to help you in your campaign nevertheless. If you do some preliminary testing with your own marketing database, you can probably draw an excellent and well-detailed profile of those of your customers who responded most favorably to your offers. You can then use that profile as a prescription for your list broker to fill to the best of his or her ability. If nothing else, the marketing database will give you a profile of the chief characteristics you want in a rented or compiled list.

USING THE DATABASE IN MODELING CUSTOMERS

The notion of cloning your customers is one of the most basic ideas of databased marketing and has been touched on several times already in these pages. That has been the general case, assuming that your customers are a relatively homogeneous group, sharing major characteristics and purchasing histories. It is a fair enough assumption if you have a fairly well-specialized business, such as one that sells home electronics products, groceries, or investment services. However, if your business has a highly diversified product line, such as office and warehouse supplies ranging from paper clips to computers, furniture, and fixtures, you are likely to have a heterogeneous assortment of customers, with a correspondingly heterogeneous assortment of marketing databases.

Not every marketer appears to recognize this marketing truth, but Jack Miller, president and founder of Quill Corporation, is an alert and knowledgeable marketer, who speaks and writes authoritatively on the subject. It is thus not surprising that among the many catalogs his company sends out are those that are general but present mostly everyday, consumable office and warehouse supplies, those that focus on office furniture, and those that focus on computers and related equipment. Presumably, the company maintains at least three separate marketing databases, as indicated by those catalogs, although I appear to be on all three, since I get all the catalogs. My purchasing history with Quill must suggest that I am a likely prospect for all those classes of items, and Quill is meticulous in sending me those catalogs regularly.

How to Sort and Classify Your Customers

One of the boons of databased marketing is that it offers the means for sorting and classifying your customers in ways that you can use in your marketing. The question arises of kinds of classifications into which to sort your customers—*main* characteristic, that is, aside from being homeowners, apartment dwellers, blue-collar workers, professionals, and other such items that flesh out the individual profiles. Here are just a few of the possible yardsticks for measuring and classifying customers by the principal characteristic that distinguishes them:

- The most obvious and probably most popular way to identify the chief distinguishing feature of your customers is by their purchases, as mentioned earlier: the new-gadget buyer, the style-conscious clothing buyer, the computer buyer, and so on.
- Another possible way is by how much a customer spends. There are 5-dollar customers, 20-dollar customers, and 100-dollar customers, or their analogues on a larger scale.
- Related to the preceding, there are "bargain-basement" customers. (On the other hand, they may be identified as being "upscale" customers.)
- Not unrelated to that is the characteristic of many individuals as being especially responsive to sales of all kinds, regardless of whether they are otherwise bargain-basement or upscale customers.
- Another variant of the customer who is susceptible to sales of all kinds is the discount customer, who finds the idea of a discount especially appealing.
- There is also the bargainer, that customer who truly believes that everything is negotiable and that he or she should never pay "the asking price." Even in mail order you may encounter such types.
- Some customers may be characterized as incurable "shoppers," always looking and taking up the time of the sales clerks but rarely—if ever—buying anything.
- Some customers are identified as "difficult" or chronic complainers. (They may also be "shoppers.")
- Some, especially in department-store sales, are returners: They constantly return most of the things they buy.)

- Another way, covered earlier, is by the customer's chief interests, as they help to indicate what the customer is likely to buy and/or what advertising and promotion is likely to be most persuasive.

Obviously, the appropriateness of these terms will vary quite widely, according to the business, and will not fit at all in many cases. There are also many cases not covered by any of these examples. Further, you want to know which are the best media and methods for appealing to various customers: Which are TV watchers, radio listeners, and readers of periodicals? What kinds of programs and/or reading material are most appealing? What, if any, are the special interests of any of your customers? You thus must continually add to the data in your database and review it continuously to update it.

A DATABASE IS NOT STATIC

A marketing database is never complete. It never has all the data, and especially it never has all data up to date. Family information changes, for example, as members of the family are born, grow up, graduate, are appointed to positions, change jobs, get engaged and married, and otherwise change their circumstances.

Obviously, interests change along with this. People become interested in collecting stamps, become golf enthusiasts, start investment programs, and otherwise develop new and different interests.

There are many ways to keep up with this information. I subscribe to and read the monthly periodical *Publisher's Weekly,* which is a trade journal of the book trade. I watch for trends and for changes in personnel, and I often send letters of congratulation to individuals promoted to new positions in their companies. Despite the basic idea of dialogue with customers and resulting feedback as input to your databases (as, for example, my automobile dealer does with a follow-up telephone call to me after every servicing of my automobile), you must also draw on all other available sources. Nor should you ever take customer approval for granted: The typical customer may have been satisfied with every purchase he or she made over many years and yet be unforgiving the first time he or she is not satisfied with a purchase. Nor can you count on that customer registering a complaint with you on that occasion. He or she may say nothing, but never patronize you again.

THE MARKETING DATABASE AS A MARKETING BAROMETER

Just as the data in your database may change, so may the niche markets defined by that data. The purchasing pattern of those in your database may indicate a response to something new on the market and reflect something of interest in that respect. For example, suppose a new board game suddenly becomes "all the rage," in the same way as the Monopoly, Scrabble, or Trivia games of the past. The reactions of your customers, as revealed by purchasing records, indicate the interest of all who respond by buying copies of that new game. All who have done so are prospects for a sudden niche market of those who buy such games. A new success inspires imitators, and those who bought the original are suddenly a promising niche market for other games of that type. Usually, such a niche is temporary because it is inspired by a sudden fad; it could be for a short or long term, but it is a niche market, nevertheless, for as long as it lasts. In fact, all markets, main ones, segments, and niches, change over time and must never be taken for granted. That reflects one of the many uses of the marketing database: It defines markets, and used properly—maintained, regularly updated, and constantly mined for new and useful marketing information—it predicts market motions and changes. In many ways, that is its most important use.

USING MARKETING DATABASES FOR MARKETING INTELLIGENCE

Marketing success depends heavily on marketing intelligence: what customers think of your products and services; how they regard and react to your advertising and promotions; what your competitors are up to; and, perhaps most important, what your customers think of your competitors and of competitive products, services, advertising, and promotion, among other things. And you want this information on both an absolute scale and on the comparative scale of you and yours versus your competitors and theirs: It is important to know in as much detail as possible what drew your customers to you. Your customers may have chosen you over your competitors for any of several reasons or even for a combination of items.

Why Is He or She Your Customer?

Your customer may have come to you because he or she:

- Simply did not know of your competitors' existence and/or their similar products and services, perhaps even thought you and what you sell were unique.
- Found you and your product or service superior in only one respect, but a respect that was important to him or her.

- Did not perceive any significant difference between you and your competitors but chose you by pure chance.
- Just found it more convenient to do business with you.
- Especially disliked something about your competitors and found you the best of several distasteful choices.
- Otherwise does not really know why or how he or she came to choose you.

This is obviously valuable information as input to your marketing planning of strategies and promotions. That the marketing database is a good key to gathering much of this information should come as no surprise. It is easy enough to read competitive advertising, and "shop" competitive businesses, and read the trade journals of your industry to learn their prices, their merchandising methods, their advertising and promotional methods, and other overt marketing operations. From the trade journals you may even get insights into the future plans of your competitors. What you cannot get in this manner in any depth or span is the reaction of the public to competitors vis-à-vis their reactions to your own offerings and promotions. In this arena, it is again the marketing database that offers the greatest aid. To structure the data items you wish to collect requires a bit of thought and planning.

The Kinds of Information Items You Need

First, you must decide just what information you want. Of course, you know that basically you need to get information on how, in the customer's mind (you are, remember, seeking *opinions,* primarily), your product or service is judged by the customer on both an absolute scale and by comparison with that of each of your leading competitor's product or service for the following:

- Function.
- Quality.
- Price.
- Packaging.
- General satisfaction with product or service.

You will also want to compare some other elements of your business with your competitors' analogous efforts:

- The appeal and effectiveness of your marketing—advertising and promotion.

- The handling of customers and fulfillment of orders.
- The adjustment of complaints and number of complaints.

These are all rather general. More specifically, you will want to develop feedback to provide more detailed information about each of these areas, such as the following few examples suggest:

- *Function.* Does the product/service do what it is supposed to do? Is it easy to make use of? Does it require time to learn? Does it have adequate instructions?
- *Quality.* If a device of some sort, is it sturdy? Made of durable materials? Etc. (Remember that answers will be subjective, reflecting *opinions.*)
- *Price.* Does customer find your price high? Low? Competitive?
- *Packaging.* Attractive? Cheap? Upscale? Good? Poor?
- *General Satisfaction with Product or Service.* Overall impression: Pleasant? Worth the price? An unusually good buy? Marginal?
- *The Appeal and Effectiveness of Your Marketing (Advertising and Promotion).* Is advertising in good taste? Does it describe the product/service accurately? Make no obviously extravagant promises? Make the guarantee clear? Explain how to order?
- *The Handling of Customers and Fulfillment of Orders.* Was service courteous and prompt?
- *The Adjustment of Complaints and Number of Complaints.*

A Few Information-Gathering Media

There are many different possible mechanisms you can use to gather this data. Here are a few suggestions that may or may not be appropriate to your business operations but will convey the general idea of some ways to get dialogues with your customers started:

- A "bonus" gift following purchase of the item, along with a brief questionnaire and a postage-paid response envelope. A message with the gift to the effect, "We appreciate your patronage and want to express it with the enclosed bottle of eau de cologne [or whatever gift is enclosed]. In the interest of serving you even better in the future, we are enclosing a brief questionnaire and invite you to use it to tell us what you think and offer any suggestions for improvement."
- A contest with a prize for the best essay, letter, advertisement, or other creative effort commenting on your product, service, advertising, or other item. To qualify, the contestant must fill out a short questionnaire and submit it with his or her contest entry.

- A telephone follow-up to each customer after purchase, asking a few questions and inviting any suggestions and/or comments the customer may wish to offer.
- A free training session in something appropriate (e.g., if you sell cosmetics, you can give a free makeover lesson to every customer; if you sell computers, a lesson related to computers). You can run these promotions over and over, interviewing the attendees.

Gauging Your Promotions' Effectiveness

Even though some of this discussion already touched on customers' impressions of and reactions to your advertising and promotion in general, they sought only general reactions of your customers and would not of themselves be very helpful in gauging the actual effectiveness of your promotions in creating customers. (We will consider here the creation of customers to be at least as important as making sales per se and thus to be an equally important objective of your marketing promotions.) Learning that some number of your customers thought your advertising or other promotion was "cute," "clever," or even "convincing" does not do the job you want done. You want to know how well each of your promotions succeeded in attracting both sales and new customers. Thus you want to use your marketing database as a medium for gathering and recording data to that effect in connection with all promotions, such as newsletters, contests, direct mail campaigns, radio and TV commercials, signs, print advertising, press releases and news stories, or other activities. You want to gather actual figures, as accurately as you can, on each of the following events that happened as a direct result of the promotion:

1. Existing customers who were induced to buy what you promoted.
2. New customers gained.
3. Number of individual sales made.

You might also wish to stratify these as the average size of sale made to (a) existing customers and (b) new customers. That would be highly useful information too.

Presumably, Item 3 ought to equal Items 1 and 2 added together, but that might not be so, since some customers may have made more than one purchase, while others may have not bought the item advertised but bought something else. However, if you can get reasonably reliable figures accounting for the three items listed, and especially if you can gather those on each advertising or promotional campaign, you will be able to compare advertising and other promotional methods to judge which are worth using again and which are not worth the effort.

If yours is a mail order business, it is not too difficult to key each campaign to identify all orders as to their origin or inspiration. For over-the-counter and telephone sales, it is a little more difficult to key the orders, but it can be done by assigning some requirement, such as a distinctive and different name, to the item for each promotion or including an admonition to the customer that he or she must ask for "special lot 23GH" to get the special discount or bonus gift. These measures may not produce precise numbers of sales and customers, but they will give you a good idea of the numbers.

Research

Postevent evaluations, such as we have been discussing, are a form of general research, and are useful guides for future marketing. It is possible, however, to use the marketing database for more sharply focused research. One method for doing this is to invite comments, complaints, and suggestions. A line in the data-gathering instrument (e.g., the questionnaire or interview guide discussed earlier) can be designed to evoke specific feedback from customers. Here are just a few suggestions to convey the general idea of items for such feedback:

- What is your pet peeve about our commercials? About others' commercials?
- How would you package _____ (name of product)?
- What is your favorite (type of product, service, other)?
- What does the slogan "_____" suggest to you?
- What are the ways in which you use our product?

Determining Customer LTV

It is difficult and perhaps even impossible to make accurate estimates of the lifetime value, or LTV, of any customer individually. It is possible, however, as the data accumulates in your marketing database, to establish average LTV with reasonable accuracy, once you have enough accumulated data to develop figures for frequency and size of purchases made by each customer. These will vary widely, of course, and they will need to be correlated with other factors, such as demographic and psychographic ones. Such stratification in estimating LTV values is highly desirable: The immediate benefits are an appreciation of how much is reasonable as an "ACO" or average cost per order, for any given niche, and a valuable measure by which to evaluate the probable worth of any new prospect, for which you might utilize an "ACP" or average cost per customer figure.

Acquiring customers is, of course, expensive, as noted a number of times already. Using some figure of merit, such as estimated LTV, to evaluate or set limits on prospecting costs is appropriate. Having gathered all the data to do the modeling of prospects with appropriate estimated LTV, however, means a more selective and more efficient prospecting process.

Your Marketing Database and Serendipity

Serendipity is Dame Fortune, making happy discoveries by accident, finding something you didn't know you were looking for. It's discovering how to make soap that floats (Ivory soap) by forgetting to turn the crutchers off when going to lunch. It's discovering vulcanizing of rubber (Charles Goodyear) by the accident of dropping sulfur into the molten mix. It's discovering how to measure volume of an irregularly shaped object by displacement of water (Archimedes). Serendipity, however, is more than the accidental happening: It is also *discovery.* For the accident to represent that discovery, serendipity requires a mind prepared to recognize the significance and usefulness of what has happened.

There is no doubt that the collection of data and the building of marketing databases offer ample opportunities for serendipity. There is also no doubt that your mind must be prepared in advance—must be always alert to make discoveries by recognizing significant events. When dealing with large numbers of items, correlations among variables are made regularly with sophisticated mathematical models of regression analysis. However, it is useful to train yourself to detect correlations by simple observation. If you were to observe a sharp peak of sales in a certain zip code, for example, you should immediately suspect that there is something worth investigating here: What is it about that area that is different and affects your sales so sharply? What are other common characteristics of the customers in that area? How have sales gone with customers in other zip codes, who share some characteristics of that first group? Perhaps you are on the verge of a valuable serendipitous discovery, but it won't happen if you do not take appropriate follow-up action. On the other hand, such fortuitous discoveries are almost inevitable if you do work at maximizing the probability of their occurrence.

Making yourself highly susceptible to serendipitous discovery is largely a matter of conditioning your subconscious mind. Professional freelance writers do this. The layperson often asks a writer, "How do you get your ideas?" or "Where do your ideas come from?" Most writers probably do not know, and many respond, predictably enough, "My head. They simply *come* to me."

So training yourself is a form of self-hypnosis, often referred to as "autosuggestion." The professional hypnotist gets into direct touch with a subject's subconscious by persuading the subject to relax his or her conscious mind as completely as possible, thereby opening a route to the subconscious. A slower, alternative route is repeated conscious suggestion. The writer consciously seeks ideas everywhere for a long time. Eventually, his or her subconscious takes over the task, and ideas come along, suggested by the subconscious, without the individual knowing why he or she suddenly thought of a useful idea.

You can condition your own subconscious in a similar manner by consciously studying your data in quest of promising correlations and other indicators. In time, your subconscious will come to your aid. (In fact, is serendipity really *accidental* discovery?)

A FEW MISCELLANEOUS USES OF MARKETING DATABASES

I have already noted several times the need to build your own marketing databases because by their nature they must be tailored to your own specific needs and conditions. Thus they cannot be rented, at least not at present.

Database Rental Possibilities

That does not mean that marketing databases will never be available to be rented or sold. Databased marketing is still in infancy, and the technology is still evolving slowly. Eventually, marketing databases are almost certain to become highly developed (i.e., highly specialized and amenable to precise definition and description). At that point, they may be adequately fitted to others' needs and thus will be rented by their owners to others with compatible situations.

Even that potential development into a highly definitive state compatible with prospective renters' needs is by no means the only possible route to future rental of marketing databases: It is possible that in the near future renters will find it sensible to rent established marketing databases that are reasonably close to their needs and need refinement to make them entirely compatible, that is, perhaps it will be practicable to rent generic or shell marketing databases as seeds to be developed into full databases. In that latter case, you could get a head start on the work and cost of developing your marketing databases.

Income from Your Marketing Databases

As you build your marketing databases, you may wish to consider renting them to other users who are not directly competitive. You may thus recover some or all of the costs of developing your databases, which represented a probably sizable investment, and you may even progress to the point of earning regular income from such rentals. And there is still one other possibility, that of swapping databases.

Database Swapping Possibilities

Many mailers trade mailing lists with each other. I built my own list of about 5,000 names into about 30,000 names by making trades with others whose lists were suitable for my needs and whose offerings were not directly competitive with my own.

Something of this sort is likely to happen with marketing databases. Once you have built up some marketing databases to a point where they are "swappable," you can cast about for others whose databases are compatible with your own and pursue exchanging databases. Nor is the speeding up of your building a collection of marketing databases the only possible benefit. There is at least one more, contributing to the serendipity potential.

Contribution to Serendipity

Acquiring additional marketing databases through swapping does not mean that you will not continue to develop your own and your newly acquired marketing databases. You will want to scrutinize the new databases carefully to see how they match your own for formats, types of data, and other points of comparison. You may get ideas from the new databases, leading you to improvements of those you have built up. You may wish to modify the new ones to match your own, but the trades should greatly accelerate the development of a complete complement of marketing databases in your own marketing database library. In general, you will have greatly increased the overall bulk of data and, presumably, raised the probability that you will have serendipitous experiences.

Chapter 14

Relationship Marketing

Even those of us who long ago learned the lesson of overhead, the lesson of credit, and the lesson of other business hazards, have often been slow to learn the lesson of customer relationships. Failure to learn it has been fatal to many businesses.

RELATIONSHIPS AND INFORMATION

More and more, as you explore and discuss databased marketing, you will encounter that companion term *relationship marketing*. It refers to an idea at the very heart of databased marketing: An indispensable element of databased marketing, pointed out again and again in these pages, is the gathering of information directly from the customer, as well as from other sources. Relationship marketing is not pursued expressly for the purpose of producing feedback from customers, but primarily because it is rewarding in and of itself in creating the right atmosphere for successful marketing. However, it certainly does encourage the development of dialogue between you and your customers as one of its benefits. That may lead some to believe that relationship marketing is almost synonymous with databased marketing, or that it is closely linked in some manner. It would be a mistaken idea: Relationship marketing is not an element or a tactic of databased marketing development, but is an entire marketing philosophy in itself. It shares much of its rationale and strategic principles with databased marketing, and it supports databased marketing, as well. But there is much more to the idea than that.

THE ANTECEDENTS OF TODAY'S MARKETING PROBLEMS

I made the point earlier that during the 1930s, the years of the Great Depression, the humblest customer was treated as visiting royalty: His or her patronage was that highly valued. During World War II, there was relatively little consumer goods, compared with its normal abundance, and much of what was available was severely rationed. The average merchant could sell readily whatever he or she was able to buy and keep in stock. Many customers worked hard at being nice to merchants in the hope that they would develop friendships and get favored treatment—preference—for whatever scarce goods were available. The merchants' attitudes were not unaffected by this; many merchants soon learned to take customers for granted and condescend to them. By the time the war was over several years later, new habits had been formed.

Thus, in the boom years following World War II, marketers tended to treat customers with a haughty aloofness that was almost contempt. In fact, for a time, when most of those in military service had not yet returned home and there was difficulty in hiring anyone for any kind of a job, a popular joke had merchants posting signs that said, "Be kind to our hired help: Customers we can get!" It was hardly an exaggeration. It was relationship building of the wrong kind.

Much of that attitude lingers yet, passively or by implication, greatly encouraged by the modern conditions of chain stores, supercorporations, prepackaged goods, self-service stores, and other conditions and practices that have seriously depersonalized commercial trade. The customer today rarely meets a salesperson in authority—rarely meets a salesperson at all, in many business establishments—and is often given less courtesy and consideration than a stray dog; if he or she has a complaint, the response is little more than a shrug. The relationship between seller and buyer is not much warmer than between vending machine and buyer.

THE GROWTH OF MASS MARKETING

Management's marketing philosophy has tended increasingly to focus on mass marketing, not only in direct marketing, which was based almost entirely on the mass-market idea, but in all marketing. The proliferation of chain stores and franchises has been one example and one of the causes. The impetus in business has been toward bigness: big stores, big malls, big shopping centers, big chains. Today, it is increasingly difficult to see much difference between one city and another: You can find a MacDonald's, a Red Lobster, a K-Mart, a Holiday Inn, a Sears, and most of their counterparts in just about every American city that is more than a wide spot in the road, nor is this confined to American cities: It is almost as true everywhere in the world today. Perhaps it is thus not surprising that the customer relations are as standardized as are the hamburgers and prepackaged merchandise sealed in almost-impossible-to-open plastic capsules. You want a half-dozen 2-inch wood screws? Sorry: They come only in packs of 24. No, we don't carry them loose. Even the mushrooms, potatoes, and celery in the produce department are prepackaged today.

Relationship marketing must reverse this trend, at least to the extent that it restores customers to their thrones, to establish a more suitable *relationship*. Relationship marketing should result in seller and buyer getting to *like* each other again, as we once did. Sellers must value customers, and customers must come to believe that sellers do respect and care about their customers enough to make sincere efforts to serve them well and be honorable in their dealings. Few customers believe that today. Even the most ingenuous customers have an almost inherent mistrust of bigness, especially when it is manifested by almost totally impersonal treatment.

Compare, for example, the problem of trying to find a clerk in a large store where everything is self-service with that of at least one chain, Wal-Mart. There, it has been my own experience in two of their stores (Hendersonville, North Carolina, and Prince Frederick, Maryland), wandering about for a few minutes with obvious uncertainty is almost certain to bring forth a store employee who offers to help you find what you are looking for. The fact that Wal-Mart operates at the lowest overhead rate in the industry and sells merchandise at greater discounts than do most retailers has not prevented the management from remembering that the customer is the entire reason for their being. The message is beginning to penetrate, but slowly, as we awaken to the cold light of a world in which consumer goods are superabundant again, some prices have actually retreated a bit, and millions of new businesses and outlets have been created, giving customers the widest ever range of choices. As far as business and marketing are concerned, we are probably entering or about to enter into a new and different world from that of the past 50 years.

ESTABLISHING RELATIONSHIPS

An obvious key ingredient of relationship marketing is the establishment of relationships. If you do not have relationships with your customers to begin with, you can hardly create an effective relationship marketing program for your business. But wait a minute: Relationships between you and your customer do exist. Are they the right relationships, however, the relationships you need? Unfortunately, they may not be; in far too many cases today, they are not. There is the mutual distrust, for one thing. You have sternly worded warnings posted prominently that Big Brother is watching (witness the closed-circuit-TV cameras patrolling the aisles from their lofty positions) and that you will diligently prosecute shoplifters. There are alarm-warning decals on doors and windows, and uniformed security guards plainly in evidence. There are signs posted about stiff penalties imposed for checks that bounce, and requirements for two "major credit cards." (It is not clear how 2 or 22 major credit cards raises the probability of a personal check being a good one.) The customer, on the other hand, is sure that any large company is coldly impersonal and is not to be trusted. Those suspicions encourage the customer to wonder how good your guarantees really are, to note the tart tongues of many of your employees, to be enraged because you would rather have long lines at checkout stations than open those that are idle and unmanned, and to become unhappily aware that all too often "self-service" really means no service. These are hardly cordial or even friendly relationships, and certainly do not benefit you as a marketer trying to please your customers. The objectives of programs to develop relationship marketing, then, are not directed toward the establishment of *any* relationships with customers, but only the kind that enhance the achievement of marketing objectives. The customer relationship program overall ought to include at least these objectives:

- Instill customer confidence and trust in you and your business organization, and thus in what you promise and what you sell.
- Develop in the customer a loyalty to you as a supplier of useful and valued products or services.
- Encourage the customer to communicate to you his or her ideas, desires, suggestions, and comments.
- Encourage in the customer a sense of identify with your business, a sense of belonging.

A FEW FIRST STEPS

The first steps will depend in part on the type of business you operate. That determines to a large degree the normal interface between you and your customer: where and how you meet to transact business. If you are in a typical retail merchandising business, you meet customers when they enter your store, whether in quest of a specific item or to look about generally and just "shop." When I go into a store where the arrangement is such that I am forced to traverse a long aisle, past shelf after shelf of merchandise and signs, I am already unhappy with the store and its owners: I deeply resent being herded down an aisle like a steer on its way to be slaughtered, for that is what such an arrangement reminds me of. It may very well terminate my interest in that store immediately and permanently. But even lacking that affront to my dignity, the store with an immediate image of a great fortune spent on fixtures and furnishings and little or nothing on customer caresses and consideration (i.e,, an obviously costly indifference) does not instantly become dear to me, either. Perhaps, the plush surrounding is intended to awe and impress the customer; if so, it fails badly in my case. I see only self-aggrandizement at my expense. Worse, I see indifference. I once shopped at a supermarket at least once and often twice a week for some 10 years. Each time, the same manager was called to approve the check I offered the cashier at the checkout counter. But not once in all those 10 years did that manager look at me, smile, and say, "How are you today, Mr. Holtz?" Why did I continue to shop there? I don't know, but I haven't shopped there in the many years since, and I have never forgotten the indifference of that store and its manager.

Admittedly, it is difficult in today's business environment of bigness to reestablish the personal touch of yesterday's individually owned neighborhood store. There is a wine and cheese shop in a nearby shopping center where the proprietor was always in evidence and was most accommodating. Whether I had need to buy cases of wine for a social occasion or just a couple of bottles for my personal use, I could count on Norman to guide me. When I needed a check cashed without formality, Norman always accommodated me immediately. He couldn't meet the discounted prices of the chains, but nevertheless, I always shopped at his establishment. His cheerful greeting, asking after my family, and his recommendations on best buys of the week were my reward for shopping there. But Norman's business grew, and with it, Norman spent less and less time in the store, until I rarely saw him and began to take my business elsewhere. What could Norman have done about it? He could have hired someone as a manager or assistant manager who knew something more than vintages and cheeses; he could have hired someone who knew how to establish relationships with regular customers and make regular customers out of others.

The first step, regardless of the kind of business you are in, is to somehow greet the customer properly. Even the smallest restaurants today have a host or hostess to greet patrons in the peak lunch and dinner hours (although they don't always do the job well or are well suited to the job). In my opinion, The Prime Rib is *the* restaurant in Washington, D.C. (although I am sure that others have their own nominees for that title). It is one of the few left where a tie and jacket are mandatory, and the restaurant actually maintains ties and jackets to lend patrons who arrive without the required apparel. (So many restaurants today, even expensive ones, have no real dress code, other than to require shoes and shirt.) The Maitre d' is, of course, quite correct, the furnishings are quietly tasteful, and the waiters are prompt and courteous—usually. It is a *class* establishment, and the ambience is much of the reward of dining there: It makes a patron feel privileged to have been admitted and catered to in those surroundings.

The principle does not change with other kinds of businesses. The high-pressure methods of direct mail obviously do work with some prospects, but they can easily backfire. I am personally put off by those sales letters that are ultrabusy with boldly interlined and marginal comments in blue and red inks, and those begging notes complaining of high costs and suggesting, not too tactfully, that if I don't start buying something I will be dropped from the mailing list. Even the most unsophisticated customers today recognize hype and are amused by it, at best, and offended by it quite often. Efforts to overpower and/or manipulate customers by such brash methods certainly make no new friendships, and a sense of friendship is one goal of relationship marketing: It is possible to make a friend of many, perhaps most, of your customers.

METHODS FOR BUILDING RELATIONSHIPS

It takes something more than your good will to begin to establish friendly relationships with customers, especially in these days when you do business in such ways that you rarely meet most of your customers face to face. No customer can divine your good will, your sincerity, or your honesty by some osmotic transference; you must have specific programs to bring the desired results about. Fortunately, there are many possible programs. There are enough to enable you to select at least one or two most suitable for your own business and need. But first let us have a closer look at what you want to bring about: Elaborating on the list of objectives offered earlier should help to clarify the nature and rationale of the programs we will discuss here to the degree that you will probably be able to infer additional programs to implement the principles.

- Everybody wants to "belong." People gravitate to association with others for some reason, probably the inherent insecurity most of us have and try earnestly to suppress. Belonging makes us feel a bit less alone in a hostile and cruel world. War veterans join one or more veterans' organization. Computer owners join computer clubs. Professionals join professional societies It is not by chance that a mail order genius found it possible to greatly step up the success of selling books by mail if he invited customers to join what he called a "book club," rather than merely subscribing to a book-purchasing program; he simply recognized the appeal of "belonging."
- Everyone wants to be recognized. We all have a basic need to be appreciated by others. Singling out someone for special recognition of any kind creates a warm feeling and a bond. That is the idea behind awards of various kinds, sometimes even with special awards dinners. But there are many ways of granting special recognition to customers:
- One special kind of recognition, appropriate here, is seeking another's opinion. To be asked for his or her judgment, to be assured that his or her opinion is valued, is recognition of a high order. It

makes the other feel obligated to you, especially if you act on that opinion. How could a customer not support any action you take based on his or her opinion?

- Accepting the judgment of another and acting on that judgment also help generate a sense of "being in this together," another desirable psychological effect. That, too, is especially relevant to these discussions of customer relationships.
- Listening to a customer's unsolicited complaints or suggestions with obvious serious consideration is still another kind of recognition that has a salutary effect on relationships with that customer.
- The mere fact of knowledge of the customer's personal interests and concerns, much less actually doing something about it (e.g., congratulations on a son's or daughter's graduation) is yet another effective bonding activity.

These approaches can be made through many organized programs, such as those described in the following pages. The emphasis here is on "organized." To be effective, any program undertaken must be adopted as a serious, long-term commitment, with absolutely clear and unambiguous objectives. Half-hearted attempts and short-lived programs often do more harm than good, and must be avoided. You must recognize that change will not come about overnight. Most programs take time to produce results, and they must be given enough time to do so.

EMPLOYEE TRAINING PROGRAMS

Employee training in the subjects important to relationship marketing is an important element in any program to establish and maintain suitable customer relationships. You can establish an in-house training program or send employees to training seminars. Many such programs are offered by firms specializing in such training. However, you can undertake many other programs toward the same end, such as the following ones.

NEWSLETTERS

Newsletters come first here because they are one of the most effective means for building ongoing communications relationships, and because they are effective vehicles for pursuing a surprisingly large number of the objectives we have postulated. You will see that as we progress. A most apparent and immediate advantage is this: You can reach your customers on a regular basis with whatever messages you want to send and whatever special offers and announcements you want to make.

Most customers, even those who customarily discard all advertising flyers and brochures as "junk mail," will read a well-designed newsletter that doesn't look like an advertising piece. The "breakthrough" rate is thus vastly enhanced when you use a newsletter to reach your customers and prospects. At the same time, the N/L (trade jargon for "newsletter") is an excellent medium for encouraging feedback from customers: Many who would never address a personal letter to you will send a "letter to the editor." Many, in fact, are especially attracted to the idea because they hope to see their letter published. (It's a form of recognition and, to many people, an achievement to have any of their very own words published.)

A newsletter is an excellent marketing tool, and a great many individuals and organizations publish free newsletters expressly because it is an excellent medium for marketing: It builds relationships, as subscribers become familiar with it and look forward to receiving it regularly. It is, in fact, so valuable a medium in this respect that many newsletter publishers for whom publishing is itself a business are willing to publish the letters at a loss (i.e., at net cost each month). They are newsletter publishers who have something else to sell—books, seminars, consulting services, and other things. Their profits come out of those ancillary sales, and they charge a nominal subscription fee primarily to give their newsletters a greater perceived value than a free newsletter commands.

Despite this, your primary purpose in publishing a newsletter should be to exploit to the fullest the innate relationship-building capabilities arising out of a good newsletter, rather than using it as a direct medium for making sales. Keep your eye fixed on that primary objective, and do not allow yourself to be distracted by the promise of early sales that are a diversion from your goal. Do careful planning before launching the new vehicle; it is far better to go slowly at first and avoid the typical mistakes.

Among the matters you must address and about which you must make decisions are these:

Publishing schedule (frequency of publishing)	Sources
	Policy
Size	Functions
Format and other design factors	Staff
Title	Production
Content	

Publishing Schedule

Probably the vast majority of newsletters are published every month, although there are newsletters published on a daily, weekly, bimonthly, quarterly, semiannual, and even other schedules. Many launch a newsletter on a quarterly basis, which means only 4, rather than 12, writing, production, distribution, and cost burdens to meet and overcome each year. Their theory is that if it goes well, they can easily speed up the schedule to a more frequent one.

That is true enough, but it is not a good answer for everyone. For someone launching a newsletter for direct profit, such a plan makes sense. It is also probably a sensible approach for someone who plans to use the newsletter primarily as a prospecting medium, searching for new clients. For someone who wants to establish and maintain a dialogue with customers, however, it is too infrequent; the monthly schedule is almost surely the right one here.

Size

There are newsletters of 1 or 2 pages, but few are smaller than 4 pages. There simply is not enough space in 2 pages—hardly enough in 4 pages, for that matter. Common newsletter size is 4 to 16 pages, although a few are even larger, with probably the majority either 4 or 8 pages. It is probably a good plan to start with 4 pages. It is easy enough to step up to a larger size. In fact, some newsletters are actually of indeterminate or no fixed size, but appear in different sizes, as many newspapers and magazines do, depending on circumstances surrounding each edition (see Figure 14–1). However, there is at least one other variable affecting this question of number of pages, as we are about to see.

Format and Design

Most newsletters by far are in an 8½- by 11-inch format, the size of typewriter sheet of paper, such as is illustrated in Figure 14–1. This is the front page of the bimonthly newsletter of the American Association of Professional Consultants, titled appropriately enough, *The Consultant's Voice*. There are 4 pages in each issue, printed on both sides of an 11- by 17-inch sheet, which is then folded, a frequently used format because it offers few complications.

Walter Vose Jeffries produces a quite different kind of publication, which he refers to as a newsletter. It is actually a bound book, of varying size. Issues may range considerably in number of pages, but are customarily somewhere in the general range of 24 to 36 pages. (See Figure 14–2.) These pages, however, are 5½ by 8 inches in size, the size you would get by folding an 8½- by 11-inch sheet. The sheets are assembled and saddle-stitched (i.e., with staples in the center). Walter is almost wildly enthusiastic about his newsletter, *The Flash*. He reports excellent results from it.

The primary business Walter is promoting is the remanufacture of toner cartridges for laser printers and copiers, but he also sells all

October - November 1991
Volume Eight/Number Four

The Consultant's

Voice

The Source of Consulting Professionalism

AAPC Membership Code of Ethics

Members of the American Association of Professional Consultants shall:

1) Maintain their client's trust at all times.

2) Treat their client's information with the utmost confidence.

3) Provide services only in those disciplines in which the AAPC member consultant is proficient.

4) Share knowledge and experience with other AAPC members.

5) Make a sincere effort to understand their client's business as part of the consulting engagement.

6) Accurately represent their experience and skills to their clients.

7) Participate in appropriate continuing education programs to maintain existing skills and develop additional capabilities to serve their clients.

8) Support the programs and activities of AAPC.

.

© Copyright 1991, American Association of Professional Consultants.

Communication Flaws Lose $150 Billion in Workplace Each Year

By Stephen Ash, Ph.D., RPC
"THE CAREER DOCTOR"

It's costly, destructive and plays havoc with the effectiveness of any organization. Every year the United States spends over $150 billion on attitude related illness, lost productivity and stress as a result of it. What is it? LACK OF COMMUNICATION.

If employers, managers, supervisors and employees communicated more effectively, the cost of doing business in this country would be greatly reduced, and we could pass on the savings to our clients and customers. That would build more business for all of us and help to stimulate the economy. Sound like a good idea? Well, let's get started...

How to Stop Saying The Wrong Thing

Most of you have had the unfortunate experience of saying something and then wishing you could take it back. In what I call, "AFTER YOUR FOOT LEAVES YOUR MOUTH," there are ways to communicate with Confidence, Clarity and Concern for those around you. When you put your foot in your mouth, it certainly doesn't intend to do harm to someone else. It's normally a case of speaking too quickly or not thinking about the words you use and how they're perceived.

Sometimes it's the result of carelessness—a slip of the tongue that hurt's someone's feelings or reveals confidential or embarrassing information. Or it might be a joke that bombs—at someone else's expense. While it's true that remarks of this nature aren't meant to be vindictive, it makes little difference to the person who is hurt or offended by your lack of "positive" communication with, or about, them.

The time may come when you, or your employees, make a slip and you find yourself faced with one of those unpleasant realities that isn't likely to go away on its own. In fact, it may escalate and get worse unless you meet it head on. Let me share with you four guidelines:

(1) Apologize

An apology is a way of communicating your willingness to accept responsibility for the harm you've caused.

If, after you apologize, bad feelings linger...

(2) Don't Fan the Flames

Perhaps the person who was offended went through the motions of accepting your apology, but is still (silently) carrying a grudge. The less you say in response to the situation, the better.

(3) Retain Your Composure

Conduct yourself in a way that consistently shows that you don't mean any harm to anyone. Be persistent in being pleasant (or at least civil) even to those who are less so toward you to show that your mistake was just that—your mistake.

(4) Forgive Yourself

Whatever it was that you said, it was undoubtedly not representative of you at your best. Human nature is such, however, that if you continue to berate yourself for having been stupid or insensitive, you won't be able to improve anything.

Dr. Ash is a San Diego-based career management consultant, author and professional speaker. Information on his publication, "The Career Doctor's" Employee Performance Bulletin, is available by sending a #10-size self-addressed, stamped envelope to "THE CAREER DOCTOR," PO Box 927, Bonita, CA 91908 or calling (619) 479-8882.

Conference Segment On Platform Speaking Lauded by Attendees

Presenting the "Speak and Grow Rich" segment of the AAPC Regional Conference in Detroit last September, Dottie Walters, RPC, C.S.P., again demonstrated why her seminar is internationally acclaimed.

An enthusiastic attendance heard the chair of the AAPC Board of Governors and president of Walters International Speakers Bureau present a wide range of practical information.

TWO PRECEDING SEGMENTS of the three-day conference were rescheduled for a new date in 1992 to be announced later.

In a full-day program, Walters shared with her audience such topics as establishing speakers' fees, structuring contracts, working with Speakers Bureaus, creating great titles, producing profitable products, developing video and audio demo tapes, preparing press kits and many other subjects designed to help consultants add highly paid professional speaking bookings to their income.

WALTERS ALSO was featured on several radio interview shows and other local media where she promoted AAPC.

As a result of the national and worldwide respect for "Speak and Grow Rich," additional seminar dates and locations are being scheduled.

Figure 14–1. Newsletter of American Association of Professional Consultants.

supplies, including spare parts, to those who wish to recharge their own cartridges and/or do so for others as a business. *The Flash* is thus devoted primarily, but not exclusively, to related subjects—how laser printers work, what toner is and how it is made, revelations on remanufacturing cartridges, and so forth. However, Walter includes a variety of other topics; among these have been a 3-part series of articles on how to develop and publish a newsletter, information about his employees and a

BlackLightning, Inc.
RR 1- 87, Depot Rd
Hartland, VT 05048

The F/ash
All the news that's print to fit.

Volume 3	Issue 1	A BlackLightning Publication	January 1991

PCmini Cleaning
By Holly Blumenthal

It takes only minutes to clean the Canon PC 3 through 7 personal photocopiers and cartridges. There are two simple keys to success: being familiar with the basic parts of the machine, and keeping the cleaning materials handy so that the job gets done.

Here we show the PC3 mini photocopier. This information and pictures (with some changes) apply to the PC3, PC5, PC5L, PC6, PC6RE and the PC7.

Cleaning, p. 10

Cost Cutting
By Tod Snodgrass, Management Consultant

Overhead is a silent killer of profits. Experience shows overhead always goes up as a percentage of revenues -- it never gets smaller on its own. Result: *lower profits due to higher costs.*

Reducing overhead can effectively and immediately improve your firm's profitability (and competitive standing). In addition, cost cutting uses less cash than trying to increase sales -- and may have a greater impact on your company's bottom line.

Costs, p. 4

Rolling Your Own
Part II: Laying It on the Line
By Walter Vose Jeffries

In the last issue we covered writing the articles and pieces for a newsletter. Now, it is time to give it form. Layout and design bring the ideas together, presenting them in an inviting format. Advertisements may add important visual breaks to the composition as well as bring in some financial backing to the endeavor. At the same time, ads are filled with product and contact information that is likely to be of interest to your readers.

Rolling Your Own, p. 12

Making Toner
By Tom Durgin
with assistance from Pat Bell of ITA

Toner is the powdery ink that seems to magically move from the cartridge to the printed page. Surprisingly, its basic ingredients are actually common materials. The method of processing and delicate mixing, on the other hand, are very exacting and not so common at all.

Monocomponent toners are already "premixed" if you will, as opposed to bicomponent toners that go through a final mixing of the two component parts in the laser

Toner, p.8

New News
BlackLightning Happenings
By Catherine Croft

These past months have heralded many developments at BlackLightning. Innovations in products, production technology, and services help us to better serve you.

We have finally reached production levels in our transfer toner after more than a year of delays and backorders. In December we filled all of our outstanding backorders and began taking new orders for this high demand, specialty toner that allows you to create full color iron-on transfers for T-shirts, caps, metal plaques and more. We have rounded out our product line with ten stock colors (Black, Red, Blue, Green, Yellow, Magenta, Brown, Orange, Purple, and Burgundy) and will be adding more in the coming months. Additionally, we are now able to do custom color mixing to match your needs. The new toner formulation has a greatly

New News, p. 14

Contents Page 3

Figure 14–2. Front page of BlackLightning, Inc., newsletter, *The Flash.*

"who we are" article about his firm, and a catalog of services, products, and prices.

Note the response cards bound into the newsletter and reproduced here as Figures 14–3 and 14–4. Walter ran a little contest for best responses and awarded prizes to readers of *The Flash*. The benefits of the responses he received are, of course, quite obvious. Incidentally, he included questions to get reader opinions and comments on the newsletter itself, as well as on other matters of products, services, quality, and prices.

He has so far found *The Flash* to be a great success. However, dynamic and imaginative businessman that he is, Walter does not rest on today's achievements. In addition to the newsletter, Walter sends out postcard mailings to his entire customer list periodically to remind them that he is still doing business at the same place and is still ready to serve their needs.

Title

I am not myself fond of cryptic titles. I think the significance of a title ought to be apparent and have meaning of its own. Nor am I attracted especially to one-word titles, such as *The Flash*. Perhaps it has some special meaning for Walter Jeffries and his customers, but it is lost on me. Nevertheless, I must admit that it seems to work for him, probably a testimonial to the quality of his newsletter, which is so high that the title has little effect on its success.

Tell Us What You Think... 8/1/90

We want to better serve you. You can help us by filling out the short questionaire below. As an added bonus, when you fill out and return the questionaire, you'll be entered in a drawing, no purchase necessary! The deadline for the drawing is 10/1/90. The **grand prize** is **$100** of your choice of BlackLightning products or services. There will also be three runner up prizes of a package of LaserColor each. Hope to hear from you soon!

Why did you choose BlackLightning?
❑ 1. Environmental concerns
❑ 2. Cost savings of remanufacturing
❑ 3. Recommendation from a friend
❑ 4. Service and experience
❑ 5. BlackLightning Guarantee
❑ 6. Other_____

What products would you like to see added?
❑ 1. Color Toner ❑ Red ❑ Green ❑ Other_____
❑ 2. Laser printer checks
❑ 3. Hardware add ons_____
❑ 4. Business Packages ❑ 5. Other_____

How many laser printers do you have?_____

How many copiers do you have?_____

What type of computers? ❑ Mac ❑ IBM ❑ Other

What business are you in?_____

Do you keep *The Flash*? ❑ 1 Week ❑ 1 Month
  ❑ 6 months ❑ 1 Year ❑ A long time ❑ No

Did you read? ❑ Flash Bulbs ❑ Inside Scoop ❑ Official File ❑ Rolling Your Own ❑ New Products ❑ Other_____

We have had many suggestions from our readers for articles in the upcoming issues. Here's your chance to rank the ideas. (1 = Best, 6 = Least Prefered)
___ Corona Wire Background and Tips
___ How Toner is Made
___ Cleaning the Series II Minicopiers
___ Transfer Materials Characterists (How To)
___ Plastics and the Enviornment
___ Rolling Your Own Part II - Layout & Publishing

When you first received you literature, did you find the following samples useful? ❑ LaserColor
❑ Toner ❑ Transfer on paper ❑ Transfer on cloth

Would you be interested in advertizing? ❑ Yes ❑ No

Would a year end compendium of all the information and articles from *The Flash* at $4.95 be useful?
  ❑ Yes ❑ No thank you

Figure 14–3. Feedback postcard enclosed in BlackLightning's newsletter.

Finder's Program
Customer Referrals and word of mouth are our best source of new business. We have established the Finder's Program to recognize the help you give us. If you are the first person to refer a customer to us, with their initial purchase of a remanufactured toner cartridge from Black-Lightning, we will send you a $5 credit coupon for your next purchase. These are cumulative. Collect enough for a free cartridge! One more way we say thank you for your business...

Name_____	Name_____
Company_____	Company_____
Address_____	Address_____
City/ST/Zip_____	City/ST/Zip_____
Phone____(_____)_____	Phone____(_____)_____
Name_____	Name_____
Company_____	Company_____
Address_____	Address_____
City/ST/Zip_____	City/ST/Zip_____
Phone____(_____)_____	Phone____(_____)_____

Figure 14-4. Customer-referral postcard enclosed in BlackLightning newsletter.

On the other hand, *The Consultant's Voice* carries distinct meaning on its own. Here are a few other newsletter titles:

Physicians' Newsletter   *Consulting Opportunities Journal*
International Coal Report   *Business Opportunities Digest*
Communication Management   *Buyers & Sellers Exchange*
The Silver Institute Letter   *Contracting Opportunities Digest*

Most of these titles rather clearly suggest the content of the specific newsletter and are also rather typical in length: Most such titles are two to four words long. For most cases, presumably the reader is motivated to read the newsletter because he or she is interested generally in the subject. However, in many cases the publisher wisely names the newsletter to suggest distinct benefits. "Digest" is one such word, suggesting information highly condensed to save the reader's time. "Opportunities" is another word suggesting special benefits, as is "exchange," although to a somewhat lesser extent. My suggestion here is to spend enough time on and give enough thought to devising a title that defines what your newsletter is about but also suggests strongly the reasons an individual should want to read it (i.e., the benefits to be derived from reading it).

Content

Walter Jeffries has a few suggestions as to the content of a newsletter, and with his kind permission, I am going to quote some of them directly:

The first step in creating a newsletter of your own is to find a focus. What is the purpose of the newsletter? Consider the issues and topics that will serve the project goal. For ideas, listen to the comments and questions made by potential readers. At BlackLightning, we spend much of our time on the phone with customers explaining the operation and maintenance of cartridges and printers. Consequently, we are careful to address these topics in every issue of "The Flash," and we always receive many thank yous for these articles.

Think of a catchy title for the newsletter that will communicate your goal creatively. Cover updates on research and current events relevant to the audience. A calendar of upcoming events may be useful. Interviews add a nice, personal touch. If product information is to be included, be very careful not to confuse product hype with news. Newsletters of pure propaganda or solicitation are a waste of the reader's time and typically land in the trash.

Of course, the content of *your* newsletter will depend on the business you are in, so your newsletter content is unlikely to resemble Walter's. One thing *The Flash* and many other newsletters do is standardize major sections. Each issue may contain items under such headings as the following:

Industry News	New Ideas
Personal Changes	Best Buy of the Week
Features	Letters to the Editor
New Products	Comments from Readers
New Services	Questions and Answers
Tips and Suggestions	

In designing your format and planning your content, remember always that your objective is to involve the reader (your customer) in every way possible. The newsletter is much more about readers than about you, for example. Its major concern is serving the needs and interests of the reader, and the reader is encouraged in every way to offer his and her comments, complaints, and suggestions. And, incidentally, if you enclose a response card or response envelope, make it a prepaid one. The average reader does not usually have a postage stamp readily at hand and therefore may not respond at all.

Sources

The content of many newsletters is generated entirely in-house, but a number of others depend on "contributors." A contributor is any outside writer who sends in usable material. If the contributor is a professional freelance writer, full- or part-time, he or she expects to be paid for the material they have contributed, if you accept it and use it. Other writers will contribute items without expecting payment, perhaps for the pleasure of seeing their writing published, perhaps as a *pro bono* act, or perhaps because it is material not normally paid for (e.g., a letter to the editor, or an essay for a contest where you will award prizes).

You can get a great deal of material by advertising your wants in a writer's magazine and/or writer's conferences in electronic bulletin boards. A portion of it will not be usable for your purposes, some of it will be hardly literate, but some will be quite worthwhile. You will, however, have to sift through the daily "slush pile," trying to select the contributions you can use, or you will have to have someone else do so.

You can read others' newsletters and make deals for mutual permission to copy from each other, with full attribution. Many newsletter publishers are willing to make such arrangements. But for this newsletter, try to rely as much as possible on your readers—your customers. As Walter Jeffries does, keep track of what they say when they call: What are their typical questions? Complaints? Comments? Suggestions?

Take active steps to obtain this kind of feedback by encouraging letters to the editor, questions to a question and answer column, prizes for outstanding suggestions and best essays, and other such subprograms of your newsletter program.

Look to your own employees for help. They can supply valuable raw input to your newsletter staff. They know the customers, the merchandise, and the problems.

Policy

Every periodical has an editorial policy. It dictates what you will and will not normally print, the editorial standards you will use, and other standards governing the publication. It is, of course, not a matter for great concern here, but it is not to be ignored either, especially if you do not yourself write and edit the newsletter. Editorial blunders can cause you a great deal of trouble, including lawsuits and lost customers. Policy, properly documented, guides anyone else working on your newsletter to ensure that it meets your own standards of conduct.

Functions

The most basic functions required to create a newsletter are writing and editing, of course, and perhaps illustrating, if you choose to use graphics. In addition, there are the functions of layout and makeup, which is the assembling of all the bits and pieces into pages ready for the printer.

That was once a tedious job, usually done by specialists, with copy-fitting and paste-up skills. Today, it is no longer necessary to do a physical paste-up; the job is accomplished by a computer with a skilled operator. In fact, the laser printer can now produce a camera-ready page. Figure 14–5 illustrates this on a simple scale. In fact, the page shown was produced by a word-processing program, WordStar, and did not require the special desktop-publishing software programs normally used for this work. It is not difficult to insert figures of various kinds here too, if desired, even halftones. Production work has thus become enormously simplified.

WRITING FOR MONEY

"No man but a blockhead ever wrote except for money."
--*Samuel Johnson, 1776*

No. 101   Editor/Publisher Herman Holtz
P.O. Box 1731   Wheaton, MD 20915   301 649-2499   Fax: 301 649-5745

EGO TRIP OR CAREER?

Getting published is always a most gratifying experience. Even the most seasoned and successful writer awaits publication of his or her latest work with great impatience and reads it with great satisfaction. Thus, in the beginning of a writing career, many writers willingly submit their work and permit it to be published without payment other than the ego gratification of getting published and a few copies to distribute to friends and relatives.

Eventually, for most who wish to make a career of writing, this proves inadequate compensation. For one thing, you find that you cannot make a career of writing without getting paid in more substantial form than ego boost and a few copies of the publication. For another and more significant consideration, the payment is, finally, the only real measure of the value of your writing. If the compensation reflects the worth, what does zero compensation say? Persuading someone to pay out cash for your writing gives you assurance that it has at least that much value!

A WRITING CAREER

There are four ways to earn money as a writer:
● Work on the staff of government agencies, companies, publishers, or other organizations.
● Write "on spec" and sell your work to commercial publishers.
● Work to order, under contract to produce custom work for clients.
● Be your own publisher.

MARKETS FOR WRITERS

You can easily combine these approaches, of course. Many staff writers and editors moonlight elsewhere, publish their own newsletter, freelance on-spec pieces, and do custom work for individual clients. Writing and editing are crafts that you can apply in many ways. One reason that more writers and editors are not working regularly at their craft and earning money thereby is that most are almost completely unaware of the total market. Of course they know about publishers who buy short stories, articles, novels, and other full-length books, but they know next to nothing about the rest of a vast market for writing and editing, or even that it exists.

Consider the market in the business world alone, for example, with both individuals and organizations as prospective clients : Individuals want help in writing and editing resumes, reports, theses, dissertations, speeches, and other papers and presentations of various kinds. Companies, associations, and sundry other organizations want help in writing and editing some of these same things--e.g., speeches and presentations--as well as newsletters, reports releases, brochures, salesletters, proposals, catalogs, manuals, scripts, articles, and many other items organizations need every day to carry on their routine and non-routine business activities. But let's have a closer look at some of the possibilities.

Plans for Business Periodicals

There are thousands upon thousands of "business publications"--trade journals (in both slick-paper and pulp magazine formats), tabloids in both slick paper and newsprint, newsletters, and some periodicals that appear to be hybrids of these styles. In fact, these represent a much larger market for writers than does the array of consumer-oriented (i.e., "general interest") periodicals that you find on newsstands in the supermarket and elsewhere. Trade journals alone, those slick-paper magazines that every industry spawns in abundance, represent a huge market with a voracious appetite for information. They want to know what is going on in their industry and in all other areas that relate to their industry--legislation, taxes, mergers, changes in personnel, labor movements, and whatever else is happening that affects the industry.

Figure 14–5. Newsletter produced by simple word processor program.

The final aspects of production are tasks you generally turn over to your printer, who will give you estimates of different quantities, using different kinds of paper, and binding, if that is a needed function. He or she will also deliver the newsletters to you flat or folded, or will deliver a quantity to your mailer and the remainder to you, as you wish.

Staff

It should not require a full-time staff to prepare a monthly newsletter. One woman who runs a computer consulting business publishes a monthly newsletter for clients and does it all herself. She says the project takes her two or three days each month. It requires the full-time service of one person for a few days or the part-time service of several people for a few days each month. Admittedly, a great deal depends on the individual skills. In my own case, I produced three newsletters alone, but I kept file folders into which I dropped material continually through the month, periodically writing up copy as galley, which I eventually cut and pasted up. Although I write other things than newsletters now, I still keep an eye open for useful items and drop them into appropriate computer files for later use.

Probably the most important staff job is that of editor. A good editor overcomes many faults and weaknesses that no other staff member can surmount; an inadequate editor almost guarantees a poor product. Look, therefore, for a highly competent editor and let him or her have a free hand.

Production

Production is not much of a concern today if you have an adequate printer and/or mailing/fulfillment house to attend to actual physical production and mailing. Incidentally, notice that *The Flash,* like a great many other periodicals, is designed as a self-mailer. If you refer back to Figure 14–2, you will see that the top portion of the front page is blank, except for the title and the mailing indicia. A label can be placed in the center of that space and the letter can be mailed sans envelope, as is the policy of most publishers. (In the post office, these mailings are referred to as "flats" and are supposed to get first-class handling, although they rarely do.)

CLUBS AND ASSOCIATIONS

More than a few companies have turned to clubs as a relationship marketing medium. Years ago the makers of products with special appeal to children—breakfast cereals, for example—sponsored "clubs" for children, with special medallions, rings, badges, and other such devices. But it is not only the youngsters who like the idea of belonging; most of us do. Banks long ago found it a popular idea to encourage customers to set up special savings accounts to meet holiday expenses, and they called them "Christmas Clubs" although there was really only the most tenuous connection with the membership idea. There are also the book clubs, mentioned earlier, the record and tape clubs, and others of a similar nature. The idea of belonging can also be turned to good use elsewhere and in other ways.

Some stores have sponsored "layaway clubs," in which the store lays some chosen merchandise away, issues the customer a payment book, and records payments made by the customer at his or her convenience until the item is fully paid for. Discount cards are another common device. I carry a card that says I am a member of B. Dalton's "Booksavers Club." It entitles me to discounts on their books. Waldenbooks has a similar program.

There was the example I used in Chapter 7, where I encouraged my newsletter subscribers to become "associates," instead of mere subscribers. That, or some variant of it, can be used by every newsletter publisher. Those who work alone as free-lancers or independent entrepreneurs often find their business existence to be a lonely one, and they are particularly amenable to joining membership associations. Most membership associations are nonprofits, organized spontaneously by enthusiastic members of professions, industries, and other activities that great numbers of people share in common, but there are also those that are, in fact, businesses or major elements of business. Some associations of writers, consultants, and other independent operators, for example, are really privately owned businesses that furnish the members the kinds of services they normally get from an association located at a distance.

A good example is the American Association of Retired Persons (AARP). It is a legitimate association, with a newsletter and another periodical, and an assortment of benefits, but its true raison d'etre is undoubtedly the insurance programs it offers members. It is a most effective medium for marketing insurance, and it addresses real enough needs of a group who probably seek highly specialized personal insurance.

That illustrates another route to organizing such associations: third-party sponsorship or tie-in, which can take various forms, often with surprising origin and unpredictable development. For example, a young woman in a Virginia suburb of Washington, Audrey Wyatt, acquired The Consultants Institute from its founder, Eugene Hameroff, of Columbus, Ohio. The Institute was dedicated to educational activities for consultants. She then organized a consultants' association, the American Consultants League, as a companion venture. She worked closely with a publisher of books for consultants, Hubert Bermont, whose own firm, The Consultant's Library, was the largest publisher of books on consulting. Later, Bermont took over the Institute and the association, and he operates them with publishing as one arm of the enterprise overall. On the other hand, the late Howard Shenson, himself the author of several books on consulting and known to many as "the consultant's consultant," had initiated several such associations and a professional society at his own initiative.

Any business owner can organize an association, if he can find the right factors to motivate his customers and prospective customers to become interested and join. There would have to be a readily apparent common interest or cause that would be served by membership in an association, and inducements to join, of course. Some entrepreneurs have shown a great deal of imagination and even wisdom in meeting these requirements.

FREQUENT FLYER/FREQUENT BUYER PROGRAMS

Other airlines have long since emulated the program conceived and initiated by American Airlines, the "frequent flyer" program that awards bonuses in free trips to those who qualify. American was inspired to do this when they became aware of how well the 80/20 Pareto principle applied to their business: 80 percent of their business was attributable to 20 percent of their passengers, the passengers who flew regularly on business trips.

Variants of the idea, in "frequent buyer" programs, have been adopted, but a great deal more can be done in organizing your frequent buyers and recognizing them in some manner—certificates of merit, gold pins, membership in your frequent-buyer clubs. At Neiman Marcus it is a "Circle Program," while the Hyatt Regency awards those who are frequent guests with a "Gold Passport." Ramada Inns long ago sent out red courtesy cards to businesspeople who had stayed at their hostelries and registered with them. More recently, Ramada has begun to issue the "Ramada® Business Card," which is actually a Visa credit card. CitiBank and Amoco offer their cardholders membership in low-cost road service plans. And Sears offers their Discover cardholders rebates on charges made against the card as motivation to be a frequent user of the card.

Such programs can deliver more than one benefit: They can help to build loyalty to products and services and/or to business establishments; they can increase average order size or order frequency from customers; and they can also attract new customers.

Obviously, such plans do not fit every business, and they may or may not fit yours. Here are a few considerations to ponder in judging whether you can make good use of some kind of frequent-buyer program:

- Your products or services must be such that customers can logically use them repeatedly or at least patronize you repeatedly. That may be because you offer a wide variety of products or services, because what you sell is a consumable product, or because what you sell is a frequent need. For airlines, hotels, automobile-rental agencies, and many others, the fit is obvious: Businesspeople travel, some almost continuously, and they need such services frequently.

- There is also the consideration of cost, and here you need to judge whether your normal margin of profit will sustain the expense of bonus or discount packages of frequent-buyer awards.

- Before you decide to undertake such a program, ask yourself first whether you are looking for short- or long-term benefit. Ask yourself, too, which of the possible benefits—building customer loyalties, increasing average order size, or attracting new customers—is your primary and most important objective, and how the other benefits rank in comparison. Then estimate the likelihood that your program will achieve the main objective. Not all such programs are shining successes, unfortunately, and they can be expensive to launch.

TRADE SHOWS

For some, exhibiting your products at a trade show is a good opportunity to get feedback from customers. One way that is employed is giving out samples, along with response cards of some kind, and inviting customers to fill out the cards. The cards have miniquestionnaires that can be filled out easily and quickly. The idea is to get the response at once. Otherwise, you will get few responses. Most people won't bother to return questionnaires later, after the show has ended and they have gone home.

Another way to get feedback at a trade show is simply to encourage questions and conduct conversations on the spot. You must provide your booth with the right representatives. That approach is of limited use, however, since you cannot usually tie the responses in with the identities of the individuals, as you would prefer to do.

OTHER MEANS FOR ENCOURAGING FEEDBACK

Remember that a prime objective of these programs is to encourage a dialogue, to inspire feedback from customers. And that is, in itself, a marketing job: You must *persuade* customers to communicate with you.

The programs we have been discussing are active, aggressive programs, with the dialogue resulting from your initiatives. However, one long-honored rule of marketing is to make it as easy as possible for the customer to do whatever it is that you want him or her to do. Here are ways to make it easier for the customer:

- A toll-free hotline. Set up an 800 number that customers can use to ask questions, register complaints, make suggestions, and offer comments. Publicize the 800 number, and be sure to include it in all your printed literature.
- Use a prepaid response envelope in your mailings that needs merely to be dropped into any mailbox.
- Use forms with suggested check-offs, boxes, and/or checklists to help the customer articulate his or her thoughts.
- Ask specific questions to which you invite frank answers. Many people find it difficult to organize their impressions and thoughts, and they need the help of being asked specific questions.

TURNING NONRESPONSES INTO RESPONSES

Those in direct marketing are usually quite familiar with testing and do a great deal of it to validate their premises on price, product, copy, and other facets of the marketing process. In some cases, the idea can be adapted to gather useful information from those who do not register. In marketing seminars with a direct mail campaign, I sent out a registration form that invited a response from those not planning to register and attend. They checked off or wrote their comments along the following lines:

I can't make this session, but . . .

☐ I would like to be invited to register for the next one. Please keep me on your mailing list.

☐ I would be interested in attending a session closer to (one or more places).

☐ I would be interested in attending a session about (one or more dates).

Comments and/or questions: _____

_____

_____

_____

INDIRECT BENEFITS

The responses to my enclosure had great value to me beyond the obvious one of adding to the databank: They had a desirable psychological effect on the customer in reflecting my concern for his or her needs and the value I was placing on his or her opinion. It thus made that individual more likely than ever to respond to my next invitation to attend a seminar. But it also inspired in me another idea for a variant of bounce-back marketing.

BOUNCE-BACK MARKETING AND BOUNCE-BACK ORDERS

Bounce-back marketing, or soliciting and winning bounce-back orders, refers to enclosing sales literature for another product with the original order when it is sent out. Quite often, that literature brings in additional orders. In fact, one marketing strategy used effectively in direct mail is to offer a loss leader in advertising (see Chapter 8) and then send out bounce-back literature (e.g., a catalog) with the item thus sold. Some mailers enclose sales literature with monthly invoices or statements sent out by others who bill large numbers of people each month (credit card issuers, for example), also seeking bounce-back orders. Other types of "piggyback" mailings are often used for the same purpose.

I turned this bounce-back idea to advantage in connection with the seminar-registration solicitation. Once I found that many people who chose not to register for the seminar responded to my invitation to comment, I began to enclose sales literature for a newsletter and two books that I was also marketing on the subjects covered by the seminar. These produced a sizable amount of additional income.

Note the several benefits then that came out of my special enclosures with invitations to register for a seminar:

- I gained useful information for future seminar dates and places.
- I turned a number of prospects into good leads for future seminars.
- I gained additional income, enough to more than pay for the mailing, thus guaranteeing a successful outcome for the seminar, even should the attendance be a modestly small one.
- I gained many new customers.
- I turned what would otherwise have been nonresponses—those who did not register for the seminar—into responses, even if the respondent bought nothing.

The latter is a most important point. "Response" does not necessarily have to be synonymous with "order." *Any* response, even a negative one, is dialogue with a customer or prospective customer and is valuable. I managed to put it to much greater use than I had ever envisioned when I first thought to invite responses from those who had chosen not to register for my seminar. Whether you call them "nonresponses," "negative responses," or by any other term that distinguishes them from orders, they are responses and still have great value if used properly.

Put this idea to work for you. In whatever marketing you do, especially direct mail but not confined to direct mail, search out ways to turn nonresponses into responses. One way to attract responses from those who resist your usual appeal is the loss leader, some product that you sell at or below your cost. Usually it is a popular item, often a small one costing only a couple of dollars or so and with presumed appeal to those you wish to reach. Another is to offer something free: a calendar, a newsletter, a booklet, or other item. And another is some variant of the idea I used, encouraging prospects to respond at no cost to themselves by using your prepaid envelopes or cards.

In the next chapter we will continue to talk about relationship marketing, among some other, related matters.

Chapter 15

Some Spin-Off Benefits of Databased Marketing

As in the case of many other new developments, databased marketing offers us many opportunities beyond those envisioned at first. One of these is the opportunity to learn the truth about many common beliefs of marketing and to create a new conventional wisdom of the field, based on the organized and objective analysis of facts gathered in an organized and objective way.

A PEARL OF GREAT PRICE

Until now we have pursued the study of databased marketing as a method for getting to know our customers better. Especially, we want to understand their wants and needs, the motivations that cause them to become and remain our customers. That knowledge will, presumably, produce an increase in business. It should bring with it both an ability to market to our customers more effectively and to clone them—to develop a greatly enhanced ability to find, select, and appeal to those prospects most likely to become our new customers.

This is accomplished through an instrument known as a *marketing database* (also referred to by some writers as a *relationship database*). The essence of databased marketing lies in the creation of that instrument, and the essence of that instrument is data—information. The data are about our customers, including as much personal, individual data as possible, as long as the data pertain somehow to marketing to that customer. That is, data that do not bear directly on the customer's wants, needs, desires, fears, ambitions, and other motivational factors are irrelevant; they are non sequiturs in the marketing database. Or are they? Should we think some more about it?

A marketing database is, in fact, a most valuable instrument, a jewel among marketing assets. But perhaps it is an even greater treasure than we have until now suspected. Perhaps we can do more with a good marketing database than be more responsive to our established customers and profile them for cloning. Surely, an instrument such as this has other uses. In this chapter we are going to consider some ways in which the marketing database can be an even more valuable gem than we have so far postulated. It has or can be so used as to have other applications of great value to our marketing capabilities.

THE FALLACY OF CONVENTIONAL WISDOM

A person entering any field that is new to him or her, whether craft, trade, profession, or industry, soon begins to learn the generally accepted truths of that field, premises upon which activities are based. These constitute the body of conventional wisdom passed on by each generation, the established veterans of that industry or profession. "Everyone knows," for example, that the June-July-August period is no time to spend money on a new promotion: Business is always slow during the summer. Business will pick up again immediately after Labor Day. Everyone knows, too, says conventional wisdom, that long copy sells better than short copy: "The more you tell, the more you sell," the pundits will assure you. A three-page sales letter will always outpull a one-page sales letter, of course. A response envelope and an order form are obligatory elements of the package of sales literature, and you must offer an explicit money-back guarantee if you want prospects to have enough faith in your offer to respond to it. Multicolor printing pulls better than single-color printing, and a better grade of paper will improve response too. Everyone knows that.

So how come business was terrific last summer and dropped dead in September? How come when I eliminated my extravagantly worded guarantee from my copy it didn't affect the response rate at all? Why did it make no perceptible difference in response when I dropped the business reply envelope from my package? Why did switching to more expensive paper and colored inks bring no improvement in my response rate?

The pundits would probably assure you that these were all aberrations, mystical and abnormal, and didn't change the general rules at all. Conventional wisdom, like most other forms of bias and dogma, does not yield to mere facts. One man I met, who claimed vast related experience, assured me most emphatically that I was dead wrong in my belief that list brokers receive a 20 percent commission from the list owners for renting the lists. List brokers pay list owners only 20 percent of the rental fees their lists bring in, and they keep the remaining 80 percent, this man assured me quite positively. He was not at all swayed from his belief when I cited verification of my figures by two well-known leaders in the DM industry, who had reported the figures in their own books. He insisted that those had to be exceptional cases.

It was characteristic. Fervently believed myth and bias obscure truth, as individuals propagate myths they have heard and choose to believe or seize upon their individual experiences and extrapolate them into alleged universal truths that they will defend to the bitter end. (Those who have never mastered the art of writing winning proposals for government contracts, for example, are a rich source of myths explaining why it is impossible for "outsiders" to win those contracts.)

Not all our beliefs are based on conventional wisdom, fortunately. We usually do some testing as a preliminary to a new marketing campaign. That testing furnishes some answers or, at least partial answers to questions we ask ourselves before launching the campaign. Unfortunately, we cannot always be sure that we know whether the answers furnished are general truths or are valid for only that one case undergoing the test. Perhaps, for example, a formal, extravagant guarantee is a must for one case, but not for another. Perhaps two- or three-color printing works better in some cases, but not in all cases. In fact, perhaps there are cases where the lengthily worded, iron-clad guarantee has a negative impact, and causes the customer to wonder why you find it necessary to be so extraordinarily emphatic about a guarantee: Is there something to hide? Something that must be painted over with such extreme assurances? Or, on the other hand, does that all-encompassing guarantee only encourage customers to return merchandise and thus vastly increase the number of returns? (That, too, is a hazard to consider: Some guarantee statements almost urge the customer to return the merchandise.)

THE LIMITATIONS OF TESTING

Testing is a must, of course. There is too much at stake in a major campaign to risk rolling out without taking some steps to verify the probability that the campaign is well conceived and the product or service will sell reasonably well. However, you can test only so much. Both time and cost limit how much of the list you can test and how many tests you can conduct. For any test to be useful, you can test only one item (e.g., cost, terms, copy, medium, guarantee, or other) at a time: Each item tested requires another mailing. Too, even that is not at all conclusive, for it tests the individual item, but not the total effect of different combinations: Perhaps with a more elaborately worded guarantee or different terms, the customer would have accepted a higher price, for example. Or perhaps the copy was a poor fit for the overall image you were trying for. Or perhaps the test indicates any of many other possibilities, which are far too numerous to test. The longer you consider it, the more possibilities for error (i.e., misinterpreting the meaning of the results you monitor) you can envision. Thus the uncertainty grows steadily, until you realize that your tests produce evidence that is useful for only this single application. It will take something more than occasional prerollout tests to produce universal truths that you can use in other campaigns.

WHAT ARE THE "UNIVERSAL TRUTHS?"

The foregoing ideas are not meant to suggest that it would be practicable for us to seek out truths of marketing that would apply to every marketing problem in every industry, even if it were possible to achieve such a goal. What we will discuss here are means for learning marketing truths that apply broadly within our own businesses and marketing needs—our individual universes—although the findings may sometimes be applicable elsewhere or even across our own industry. However, for most of us, our marketing revolves around some well-defined class of products or services. In my own case, for example, the products I sell are written information, and the services are writing and related editorial services. Thus, although I offer a variety of products and services, there is enough similarity among them to market them with common strategies and tactics. "Universal" marketing truths are, to me, those strategies and tactics that work best for me in marketing my products and services.

The same philosophy applies to all others, of course, even if there are a few exceptions. Most of us market reasonably uniform kinds and classes of products and services, and thus "universal" means common to our own, individual marketing needs.

CREATIVE VERSUS LIST VERSUS OFFER

Among the many uncertainties in marketing is the relative importance of the several major elements. In marketing generally, we can explore the influence of three major elements: The offer, the sales/advertising copy (commonly referred to as the "creative"), and the medium. The medium is, for all practical purposes, the population, or prospects, reached by the medium. If you use TV, for example, the prospects are those who are watching the channel you have chosen at the time you have chosen to air your commercials. In the case of direct mail, which I will use as a base of reference for discussion, the medium or population of prospects, is the mailing list or lists used.

You can assign relative values to each of the three elements. Undoubtedly, the copywriters or creative people are certain that when a campaign is successful, it is creative that has made it so, and when a campaign is not successful, the weakness lies in the offer or in the list. Of course, those responsible for the other elements have their own rationalizations, which make them responsible for successes and guiltless in failures. Testing helps to prove or disprove some of these understandable biases and bring at least some light to shine on the truths. However, there are still many who insist on offering average figures or their own estimates as conventional wisdom upon which to base future plans and decisions. One recent writer, Camille McDaniel, states as today's conventional wisdom, in this era of relationship and databased marketing, that 40 percent of the effectiveness of a DM campaign today is determined by the quality or aptness of the list, 40 percent more results from the offer, and only 20 percent is the product of "creative," that is, the copy ("Relationship Marketing & Demands of the 90s," *DM News,* December 16, 1991). Unfortunately, the author offers no basis for these figures, although they are far more balanced than the position of many to whom all DM failures are due directly to using the "wrong" mailing lists.

The major thrust of the argument made here is that creative was once of great importance in a marketing campaign but is far less of an influence today, in this "relationship" environment of greatly enhanced knowledge of the customers and their wants. Creative is now only half as important as the list and the offer are in producing responses to the appeal. The rationale is, apparently, that greater importance should now be assigned to the list and the offer, as marketing focuses more and more on relationships and the building of marketing databases. Presumably, the argument suggests, in this enlightened age you can shape the offer to fit the customer's goals and perceive the customer's wants and needs as he or she perceives them; thus, in this era of enhanced marketing insight, knowing as we do what customers really want, you need not rely on creative to persuade customers to want what you want them to want.

True or not, at best the quoted figures can be accurate on only the most general basis (i.e., across the board for all industry). Obviously, the figures can and will vary quite a lot for any individual case, for example, creative may represent 75 percent of the influence in your own marketing appeals, and only 10 percent in some other individual case.

CHARACTERIZING MARKETING

Marketing has been and is characterized by many factors that reflect the strategy or rationale of a given marketing approach. We have read and heard the arguments of those advocating various approaches, such as those we discussed in the previous chapter. There was mention of "loyalty marketing," for example, an approach that seeks to build in the customer a sense of loyalty to a product name or a given supplier. That basis for building customer loyalty might well be called "name brand marketing," since it essays to trade on the prominence and perceived value of the name as the basis for a sales argument. There is also discount marketing, trading on the desire of all of us to save money by buying things at the lowest prices possible. (For some customers who patronize discount sales, the motivation is not saving money per se nearly as much as it is a sense of satisfaction in being a shrewd buyer. Never underestimate the motivative power of enhancing the prospect's self-esteem.)

There is the opposite phenomenon of those who prefer to pay high prices and who, quite often, brag to others about how much they paid for some prized possession. (In fact, the potential for bragging to others and pumping up their own self-esteem are factors that drive certain customers to the higher priced items in impressive salons.) That might be called *prestige marketing,* perhaps vaguely akin to loyalty marketing, because it is based at least partly on creating an upscale image for a store or product. Such an image tends to make customers feel especially privileged and distinguished to patronize such an expensive and elegant product or place of business, and they take great pride in assuring themselves that they are so discriminating. There is premium or incentive marketing, which attempts to sway the customer by focusing on a bonus or gift of some sort that will accompany an order, almost as a bribe. There is also consensus marketing, which appeals to the herd instinct by assuring customers that the product or the seller is one that is hugely successful and chosen by great numbers of customers; it thus attempts to instill in the customer a sense of security in patronizing the seller. Most of us do tend to follow the crowd, which probably reflects a common fear of being alone and a sense of comfort in being with our fellows. I suppose that we might fairly call this herd appeal.

GAINING ANOTHER KIND OF INSIGHT

Marketing databases should be repositories of data that help you identify these various kinds of motivation and so get a good look at your business as your customers see it. Robert Burns's "To see oursels as ithers see us" is as difficult to accomplish in business as it is in personal life. As a business owner, you have a view of how you want your business to appear to customers, and you undoubtedly think that it does so appear to them. The truth may shock you: It may be that customers perceive your business in a drastically different light than you do. It is very difficult to know the other's view from casual observation. What you think is gaudy might be tasteful to another. What to you is a comfortable, relaxed atmosphere may be an overly formal, uptight atmosphere to someone else.

The marketing database can enable you to get insight into your customers' view of your business—what that view is and what they would like your business to be, as far as they are concerned. (*Reader's Digest,* in a current contest for new and additional subscriptions, includes among the response devices a card listing a wide variety of choices of reading matter that entrants are asked to check off. This, they say, will help them bring readers more of the kinds of reading material that they prefer.) Of course, customers are individuals, and you will find a number of views, some of which will conflict with each other. However, you can analyze the data you collect to project a profile of your business as most of your customers see it. Or, if you cannot find a consensus or majority opinion, you may have to work with several profiles, but you do have first to find out what those profiles are. Start by projecting appropriate questions, such as the following few examples (modify these and/or add your own questions, of course) to which you will seek answers:

Do customers see your business as a friendly, unfriendly, or austere place to do business? As an upscale or prestigious emporium? As a seller of strictly high-quality merchandise? As a place to get bargains or great values? As a place where return privileges are such they need not worry about a purchase proving to be a disappointment? As a place where it is difficult to return purchases and thus one where they must be very careful in making purchase decisions? As one offering hard-to-find merchandise? As one with limited selections? As one handling a wide variety of items, both high and low in quality and price?

THE OFFER

At the heart of most marketing strategies is the offer. In broad terms, marketers tend to regard this as a statement of the product or service, the price, and the terms, including any incentives. I believe there is a bit more to it than that; for example, if the offer also promises a sense of security, a feeling of prestige and privilege, or other such reward, I consider those to be incentives and also significant elements of the offer. I believe that the offer is truly your promise to customers of what your goods or services will do for them (bring joy, help them like themselves better, make them feel more secure, etc.), even more than it is the specific price, terms, and conditions you stipulate. Actually, it is not a simple matter to segregate these various approaches: Many of them overlap or include elements of others. Be prepared for many surprises. Learning the truth of how others view you (as a business, as well as an individual) almost inevitably brings surprises. Many of the surprises will be unpleasant ones, but they will be valuable data to help you formulate the proper image for your business, the image your customers want.

THE MURKIEST AREAS IN TESTING

None of the three principal items or of the many subitem factors exists in total isolation from the others, as already noted. Thus, none can be tested on an absolute basis. However, to the extent that the individual areas can be tested, the easiest to test of the three major areas is the medium, or list. For any given offer and campaign, you need merely address representative samples—usually random samples that are large enough to furnish statistical significance—to determine two things: the relative response to your offer of each list or medium and the economic viability for your purposes of the best response rates found.

Much the same consideration applies to testing the offer itself. You can vary major items of the offer—cost, terms, guarantee, promises, and proofs, probably in that order—and determine which produces the best results for you. Note that wording: *best results.* That is not necessarily the largest response rate: 100 orders at $12 each is not better than 90 orders at $15 each. For that matter, it is not an unknown phenomenon that raising a price actually increases the response rate. The customer is likely to mistrust what he or she sees as an unrealistically low price and therefore shun your product if it is "too cheap." You probably should test three prices, high, low, and medium to see how customers react.

What is most difficult to test is the copy, the "creative" element of the marketing program. There are definite practical limits to the variations you may test in media (simple judgment rules out many) and the many items among which you choose are usually discrete ones. Similarly, you have a limited range of prices, terms, and other separate and *quantifiable* factors of the offer that you can test. But in copy, the range is almost infinite, and the possible choices to test are virtually continuous and nonquantifiable, rather than discrete, items. Creative is undoubtedly the most subjective, personal-opinion-based area of all, and thus by far the most difficult to test and the most difficult about which to uncover truth. ("Truth" is here defined as the information that identifies the most effective presentation.) Here is where databased marketing can produce information almost impossible to gather by other means available to us.

A GIANT STEP BEYOND CONVENTIONAL TESTING

How is it possible to arrive at truth in any matter of uncertainty? Generally speaking, we collect data and decide from it what is true. We make our decision both objectively and subjectively, the latter when we do not have enough factual data to force conclusions on us. In the matters we have discussed here, the data derive from two sources: the results of testing and the observations of individuals conducting marketing campaigns, including their records of results. The limitations of these are already apparent: For one thing, the data have been limited in both scope and volume. Now a new avenue is at hand: the data collected from customers and campaigns, not as personal impressions of individuals and not confined to the fragmentary data from prerollout testing, but the masses of quantified, factual data steadily accumulating in marketing databases. The instrument itself, the computer with its capabilities for use in analyzing masses of data, is readily at hand, and the data are already being collected in various databases. They may be assembled in any good relational database and analyzed objectively to test the beliefs of conventional wisdom and discover new truths.

There is a special significance to this: We have been discussing the development and use of relationship/databased marketing to improve marketing results directly and specifically by understanding our customers and appealing to their individual wants and needs. We have the opportunity, however, to go well beyond this immediate goal and to seek some truths that will increase our marketing effectiveness overall. The data produced by each test need not be confined to the single campaign that it preceded, nor need the data be discarded when the campaign rolls out. Rather, they should be entered into a special database and added to data resulting from earlier tests and experience, and become part of a general bank of data useful for your marketing in general.

In the remainder of this chapter I will explore in greater detail than previously the kinds of information we ought to gather and study for both purposes. That is, until now, I have discussed only data affecting your relationship with individual customers in your marketing database. Let us now expand that to see what we can learn about fundamental truths in all your marketing—for example, does long copy sell better for you than short copy? Always? Never? Sometimes? And if "sometimes," when and under what circumstances? What about the usefulness of business reply envelopes? Colored paper? Multicolor printing? Other factors about which there is so much conventional wisdom and mythology?

HOW TO EXAMINE CREATIVE COPY

Generally in testing, you seek to discover what is truth for a given campaign or offer, and you carry out your testing in those terms. In testing creative—copy, primarily—you also seek to find out what will do the job for you in the campaign planned. However, you can and should also seek to test the common and accepted premises on which you base your creative efforts, such as the popular beliefs concerning long versus short copy and the relative merits of many other features and characteristics of creative efforts. To achieve a more global understanding of all these matters, however, it is necessary to build a large enough body of data in your marketing databases, and to evaluate the data repeatedly, as they accumulate. We will discuss some typical cases here to illustrate the concept

LONG COPY VERSUS SHORT COPY

Among the most debated of topics is the appeal of long copy versus short copy (e.g., multipage sales letters versus single-page sales letters). Some proponents of long copy simply state flatly that longer letters produce better response. Others point out that this is a sometime truth, and they envision situations and cite case histories to support this hypothesis. In a round-robin discussion among professionals in the field of direct marketing, a number of comments and observations illustrated sharply the importance of "it depends" (on individual cases and circumstances) in reaching conclusions.

One participant asked a simple question: Would you send a lengthy letter to a busy executive simply to introduce yourself and advise him or her that you will be calling in a few days to request an appointment? "Probably not," was the answer. You might, in fact, only antagonize your prospect with a tediously long letter to deliver such a simple message.

Another comment that aroused many responses from others participating, was this: What is a "letter" for purposes of this discussion? Is it the letter literally, or is it everything in the package: the brochure and whatever other sales pieces (catalog sheets, specifications, news releases, and or other items) are enclosed?

Again, what is in the letter? Is it page after page of smug assurances, boastful claims, and other assorted hyperbole, or is it an organized presentation of useful information? There is ample evidence that no copy is too long if it succeeds in holding the reader's interest, and the best way to do that is to write about the reader (i.e., the reader's wants, fears, hopes, dreams, ambitions, and other concerns). You can't help but hold the reader's attention if you offer information of direct interest and utility to him or her.

It is almost inevitable at this point to be reminded of an analogous and equally ancient popular argument about copy set solid versus copy set with ample white space in print advertising. For many, conventional wisdom is that the reader is repelled by text set solid in formidable blocks on a page, and he or she simply rebels emphatically and automatically at reading such copy. Those marketers and copywriters who are believers in short blocks of text and generous amounts of white space are quite confident that theirs is a correct print-advertising philosophy. However, some of the most successful print advertisements have been full pages of text, line after line and paragraph after paragraph, relieved only by an occasional indent for a new paragraph or sidehead. One such advertisement, a full-page letter headlined "I Want You to Have This Before It Is Too Late," and featuring a photo of (presumably) the advertiser, ran successfully for years in *Popular Mechanics*. The late Joe Karbo was extremely successful with another such print advertisement, headlined, "The Lazy Man's Way to Riches." These are by no means the only cases nor are they exceptions; they are merely two of the most outstanding examples.

The rationale supporting long sales copy and its print advertising counterpart, lengthy text set solid, is simple enough: If the copy "strikes a nerve" in the reader—arouses and sustains the reader's intense interest—he or she will endure until the last word of the last paragraph, no matter how far that is from the first word of the first paragraph. Those other matters are irrelevant: Short text and lots of white space do not induce a reader to become interested; only the right *copy* or *content* does. And when the copy is right for the purpose, you need no other inducements.

It is clear enough now that there is no universal rule about this, except that what is relevant is whatever engages and sustains the customer's interest. You can't pry a reader away from copy that, he or she is convinced, is important to his or her happiness, prosperity, security, or other aspects of well-being. And, yes, they are emotional issues more than rational ones.

Thus the real point is simply this: What kind of offer justifies the equivalent of that lengthy solid text or long sales copy? If you are inviting respondents to use an enclosed coupon to get two dinners for the price of one, how long a presentation is required? What can you say about that offer that would hold the reader's attention for several pages? On the other hand, if you are offering a costly wristwatch, you might very well have a great deal of useful information to provide about the product, its manufacture, and your guarantee.

Then again, as one veteran of the industry at the conference observed, What *is* long copy? Is it a lengthy parade of new facts and new ideas? Or is it the same main claim made over and over, each time with new benefits and new proofs, and finally repeated in a postscript? For that matter, is that really long copy, or is it short copy repeated to persuade those who weren't persuaded the first time? (Of course, a corollary question not raised at the conference is, Why would repeating the argument work a second, third, or nth time when it didn't work the first time?)

One participant even introduced a case of one of his clients who had gotten excellent results with unusually short copy—three lines surrounded by a generous amount of white space, as an extreme exception. Unfortunately, it was only a conversation piece; nothing useful was drawn from it.

One point that was not raised in connection with the question "What is long copy?" is that "long" is a relative term. What represents long copy for one case may not be long at all for another. That is, there is no absolute definition, such as number of pages. "Long" and "short" must be defined for the individual case. However, there is yet another aspect to the question: What is the *optimal* length of copy for any given case? Or, as the corollary to that question, what is the point of diminishing returns? Presumably, even if it is a general truth that copy sells better as it is lengthened, at what length is the copy maximally effective? That, too, is a question to which an answer is useful, but the answer is definitely one that must fit your individual marketing situation. Overly long copy is much like the salesperson who talks too much and is still selling when he or she should have shut up and asked for the order. That mistake often has the unfortunate result of unselling the customer who was ready to sign an order before the salesperson said too much.

Other matters raised as possible variants that would affect the perceived need for long or short copy included the overall purpose of the solicitation (e.g., sales versus leads and a cold list versus one of prequalified leads) the kind of response wanted, and the nature of the recipient.

The net result of the discussion illustrated clearly enough that no one has clear answers, and that an unqualified answer is simply not possible. But even qualified answers expressed here were heavily laden with personal opinions and "for instances" that were clearly individual cases, probably atypical. Obviously, we cannot draw firm conclusions based on a small number of individual cases, especially when the events in those cases are interpreted subjectively by individuals citing the cases to support a position. We need enough data, based on objective reporting, to draw conclusions with some degree of confidence in the conclusions. What we ought to investigate is not the merits of long versus short copy, but how to know which to use for any given case.

The concept overall is to gather and include in your marketing database the kind of information that will enable you to determine in advance what kind of copy will work best. How can you judge in advance, for example, just how long or short your copy ought to be for any given campaign?

First of all, it appears obvious that such a question does not exist as an absolute one, independent of other factors. To do any kind of organized research without starting from a base of total and absolute ignorance, it is necessary to establish one or more premises, and then test the premises in gathering the data. For this question, I suggest as a premise that the optimum length of the copy depends on the following factors:

1. The nature of the product or service.
2. The cost of the product or service.
3. The importance (to the customer) of the product or service.
4. The promised benefit and the proof required.
5. The action you want.

The Nature of the Product or Service

Questions to ask yourself in advance, regarding the nature of the product or service, is how much explanation of it is needed for the customer to gain a full understanding. If, for example, the product is a familiar one, such as a wristwatch, the copy does not focus on what wristwatch is but on what *this* wristwatch is—what makes it better, more valuable, more comfortable, more prestigious, or otherwise especially desirable. How much copy does it take to make the case? That is something you must judge and then test.

The Cost of the Product or Service

It seems fairly obvious that it takes more effort to sell a $1,000 item than it does to sell a $10 item. The length of the copy is thus inevitably linked to the size of the sale (i.e., to how much persuasion is required). But there are other factors, such as the brand name. You need not strain to persuade a customer of the value of a well-known expensive watch, as you must if the name is not well known.

The Importance of the Product or Service

Cost is not the only factor that affects how important an item is in a customer's mind. There are both practical and emotional elements involved in how a customer views the importance of an item offered. Life insurance on a person's spouse, for example, is most likely to be viewed with much greater gravity and longer deliberation than automobile insurance. Moreover, wives are likely to view life insurance on a spouse more seriously than husbands for the obvious reason that life insurance may be all a wife is left with when her spouse departs, whereas a husband does not usually face this problem.

The Promised Benefit

The promised benefit was postulated earlier to be part of the offer. However, the benefit or how it is expressed, is also a part of the copy. (None of the many elements are totally isolated from each other.) Losing weight is likely to be a more influential promise with a woman than with a man, and thus would justify longer copy to prove the case. Many individuals, and, again, usually women to a larger extent than men, will buy, try, or subscribe to almost anything that they are convinced will help them lose weight or keep it off.

The Action You Want

If you are selling magazine subscriptions, you want the customer to place an order. If you are selling houses or automobiles, you want to persuade the customer to come visit and look at the models. You need totally different kinds of motivation for each of these objectives.

All these items vary widely with the individuals, and all affect each other. No one ponders very long about buying a $20 wristwatch, but even the wealthy do not buy watches costing thousands of dollars without a great deal of deliberation. Persuading someone to come visit your model houses or automobile showroom is another matter. You aren't asking for money, but you are asking people to give you their time. For many people, this is as serious a request as one asking for money; time is a valuable commodity too.

OTHER ITEMS TO BE TESTED

You pursue and validate or invalidate these premises in your testing and in gathering data through dialogue with your customers. Just as you enter into your marketing database data derived from dialogue with customers, you should enter data derived from tests. Test data should be accumulated from one campaign to the next, to form a growing body of information that can be analyzed and applied effectively to the general case, as well as to the specific case. Of course, there are many other factors to be tested similarly. Here are a few typical items and some suggested premises to test for each one.

Business Response Envelopes (BREs)

The theory is that the average individual often does not have a stamp and envelope conveniently to hand, and is thus much more likely to respond promptly if you furnish a stamp and envelope. Probably that is a sound idea when you are appealing to the average individual in his or her home. However, that is not the case in business-to-business marketing. Most executives will simply turn their responses over to a secretary to mail, and the secretary will use company stationery and postage. At least, it has been my experience that responses by businesspeople rarely have arrived in the BRE I furnished. But it is worth testing for your own case.

Multicolor Printing and Paper

Whether multicolor printing produces better response than single-color printing does is a moot question in my mind. Certainly, printing in red ink on brown paper will not endear you to the reader because such printing is most difficult to read. My own candidate for greatest legibility is black ink on yellow paper, but black ink on white paper is usually quite satisfactory. It will take testing to discover whether colors really produce significant increases in response, and even then the differences may not be statistically great ones.

Paper Quality

A mail-order expert soundly condemned my copy as being printed on cheap and even cheap-looking paper, too shoddy (in his opinion) for the $79.95 I was asking. Unfortunately, I had already prepared the mailing, so I crossed my fingers and consigned it to the U.S. Postal Service. Fortunately, my customers were less critical or less discerning than the expert, and the mailing was quite successful. "Cheap" and "cheap looking," by the way, are not the same. I recall a case where the U.S. Air Force required us to use a costly paper that *looked* cheap (in their opinion) because they were being criticized by members of Congress for being a bit too profligate. In marketing, as in public relations, appearance is often more important than reality.

Other Response Devices

There is a popular theory that getting a customer "involved" somehow improves response. Publisher's Warehouse, *Reader's Digest,* and many others running multimillion-dollar contests obviously subscribe to this idea, and they enclose a variety of seals, stamps, and emblems that the contestant must find, detach, and paste somewhere on the entry forms, while contestants are also encouraged to rub off overprinted inks to reveal still more opportunities for prizes. How valid is the theory? Who knows; verifying data are quite hard to find, if they exist at all. The response devices are quite expensive, and it seems to be worthwhile to do at least some testing to validate or invalidate the premise under which all the activity and expense are required.

WHERE TO ACCUMULATE SUCH DATA: THE TACTICAL DATABASE

The information called for here has far-reaching significance. Philosophically, it is part of the relationship/marketing database because it is part of the dialogue stream that represents feedback from customers. In practice, it need not be entered physically into that database and probably is more efficiently handled by setting up a separate database for it. Because your marketing database is a relational database, you can install this other, more generalized data into a separate database and still import it into and use it as part of your marketing database.

However, this database will also contain the data gained from tests and from rollouts. Overall, it should be handled as a constantly growing bank of data that you can and should analyze periodically to infer new general truths on which to plan marketing strategies and tactics. As this database grows and you infer information from it, you will see more and more clearly what strategies and tactics work most effectively under various sets of conditions.

I suggest that you find a distinctive name for this new database to remind you of its purpose. I regard it as a "tactical database" and would so refer to it in order to distinguish it from the marketing database.

This raises an issue mentioned several times in passing, but not seriously addressed yet, which we will discuss in the next chapter.

Chapter 16

Hardware and Software Problems and Answers

Databased marketing is only one of the many developments growing out of the computer revolution of the eighties. The many technological breakthroughs in hardware and order-of-magnitude advances in software have slowed slightly, but they continue. New developments are difficult to predict, but they will certainly occur. To the extent that we can, we ought to consider where we are now in terms of the latest realities in both arenas of the computer revolution.

DATABASED MARKETING AND MAINFRAMES VERSUS DESKTOPS

Our main focus in the prior chapter was on uncovering general truths about our marketing methodologies, especially those on the creative side, by taking advantage of the unusual suitability of our marketing databases for such truth-finding researches. Prior to that chapter, we had concentrated our attention on collecting individual and personal data of marketing significance on each customer, as part of the relationship/databased marketing concept.

In pursuing the underlying idea of gathering information about individual customers, there is some tendency to forget that despite this revolutionary new way of gaining a greater understanding of your markets, ours is still a mass market (i.e., our whole economy is based on mass marketing). Without mass marketing, we could not have mass production, and we would not then have a generation of customers who are the best-fed, best dressed, best-educated, and best-supplied with material comforts in all history. Our entire socioeconomic system is based on an ever higher standard of living, and mass marketing has been a key to achieving this.

Inevitably, then, we have considered what databased marketing represents to mass marketing. We explored our databased and relationship-based marketing to expand the concept, and we added another dimension to the system: That was to utilize the growing bank of data resulting from our efforts in building marketing databases, testing, and rolling out campaigns, to learn the truth about many popular beliefs in marketing (e.g., copywriting principles and sundry other strategies and tactics commonly employed by all marketers) as they apply to your own marketing needs.

However, another subject related to this, perhaps indirectly but nevertheless too important an element of such studies to be ignored, is the issue of the hardware and software required for relationship and databased marketing generally, and for the main purpose of the studies postulated in the previous chapter. That is, just what computer capabilities are required for the tasks, including that of managing the tactical database proposed here as an element of the greater subject of relationship marketing?

The question of whether mainframe computers are a requirement for relationship and databased marketing generally has been noted and addressed briefly several times in previous chapters, but without a serious probe of the issues involved. There are those who are staunch defenders of the mighty mainframe computer: They are quite insistent that only a mainframe, with its massive memory and great storage capacities, can handle the data requirements of databased marketing. In fact, the vehemence with which some "old-timers" defend their arguments of mainframe supremacy and indispensability suggests that they consider themselves threatened directly by the PC, as it encroaches on the domain of the once dominant mainframe. (There are, in fact, many who believe that the existence of the mainframe computer is indeed threatened by the modern PC, but for this discussion we shall assume that the mainframe computer is an entity unto itself, firmly ensconced in its own niches in the business world, and, at best, only challenged by the PC for some kinds of duties. It is not my purpose here to predict the future of the mainframe, but only to assess the necessity for its use in databased marketing.)

Here, as elsewhere, there are probably few, if any, universal truths. Perhaps there are individual cases where only a mainframe computer can do the job efficiently and reliably. That might well be the case for General Motors, General Foods, and other supercorporations. But they represent only about 3 percent of all the 15 million companies in the United States, most of whom would be hard pressed to justify using a mainframe computer if, indeed, they could afford it at all. On the one hand, there is the question of absolute necessity for mainframes today: Isn't it possible for desktop computers to handle the job? On the other hand, there is also ample evidence of the still-growing ability of the latest desktop computers to handle major masses of data for important programs. The capability of the desktop computer is still growing steadily, is ample for today, and more than ample for tomorrow. If memory and storage capacities are the main areas of qualification or distinction between the two, the PC is indeed still a somewhat lesser power than the mainframe, but it is closing the gap steadily.

Costs Are Always a Consideration

One important consideration that does appear to be undeniable is the wide cost differential: Mainframe computer hardware and software are many times more expensive than are desktop computer hardware and software. "Many times more expensive" is not hyperbole, but a deliberately chosen comparative: Where a software item (e.g., a relational database) for a PC costs $2,000 or even $20,000, its counterpart for a mainframe computer is likely to cost $50,000 or even $150,000; and the cost of even the smallest mainframe computer is astronomical, compared with that of a desktop computer. (Although we have come to refer to every desktop computer as a "PC" (personal computer), they have long since outgrown that early status and are used increasingly by companies as central computers.) For example, the Adabas relational database system, designed to operate on mainframes and a product of Software AG of North America, Inc., ranges in price, according to several factors, from about $25,000 to about $175,000. The range typical for mainframe software.

That factor alone, cost, is likely to be a controlling factor in determining who can and who cannot put relationship/databased marketing to work effectively in their own marketing activities: A great many of the smaller organizations cannot afford the use of mainframes on even a time-sharing or rental basis, let alone the ownership of a mainframe system. For many of the smaller organizations, databased marketing must be with a desktop computer or there will be no databased marketing for them at all. Thus the critical importance of these issues.

Storage Capacities

The desktop computer has not yet caught up with the mainframe for total storage capacity but can offer adequate storage for all but the most extreme needs of databased marketing. If you wish to build a database of one million records, for example, estimating about 600 characters (bytes) of information for each record, you will need about 600 megabytes of storage. Add perhaps 25 or 30 percent more storage for software, ancillary data, and space to manipulate files, and you have a nominal requirement of 750 to 800 megabytes of storage. That is not difficult to achieve today in a desktop computer. In fact, aside from the several ancillary methods of storage, desktop computers today already offer hard-disk storage of five to six gigabytes, and are still growing in size. (A gigabyte is one billion bytes, e.g., 800 megabytes = 0.8 gigabyte.) Thus storage is itself not likely to be a problem for the average database need. Relatively few of us are likely to suffer from a shortage of storage capacity. In practical terms, the mainframe offers little advantage. The Adabas program mentioned here, for example, is mainframe software but requires only 450 kilobytes of memory, which is easily supplied by any modern PC.

Magnetic Tapes and Conversion Problems

One argument raised by mainframe champions is that so much of existing data today is on the large 9-track magnetic tapes characteristically used by mainframes. These must be converted for use by desktop computers. The fact is that several manufacturers offer equipment to enable a desktop computer to use these tapes directly, but there are also many services available to convert these tapes to one of the media used regularly and routinely by desktop computers. These media include floppy disks that can hold as much as 10 megabytes each, and several kinds of laser and optical compact disks that can hold several gigabytes each. Data from the tapes can also be transferred directly from a mainframe computer to the hard disk in your desktop computer via modem and dial-up telephone line. Thus it is no longer a problem to convert original data on the large magnetic tape reels and transfer it to PC-compatible storage media.

Processing Speeds

One way in which the mainframe is faster than the desktop computer results from the mainframe's wide data track or bus, which confers on it an ability to accept a large number of simultaneous inputs. Desktop computers are somewhat more limited in this capability, but it is of relatively minor importance, inasmuch as there is rarely a need for online processing of data in building marketing databases; the work is essentially an offline operation. In terms of their internal data-processing speeds and access speeds, on the other hand, the latest desktop computers are quite fast, often much faster than mainframes.

Printing Speeds

Another argument raised by the champions of mainframes is that many applications need the high-speed printers normally run in conjunction with mainframe printout operation. That, too, is an irrelevant argument: Any printer that can be driven by a mainframe computer can be driven by a desktop computer, even if tape drives are needed to get maximum printer speed. Thus printing speeds and capacities are really not a computer problem per se. Printing production rates of 2,000 pages per hour and even higher are possible with desktop computers and high-speed offline printers.

Multiple Access

In database marketing, it may be necessary for a number of people to have both input and output access to the central computer from their own remote stations. That would have been a legitimate argument for the mainframe computer a few years ago. It is not today. If it is necessary to provide many people with access to the central computer, a large number of desktop computers may be linked by any of several available LAN (local area network) systems. The remote stations from which access to and from the central computer is provided may be either dumb terminals or they may be fully operable desktop computers. The tendency is toward the latter because the cost differential between the PC and the dumb terminal is small, so it is entirely practicable to use desktop computers as terminals, and this is probably more cost effective than using dumb terminals hardwired to a central computer.

One rationalization offered to justify requiring a mainframe for databased marketing is that there is a need for a bank of telemarketers to have online access to the central computer. Presumably, many individuals (who knows how many) will be making calls to and accepting calls from customers all day, and will be inputting data as they talk to the customers. Presumably, the operator will call up the customer's file from the central computer's database and display the file on the remote terminal, updating it as the conversation with the customer proceeds. There is, however, no reason to suppose that the capability is limited to mainframes. Desktop computers linked together by any of the LAN systems (ARCNet, Ethernet, Token Ring, and others) are capable of providing similar multiple access, and are in quite common use today.

Operators

One other major consideration is that of the need to hire a computer operator when running a mainframe computer with all its peripheral devices versus the convenience of running desktop computers that just about anyone can learn to operate with brief instruction. This can be a major consideration, especially in emergency situations, when an unexpected need arises to run the system in the evening or on a day when the offices are normally closed down (e.g., a holiday or weekend). Such situations arise all too often and, perversely enough, often at the most inconvenient times, when it is all but impossible to bring a computer operator in and no one available knows how to even turn the computer on, let alone operate it.

It is not by chance that this is the case. One reason for this difference is that the manufacturers of mainframe computers and those writing software programs for mainframe computers expect you to have a trained computer operator and other professional data processing experts available: The hardware and software are designed on that premise. However, the manufacturers of desktop computers and those writing software for desktop computers design their machines and software to be used by the general public (i.e., by those trained only briefly or self-trained with the aid of the computer hardware and software manuals).

DESKTOP SOFTWARE

We have considered a number of kinds of software you need in connection with your marketing. Most of it has been the conventional kind used in all direct marketing, whether databased or not, and consists of three primary types of programs: One is software for merge/purge, used to merge lists, purge duplicate names and addresses, and standardize formats. A second type of program that we have discussed is mail/merge, software that merges names and addresses from your mailing list with form letters, so as to address each customer individually, despite the letter being the same for each. (We also discussed variants of this application, as in some of the major contest mailings.) Most significant to the subject of databased and relationship marketing, however, has been the database management software.

Databased Management Software

There are two basic kinds of DBM system, the flat-file and the relational. Flat-file systems enable you to work with only the records already on file in that system. Relational systems permit you to go to other files and other databases as though they were themselves part of the system.

That is nominal truth, but it is also an oversimplification; as in most other things, the definitions, differences, and distinctions are not that black and white. It is possible in a flat file, for example, to import other files. That doesn't mean to move those other files, however; it means to copy them. But the copies of those other files would then become part of the DBM and would be redundant with the originals from which they were copied, wasting space and time. The main point of the relational database is to eliminate the redundancy of keeping copies of files in more than one place (i.e., to avoid the necessity for adding copies of other files to the DBM). In the case of databased marketing, one objective is to continue to add new data to records indefinitely. Keeping all of it in one DBM would soon make it so large as to be awkward to handle. Thus there is no question but that a relational database is the right one for relationship and database marketing. Still, that doesn't mean that the relational database is ideal; the best relational database still has its shortcomings for databased marketing purposes.

Structured versus Unstructured Data

The most popular use of desktop computers is for word processing and similar functions: writing reports, manuscripts, speeches, lists, presentations, and all other paperwork of the business and professional world. Such software programs are free form in type, suitable for totally unstructured data. That is, the data are as structured as the writer may desire and amenable to endless restructuring, redesign, and other manipulations.

Mailing lists are at the other extreme. Their usefulness is dependent in large degree on some practical and uniform structure (e.g., a 5-line address, with telephone numbers and other fields) to code the lists. One problem with conventional database management systems, even of relational databases, is the rigidity of their structure. All conventional database management programs impose some degree of rigidity on the structure of the data. although this varies, from one DBM to another: In some systems, for example, you cannot have two fields with the same name. If you want two fields (i.e., two lines) for a street address, you have to call them "address1" and "address2," or otherwise distinguish one from the other. This is only one of the many difficulties of structure you are likely to encounter in typical database managers: You must create a separate field for each item by which you might wish to retrieve or sort the records. as one example. It is usually impracticably difficult to add new fields to an existing database. And there is usually no way you can add narrative remarks to a record beyond brief notes.

It is inevitable that there are limits on how flexible any database manager can be, although some are far more flexible than others. But all conventional database managers are based on the principle of working with essentially structured data (i.e., organized according to the master plan of the DBM designers and following a set of rules to ensure that the data are so structured).

There is an alternative, today, in programs that are designed for use with unstructured data. These essentially free-form programs can be used as relational database managers of exceptional flexibility. In some respects, they are better suited to databased marketing applications than the most sophisticated and popular conventional relational database management systems. A number of these systems are available, but I shall describe one, a system called "askSam" (Version 5), which I investigated especially to evaluate its suitability for data-based marketing.

The askSam System

askSam is the product of askSam Systems, to whom I am indebted for their generous permission to quote freely from their manuals, which describe the program as one that "can be used as both a database manager and a free-form information manager." In fact, askSam is an almost bewilderingly sophisticated and complex program, with far too many features really to do it justice here. I shall present the most relevant highlights to illustrate the advantages of using a database management program that can handle unstructured data in creating marketing databases and otherwise supporting relational and databased marketing generally. In askSam's own words, "askSam is an information storage and retrieval system for use with both textual and numeric information."

The program is a database manager with many word processing or text editor features. It accommodates both structured and unstructured data, which can even be mixed in the same records or other files. You can set up records with fields, structured fully as in conventional database managers, but you can also enter data in any way you like and retrieve it by searching for any field, word, term, phrase, number, or almost any other test string or identifying item. In fact, I found it possible to access records almost instantly with only a part of an address or telephone number. If I recalled only that the address was on Broadway, using "Broadway" as a search term presented all items with "Broadway" as part of the record, and I could scroll through them to find the one I wanted. Following are just a few of the other significant attributes of such systems, as represented by askSam. *Note:* I list here only a few functions that are obviously of interest for building marketing databases. There are many other functions and capabilities that I will not mention here, although some individuals might find them useful in marketing applications.

Types of Field. Most database systems require designating a field as alphabetical or numerical. askSam does not require fields to be so designated, and will accept textual, alphabetical, or numerical entries in any field. In fact, you don't have designate fields at all: You can keep the data in totally unstructured form and, if you wish, reorganize it and add fields later.

File Sizes. This program can accommodate file sizes limited primarily by the storage capacity of your system. (Theoretical sizes are up to four gigabytes.)

Fields. You make fields whatever you want them to be. There are no mandatory fields, and no mandatory number or size of fields. You can add fields later, if you wish, or make changes to them at random.

Text Editor. The program has its own text editor that does all the normal functions of a text editor, including cut-and-paste operations.

Random Entries. You can enter notes or memoranda at random anywhere. The program has three modes of operation: RECORD, DOCUMENT, and FREE mode, and you are free to switch to any at your convenience. A record is limited to one screen in size; 20 lines of 80 columns, and so a maximum of 1600 characters. It is the most suitable mode for structuring your data, as in conventional database management systems. Records can be linked to each other to form a document, so the one-screen limitation is not a problem. The FREE mode, for free-form entry of information, has no boundaries: The record can be as long as you wish it to be. It is also the most useful mode for writing generally, since it is entirely amenable to completely unstructured data. You can thus work with structured records and unstructured data in the same file or document.

Programming. As in the case of most sophisticated database management programs, askSam has its own programming capabilities, adding further to its general flexibility.

To illustrate some of the relevant flexibility and advantages of being able to combine structured and unstructured data, consider Figure 16–1, which presents several examples from askSam's demonstration program. These files have both structured and unstructured data in them, providing a ready facility for adding as much information as you wish, in almost any form you wish. However, you need not structure the data completely, but may use the form of Figure 16–2. In either case, you can sort, retrieve, print, add to, edit, or otherwise use and manipulate records and the data freely, to suit whatever needs you perceive, based on any word, term, numeric, or string you choose. You can also modify and alter the forms, and send data to screen, printer, or disk.

The field names in the first figure have a left bracket ([) following them, which makes them *explicit* fields, identified by the program as "NAMES." The data following field names are *values.* The other two types of fields are *implied* fields and *contextual* fields. A field such as "Attorney Jane Smith," uses "Attorney" as a contextual field, and this then can be utilized in contextual commands such as "{AFTER[} Attorney" to define the field value "Jane Smith." (You may also send values with or without names to disks, reports, printers, or other destination.) The symbol $ is an implied field in an entry such as $500, and may also be utilized searching, sorting, and generating reports.

```
      NAME [ Edward Martin
   ADDRESS [ 111 E. Broadway
CITY/STATE [ New York, NY
       ZIP [ 99999
     PHONE [ 555/123-4567
     NOTES [ Ed's wife is named Leslie, and he is a CPA.
```

He called 10-16-88 about changes in tax code impact on short-term buyouts.

His latest venture is in graphical interfaces based on zoological design submitted by Lisa Ruffolo, of Madison, WI.

```
      NAME [ Rapid Transport
   ADDRESS [ PO Box 2386
CITY/STATE [ Carlsbad, NM
       ZIP [ 79770
     PHONE [ 505/555-4421
     NOTES [ Notify of upcoming shipment of imported chocolates.
```

```
      NAME [ Suzanne Lindsey
    ADRESS [ Nautilus Drive, NE
CITY/STATE [ Palm Beach, FL
       ZIP [ 32333
     PHONE [ 555/333-1111
     NOTES [ She is partner in accounting firm with headquarters in
             Brussels.
```

Talked to her 10-16-88. Call back on 11-16-88. Her birthday is December 16, and her son's name is Kevin. He plays the cello.

Figure 16–1. Conventional record with structured and unstructured data.

Here are a few such possibilities suggested by the designers:

Retrieve and route to screen, printer, or disk: documents, records. field contents, paragraphs, sentences, or lines . . .

. . . with searches against: a "remembered" subset of words, word groupings, symbols, field names, interchangeable calendar dates in any format and/or their context in a record

. . . using: sort option codes; Boolean operators (and/or/not) and "wildcards"; arithmetic comparisons; proximity searches within a specified number of words, lines, sentences, or paragraphs.

There are many other possibilities: various other combinations of structured and unstructured data, and many other possible forms and reports. Most important, however, is the freedom with which data may be entered and manipulated in both formal and informal means and

Ben Neel Blalock
10001 Conch Lane
Key Largo, FL
33333
904/584-6589

Last called on 10-16-88, 16:44:36.

He has controlling interest in shrimping fleet located near Aruba. Attended meeting in Los Angeles in August. Interested in advertising the shellfish import business in California, if needs can be met by marketing firm of Jensen and Meyerson. Check with Randy Herndon on balance sheet. $8,000 payment due 10-16-89.

Marie Mitchell
MITCHELL & ASSOCIATES
PO Box 1356
New York, NY 10011
212-903-2145
Ms. Mitchell

5-9-88: Thought we should use customer profiles in our advertising. Is willing to provide a testimonial.

DONE: Seaside Advertising has helped me increase our client base through a well-executed direct mail campaign. The professional brochure reached the right people, and we are now providing financial counseling in three states. March 15, 1988. Pub Sept 1988—Get Mary Lane to write the piece on MITCHELL & ASSOCIATES.

Figure 16–2. Records with completely unstructured data.

formats. This, with the relational nature of the system design, makes it easy to build and maintain a large number of separate customer files that can be used as elements of the marketing database. You thus can have the efficiency of specialized databases for accounting, inventory, project status, customer complaints, delinquent accounts, calendar (appointments), scheduling, marketing, and other needs, while still enjoying ready access to all the others from the marketing database. But even that is not the whole story of the versatility offered by such newer systems.

Hypertext

An outstanding example of the versatility possible is that, in addition to the conventional account files for invoicing and crediting payments, you can utilize such a program as a kind of electronic read file by using the hypertext capability. Instead of spending an hour or two flipping and reading sheets of bound correspondence and attached records to find an item or absorb the history of a project of some kind, you sit at a keyboard and use any of several hypertext methods to search quickly through various documents and records. (Hypertext is an exceptionally versatile search capability that furnishes, for this purpose, a function somewhat like an electronic encyclopedia, with indexing and cross-indexing.) Should there be notes too lengthy for addition to a record, a notation in the record can refer the reader to a read file.

We have not done a great deal more than peer under the outer skin of the new art of databased relationship marketing, but its future looks quite bright indeed, if it keeps pace with the burgeoning technology of today's data handling hardware and software.

Glossary

ACTIVE BUYERS OR ACTIVE CUSTOMERS Those who have made a purchase, usually within the year.

ACTIVE MEMBER Member of book or record club still ordering.

ACTIVE SUBSCRIBER Subscribers to periodicals still receiving their copies.

AD HOC REPORT Informal report in response to casual query made of database (e.g., how many buyers of wrist watches last year were over 60?).

ALPHANUMERIC Including both alphabetical and numerical characters.

ALGORITHM A rule, procedure, or formula for processing data.

ANALOG Of continuous form, opposite of digital.

ASCII American Standard Code for Information Interchange, a de facto standard for data format, recognized by all computers.

BACK END Additional business from customers after initial orders.

BACK TEST Additional test for verification.

BAD PAY (also nonpay) Orders (e.g., subscriptions) entered but not subsequently paid for.

BATCH PROCESSING Processing large quantity of data in one pass.

BATCH PROGRAM Short program that runs procedure or invokes a larger program automatically when invoked by a brief command.

BAUD Unit of speed in transmission, equal to bits per second.

BINARY Two-state (e.g., 1,0) language used by computers; computer language.

BIT Smallest unit of data in computer systems.

BOUNCE-BACK Sending sales literature for other products with fulfillment of original order or otherwise following up a sale with a try for a bounce-back order.

BPI Bytes per inch, measure of magnetic tape density.

BPS bits per second. *See also* Baud.

BRC/BRE Business reply card or business response envelope, supplied to customer to use for ordering or querying further.

BREAKEVEN The volume of sales that returns all costs.

BROKERAGE COMMISSION The commission, usually 20 percent of the rental fee, paid by a list owner to a list broker for marketing the list.

BUGS Errors and problems in computer software.

BULK MAIL Third class mail.

BYTE Units of data (8 bits) equal to alphanumeric character.

CARD PACK/CARD DECK Package of postcards mailed as direct mail advertising.

CARRIER ROUTE Arrangement of addresses grouped by mail carrier's route.

CARRIER ROUTE PRESORT (also presort) Presort of mail to carrier routes for reduced postal rate.

CHESHIRE LABEL Continuous form on which names and addresses are printed and which is then cut into labels and fixed to envelopes or packages, all by machine.

CHIP The modern electronic component containing all the circuits.

CLUSTER Grouping of individuals according to demographic characteristics.

COBOL (Computer Business Oriented Language) A computer language for business use.

CODE *See* Key.

COMPILED LIST List gathered from directories and other published sources.

COMPUTER LANGUAGE Any of several sets of codes and terms for writing computer programs.

COMPUTER RECORD Information about any individual or organization, usually an element of a database.

CONSUMER DATABASE/LIST Undiscriminated list or database of customers and/or prospects.

CONTROLLED CIRCULATION The subscribers to a publication whose circulation is limited to readers of a given interest (e.g., a profession, trade, or industry) and audited for accuracy; usually a trade journal with free subscription.

CONVERSION RATE (or response rate) Percentage of addressees who order.

COPY The written sales or advertising material.

CPI Cost per inquiry.

CPM (cost per thousand) Cost of mailout or other promo arrived at by dividing total cost by numbers of pieces mailed in thousands.

CPO (cost per order) Calculation of advertising/promo costs to get each order.

CPU (central processing unit) The central operating circuits of a computer.

CRT (cathode ray tube) The central element of a TV or computer monitor.

CUSTOMER DATABASE/LIST List or database of actual customers.

CUSTOMER PROFILE Chief characteristics of customer as related to marketing.

DATA Information, usually in computer form.

DATABASE (also data base) A special compilation of names and addresses arranged for analyzing, sort, and/or retrieving by any of many assigned codes.

DATA ENTRY (also keyboarding) Entering data into system (on tape or disk).

DEBUG Find and correct problems in new computer program.

DECOY NAME Names rented lists are "salted" with to detect unauthorized use.

DEMOGRAPHICS Statistical characteristics of groups of people (e.g., census data).

DIRECT ACCESS Ability to go straight to desired data item, as on a disk, in comparison with gaining access on a tape, which must be traversed to get to the item.

DISK Most popular and convenient device for storage and retrieval of data. Most computers today have built-in "fixed" drives (also called "hard drives"), which are the fastest variety. But there are advantages to other drives, with removable disks, called "floppies."

DMA Direct Marketing Association.

DUMMY NAME same as decoy name.

DUPE Duplicate item, generally name and address.

DUPE ELIMINATION Removal of redundant names, as in merge/purge.

EXCHANGE Swap of name lists between mailers.

EXPIRE Subscription that has not been renewed.

FIELD Individual entry in a record.

FILE MAINTENANCE Keeping lists clean and accurate. *See* List cleaning; Merge/purge.

FLAT Postal term for any package mailed flat, but usually refers to brochures, magazines, and other periodicals mailed flat and without envelopes.

FLAT FILE Simplest kind of database manager, one that can handle only one file at a time.

FLOPPY (or floppy disk) Disk coated with iron oxide and used as storage device and as input/output media with desktop computers.

FORTRAN Formula Translation, a computer language.

FREQUENCY Number of times a customer buys.

FRONT END Initial response to a solicitation.

FULFILLMENT Responding to customer's order; processing and filling orders.

GEO CODE Symbols used to identify geographic locations.

HARDWARE Computer equipment, as distinct from software. *See also* Software.

HOTLINE Current and recent transactions.

HOUSE LISTS Lists owned by the mailer or broker.

INDICIA Postal permits imprinted on envelopes.

INFORMATION RETRIEVAL Bringing selected data up on screen, printed out, or transferred to disk or tape.

INQUIRIES Requests from prospects for information.

INQUIRY ADVERTISING Soliciting inquiries to build mailing lists and sales leads.

INSERT (also package insert) Promotional item added to literature package.

INTERFACE Point of information exchange between machines, humans, or humans and machines.

KEY Distinctive item added to address or order form to identify source of order.

LAN Local Area Network, a method for linking desktop computers in a given location with each other to share printers, programs, and other utilities and ancillary devices.

LASER Adjective for laser printer and for laser letter, one printed on a laser printer.

LEADS/SALES LEADS Prospects who have been qualified.

LETTER SHOP Vendor providing various services with reference to mailing and promotion.

LIFESTYLE A presumption that everyone within a cluster (a demographically defined group) shares certain values and patterns of living.

LIFETIME VALUE   A presumption as to the total contribution to the company a given customer represents.

LIST BROKER   Vendor who rents mailing lists.

LIST CLEANING   Maintaining mailing lists by removing nixies and dupes.

LIST COMPILER   One who assembles lists from published sources.

LIST EXCHANGE   *See* Exchange.

LIST MAINTENANCE   Keeping a mailing list up to date and free of errors.

LIST MANAGER   One who markets lists for list owner; list broker.

LIST OWNER   Publisher, mail order house, or other owner of lists.

LIST RENTAL   Arranging to permit one-time sue of list for fee.

LIST SEGMENT   Chosen portion of a list.

LIST SEQUENCE   Order in which list names are kept (e.g., by zip code).

LIST TEST   Mailing to a part of a list to judge the list, the copy, the price, or other element of a promotion.

LTV (lifetime value)   The dollar volume of an individual customer over his or her "lifetime" as a customer.

M   Symbol used to represent 1,000.

MAGNETIC TAPE (also magtape)   Reel of tape used to store information; usually with reference to mainframe computers.

MAIL DATE PROTECTION   Agreement by a list owner, when renting a large list, to refrain from renting to anyone else for some period prior to and following the renter's stipulated mailing date.

MAILER   Anyone who sends out material by districts.

MAIL/MERGE   Computer capability of printing out a form letter but addressing each copy to an individual by taking the individual's name from a mailing list stored in the computer. *See also* Personalization.

MAIL PREFERENCE SERVICE   Consumers who have requested that their names be removed from mailing lists.

MAIL SHOP   An organization that supports mailers by assembling literature packages and performing sundry related services.

MAINFRAME   Large computers that require raised floors (to accommodate cabling beneath them) air conditioning, and other special features.

MARKET PENETRATION   The percentage of buyers who are your customers as compared with the total size of the market you choose to address.

MATCH CODE   Identification items used on records to enable sorting and retrieval by any of several items (fields).

MB OR MB Megabyte, or one million bytes.

MEMBERS Active member of book club, record club, or similar club; active credit card holder.

MEMORY The temporary storage area of a computer, in which data is manipulated, as compared with its areas for permanent storage of data.

MENU Presentations on computer screens to help users find their way.

MERGE/PURGE Combining lists to remove duplicate names. Also refers to programs that permit lists in different formats to be combined in a common format.

MODELING A statistical operation, the purpose of which is to examine all the customers in a database for common factors and project a representative model.

MODEM A device that allows communication between computers via dial-up telephone lines.

MOUSE A mechanical device that, by rolling it about and pressing a switch, issues commands to the computer.

MULTIBUYER A buyer whose name appears on completely different lists.

MULTIHITS Multiple matches in a merge/purge.

MULTIMEDIA Advertising and promotion that uses more than one medium at the same time.

MULTIPLE REGRESSION Statistical analysis and manipulation of data to develop the formula explaining correlations of variables in customer behavior.

NEGATIVE OPTION A plan such as the book club in which the item is sent and billed each month unless the member opts to block it.

NET NAMES The number of names remaining after merge/purge of dupes.

NET-NAME ARRANGEMENT Agreement to accept payment for less than total number of names shipped to compensate for dupes.

NICHE/MARKET NICHE Specialized segment of a total market.

NIXIE Mail returned for incorrect address, addressee moved, etc.

NTH NAME SAMPLE Sampling a list by 10th name, 20th name, other nth name.

OFFER Usually product, service, terms; may also be benefit promised.

OFFLINE ACTIVITY Computer operations when not connected to another computer.

ONE-TIME USE Rental for single use.

ONLINE ACTIVITY Actions while communicating with another computer.

ORDER CARD/ORDER FORM   Form for customer convenience in placing order.

PACKAGE   Package of literature and inserts in mailing.

PACKAGE TEST   Tryout of package on portion of mailing list.

PAID INQUIRIES   Prospects paying for catalog, other response to inquiry.

PC   Personal or desktop computer.

PENETRATION   Percentage of total category represented by names on list. Also portion of a given market or niche captured.

PER INQUIRY (PI)   Special arrangement whereby mailer gets free advertising and pays fee for each inquiry.

PER ORDER (PO)   Special arrangement whereby mailer gets free advertising and pays commission on each order.

PERSONALIZATION   Addressing a customer by personal name in literature, usually by means of a "mail/merge" process.

PRESORT   Separating and packaging mail to take advantage of postal discounts.

PRESSURE-SENSITIVE LABEL   Label with sticky back exposed by peeling off backing.

PROSPECTS   Prospective customers.

PSYCHOGRAPHICS   Array of lifestyle characteristics.

QUALIFY   Establish viability of prospects for becoming customers.

RANDOM SAMPLE   One or more names chosen at random from a list.

RATE-OF-RETURN CURVE   Estimate of how response to a mailing will decline to the point at which a reasonable measure of results may be made.

RECENCY   Term for most recent date customer has purchased something.

REFERRAL   Promotion offering bonus or gift to a member who brings in another member.

REGRESSION/REGRESSION ANALYSIS   A study of variables to correlate them and so be able to make predictions of the results of various combinations. (*See also* Multiple regression.)

RELATIONAL   Refers to relational database manager, which permits you to work with several files at a time.

REPEAT MAILING   A second, follow-up mailing to the same list.

REPLY DEVICE (also response device)   Any device facilitating a response from addressee.

RESPONDENT   Anyone who responds to a mailing.

RESPONSE DECK   *See* Card pack.

RESPONSE RATE   Percentage of addressees who respond.

RETURN DATE   The date the mailer says the names are needed.

RETURN PERCENTAGE   *See* Response rate.

ROI (return on investment)   A method (other than response rate) to calculate results by using actual profit versus costs of campaign.

ROLLOUT   Mailing the rest of the list after initial testing.

SALT NAME   *See* Decoy name.

SAMPLE MAILING PIECE   A sample of the package to be mailed, submitted for list owner's approval.

SEED NAME   *See* Decoy name.

SELF-MAILER   Periodical, brochure, or other piece mailed with a label but without an envelope.

SEGMENTATION   Division of mail into coded groups for testing and/or improvement of response.

SEQUENCE   *See* List sequence.

SEX SELECTION   Capability for sorting names by gender.

SIC   Standard Industrial Classification. All industries have an SIC.

SOFTWARE   Programs used by the computer.

SORT   Order in which names are arranged by computer command.

SOURCE   Media by which names are gathered or acquired.

SPLIT TEST/SPLIT RUN TEST   Testing two versions of offer by running each in one half of mailing list or one half of periodical run (where publishers offer such features).

STATE COUNT   Number of names in each state of interest.

TAPE DUMP   Printout of data on tape.

TAPE FORMAT (layout)   The arrangement of the data in tape files.

TEST   *See* List test.

TEST PANEL   Selection of names to be used for test.

TITLE ADDRESSING   Inclusion of titles of individuals on list.

TRIAL SUBSCRIPTIONS   Special, short-term subscriptions.

UNIQUE NAMES   Names surviving merge/purge.

UNIVERSE   Total mailing list.

UPDATE   *See* List cleaning.

USPS   United States Postal Service.

ZIP CODE   Numerical code assigned to each geographic entity by USPS.

ZIP CODE SEQUENCE   Frequently used order of arrangement of names.

ZIP COUNT   Number of names for each zip code of list.

Bibliography

DAVID SHEPARD ASSOCIATES The New Direct Marketing How to Implement a Profit-Driven Database Marketing Strategy (Homewood: Business One Irwin, 1990).
Other Entries: Direct marketing—Data Processing; Marketing—Data bases; Data base management; Direct marketing—Statistical methods.

HUGHES, ARTHUR M. The Complete Database Marketer, Tapping Your Customer Base to Maximize Sales and Increase Profits (Chicago: Probus Publishing Co., 1991).
Other Entries: Marketing.

RAPP, STAN AND COLLINS, THOMAS L. MaxiMarketing: The new direction in advertising, promotion, and marketing strategy (New York: McGraw-Hill, 1987).
Other Entries: Marketing; Advertising; Sales promotion; Collins, Thomas L.

RAPP, STAN AND COLLINS, THOMAS L. The Great Marketing Turnaround: The Age of the Individual—and How to Profit from It (Englewood Cliffs: Prentice-Hall, 1990).
Other Entries: Marketing; Advertising; Sales promotion.

HARPER, ROSE Mailing List Strategies: A Guide to Direct Mail Success (New York: McGraw-Hill, 1986).
Other Entries: Mail-order business.

FIDEL, RAYA Database Design for Information Retrieval: A Conceptual Approach (New York: John Wiley & Sons, 1987).
Other Entries: Data bases; Information storage and retrieval systems.

SHAW, ROBERT AND STONE, MERLIN   Database Marketing: Strategy & Implementation (New York: John Wiley & Sons, 1988, 1990).
Other Entries: Marketing—Data bases; Database management.

GESSFORD, JOHN E.   How to Build Business-Wide Databases (New York: John Wiley & Sons, 1991).

SAVINI, GLORIA   24-Karat Database.
Summary: How a long-time retailer used marketing database to cultivate its customers and double its number of stores. In Direct Marketing, MAR 01 1989 v 51 n 11, page 36.

STORING DATA
Summary: An expert explains how to develop and maintain a retail store's database of customers and prospects. Interview with Fred Allen and Pete Hoke. In Direct Marketing, APR 01 1989 v 51 n 12, page 22.

CARNEY, JIM   Glamorous Database.
Summary: Supporting its sales force is paramount at Mary Kay Cosmetics—just how they do it is, well, beautiful. In Direct Marketing, JUL 01 1989 v 52 n 3, page 54.

WOJTAS, GARY W.   A Perfect Fit.
Summary: Using customer information gleaned from its retail sales outlets, this established shoe manufacturer has discovered the marketing power of database. In Direct Marketing, NOV 01 1989 v 52 n 7, page 26.

WHEATON, CYNTHIA BAUGHAN   How To Create A Customer Database.
Summary: Follow these basic design rules and the result will be a powerful business tool. In Direct Marketing, FEB 01 1990 v 52 n 10, page 34.

PASSAVANT, PIERRE   The Strategic Database.
Summary: Investing heavily in your database, with lackluster results? Here's how to get more value for your money. In Direct Marketing, MAY 01 1990 v 53 n 1, page 40.

FREEHLING, JOHN S.   Simpson's Paradox and Database Profiling.
Summary: Two rights can make a left. In Direct Marketing, SEP 01 1990 v 53 n 5.

DATABASE MARKETING FROM PAST TO PRESENT
Summary: From its primitive beginning to its sophisticated uses today, you'll see what the database is so important to your marketing efforts. In Telemarketing, NOV 01 1990 v 9 n 5.

HAVLICEK, CHUCK   Demystifying Database Marketing.
Summary: Using computers to organize data lets programs target mailings based on learners' interests and demographic factors. In Adult Learning, SEP 01 1990 v 2 n 1, page 13.

RAPP, STAN AND COLLINS, TOM   Turnaround Marketing.
   Summary: Forget creative, think database. In an adaptation of the new book by Stan Rapp and Tom Collins, the authors discuss "The Great Marketing Turnaround" to be achieved by pinpoint consumer profiling. With specific examples from database success In Adweek's Marketing Week, AUG 27 1990 v 31 n 35, page 20.

MANN, DONALD C.   Database Marketing: How It's Changing Your Business.
   Summary: Applying the information contained in your MCIF. In Bank Marketing, AUG 01 1990 v 22 n 8, page 30.

VAN DOREN, DORIS C. AND STICKNEY, THOMAS A.   How to Develop a Database for Sales Leads: Specific steps for developing a sales leads database.
   In Industrial Marketing Management, AUG 01 1990 v 19 n 3, page 201.

SCHWARTZ, JOE   Databases Deliver the Goods: Building personal relationships with customers is what database marketing is about. Here's how to bring customers along the "loyalty continuum."
   In American Demographics, SEP 01 1989 v 11 n 9, page 22.

TOWNSEND, BICKLEY   Lifelong Learning. Database marketing is working for New York University's School of Continuing Education.
   In American Demographics, FEB 01 1990 v 12 n 2, page 38.

DATABASE MARKETING DEMYSTIFIED
   Summary: Linking names, addresses and other data about individual customers to their purchases can open all sorts of possibilities. But where do you begin? In Progressive Grocer, NOV 01 1989 v 68 n 11, page 21.

MILLER, STEVEN   Mine the Direct Marketing Riches in Your Database.
   In The Journal of Business Strategy, NOV 01 1989 v 10 n 6, page 33.

REISBERG, GERALD AND GILBERT, SAMUEL   Finding Quality Prospects: Making the most of your business database.
   In Target Marketing, FEB 1991, page 59.

GEIGER, CHRISTOPHER W.   Database-Building Requires Firm Commitment.
   Summary: A minuscule budget and a short-term commitment will only undermine the process of enhancing the database. In DM News, JUL 30, 1990, page 28.

HUGHES, ARTHUR MIDDLETON   How to Build a Successful Marketing Database.
   Summary: (Excerpted from The Complete Database Marketer.) The path is long and hard but worth the trouble if you know where you want to go. In DM News, MAR 18, 1991, page 27.

JACKSON, ROB   Package Goods' New Target: Database Marketing.
   Summary: How a manufacturer can get a database marketing program under way and looks at advantages of targeted coupons over FSI coupons.

DIETZ, ALEX   Why Accounting Database Systems Won't Work.
   Summary: Discusses the limitations of accounting databases and the greater specificity that marketing databases provide. In DM News, JUN 24, 1991, page 21.

BARTKO, MAX   How to Build a "Smart" Prospecting Database.
   Summary: Replacing the traditional practice of mailing to rented lists with special, private lists. In DM News, JUN 24, 1991, page 23.

GROSS, MARTIN   Financial DM Moves from Disaster to Databases.
   Summary: Adapting the examples set by banks for direct marketing of securities by Wall Street brokerage houses. In DM News, JUN 25, 1990, page 27.

WHITE, DON   Conversational Databases Are DMers' Future.
   Summary: Using existing databases to increase bank and insurance sales. In DM News, JUL 1, 1991, page 23.

EMERICK, TRACY   The Power and Glory of Desktop Marketing.
   Summary: Using your desktop computer for information management and related marketing activity. In DM News, FEB 18, 1991, page 57.

BIRT, RICHARD AND COOPER, CATHY   Bracing for the Coming Sea Change in Marketing.
   Summary: On the increasing complexity of marketing in the database marketing age. In DM News, JUL 30, 1990, page 25.

SHEPARD, DAVID   What's Different About Database Marketing?
   Summary: The difference between focusing on the individual and focusing on the group, and how the difference affects decision-making, profit projection, and creative strategy. In DM News, DEC 3, 1990, page 25.

MANN, DONALD   Why You Can Bank on Database Marketing.
   Summary: A bank's customer application files can be built into a true relational database. In DM News, APR 8, 1991, page 29.

STAFF WRITERS: Database Marketing Has to Prove Itself.
   Summary: Corporations like the concept . . . but still wonder how it will pay off. In Target Marketing, SEP 1991, page 18.

KEEFE, MARK   Tips on Developing a Double-Duty DM Database.
Summary: How to model a marketing database to enhance relationships with your customers. In DM News, SEP 23, 1991, page 19.

MCQUAID, JAMES D. AND BONELLO, PHILLIP H.   Putting the Relations in Relationship Marketing.
Summary: All those sophisticated modeling programs will do little good if they are not integrated with printing, creative, and other marketing functions.

JASINSKI, RICH AND MORRIS, MARK   Save Money: Run Your Database from a PC.
Summary: Not only can today's pc handle your database marketing needs, but it can probably do so more efficiently and certainly at less cost than a mainframe computer. In DM News, Dec 16, 1991, page 23.

SHEPARD, DAVID AND DEUTCH, ANDREW   You Can Have the Last Laugh Now.
Summary: Don't be misled by conventional wisdom, which may be only mythology, but be prepared to question premises and seek new truths. Especially, design systems for adaptability to change. In DM News, Dec 16, 1991, page 16.

CAMILLE MCDANIEL   Relationship Marketing & Demands of the 90s.
Summary: Emphasis has shifted in marketing approaches as a result of relationship marketing. Many other factors emerge as dominant forces in customers' decisions. In DM News, Dec 16, 1991, page 27.

MCQUAID, JAMES D., AND BONELLO, PHILIP H.   Putting the Relations in Relationship Marketing.
Summary: Introducing a new term, "transpositioning," which refers to communicating with your customers on the basis of the information you have collected about them—i.e., making your positioning a proper match for the data you have. In DM News, Dec 2, 1991, page 23.

LIBEY, DONALD R.   Relationship Marketing and Credit Collections.
Summary: A new approach to collections, softening the demand for payment and integrating it with relationship/databased marketing methods as part of a continuum of relationships with customers. In DM News, Nov 25, 1991, page 18.

WILSON, DAVE   Let's Not Forget the Database Basics.
Summary: A few sobering thoughts on facing realities before you plunge in and start flailing away blindly: You need commitment and planning. In DM News, Nov 25, 1991, page 46.

Index